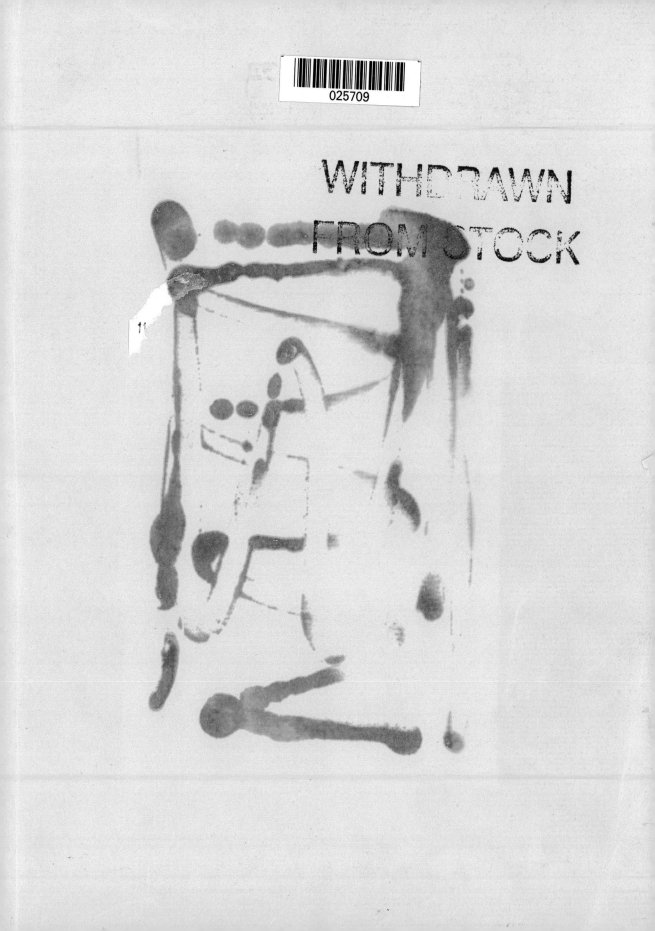

THE BIG
FAMILY
COOKING
SHOWDOWN

BOOKS

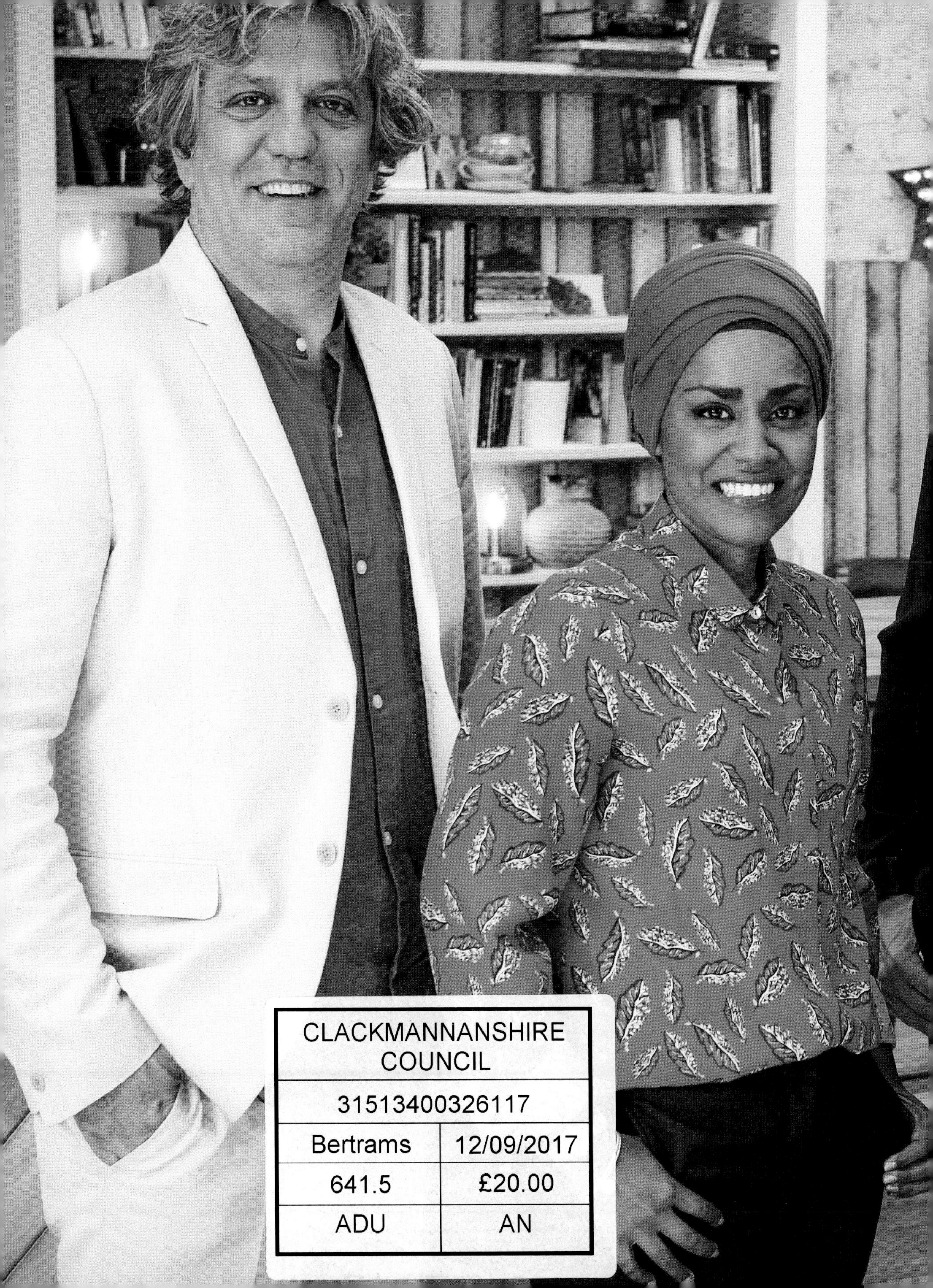

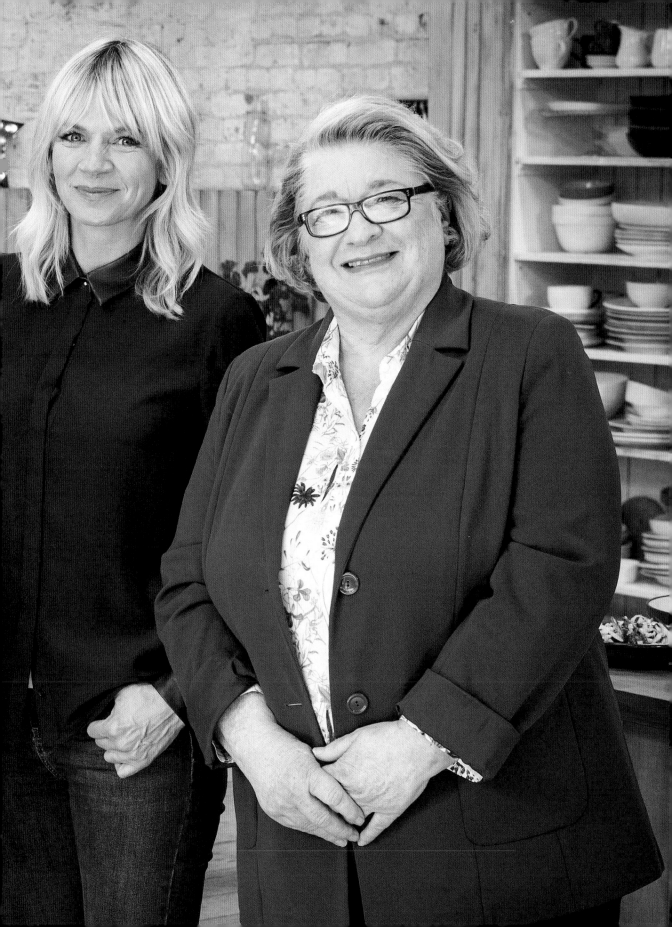

10 9 8 7 6 5 4 3 2 1

BBC Books, an imprint of Ebury Publishing
20 Vauxhall Bridge Road, London SW1V 2SA

BBC Books is part of the Penguin Random House
group of companies whose addresses can be found
at global.penguinrandomhouse.com

Penguin
Random House
UK

Recipe copyright © Voltage Productions 2017
Photography and design copyright © Woodlands
Books 2017

This book is published to accompany the television
series entitled The Big Family Cooking Showdown
first broadcast on BBC Two in 2017. The Big
Cooking Showdown is a Voltage TV production.

Executive Producers: Sanjay Singhal,
Kathleen Larkin
Managing Director: Steve Nam
Series Editor: Gary Broadhurst
Series Director: Sarah Myland
Line Producer: Nina McIntosh
Production Manager: Samara Friend
Producers: Hayley Cartwright, Ollie Scarth
Food Team: Rashid Khalil, Martha Swales
BBC Commissioning Editor: Catherine Catton
Head of Production: Amanda Hibbitts
Series Home Economist: Lisa Harrison

First published by BBC Books in 2017
www.penguin.co.uk

A CIP catalogue record for this book is available
from the British Library
ISBN 9781785942808

Publishing Director: Lizzy Gray
Editor: Charlotte Macdonald
Project Editor: Jo Roberts-Miller
Home Economist and Recipe Developer:
Lizzie Kamenetzky
Design: Smith & Gilmour Ltd
Recipe Photography: Andrew Burton
Stills Photography: Andrew Hayes-Watkins
Illustrator: Jane Farnham
Food Styling: Aya Nishimura
Assistant Food Stylists: Nicola Roberts &
Charlotte O'Connell
Prop Stylist: Olivia Wardle
Production: Alex Merrett

Printed and bound in Germany by Mohn Media GmbH

Penguin Random House is committed to a sustainable
future for our business, our readers and our planet.
This book is made from Forest Stewardship Council®
certified paper.

FSC
www.fsc.org
MIX
Paper from
responsible sources
FSC® C018179

CONTENTS

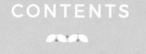

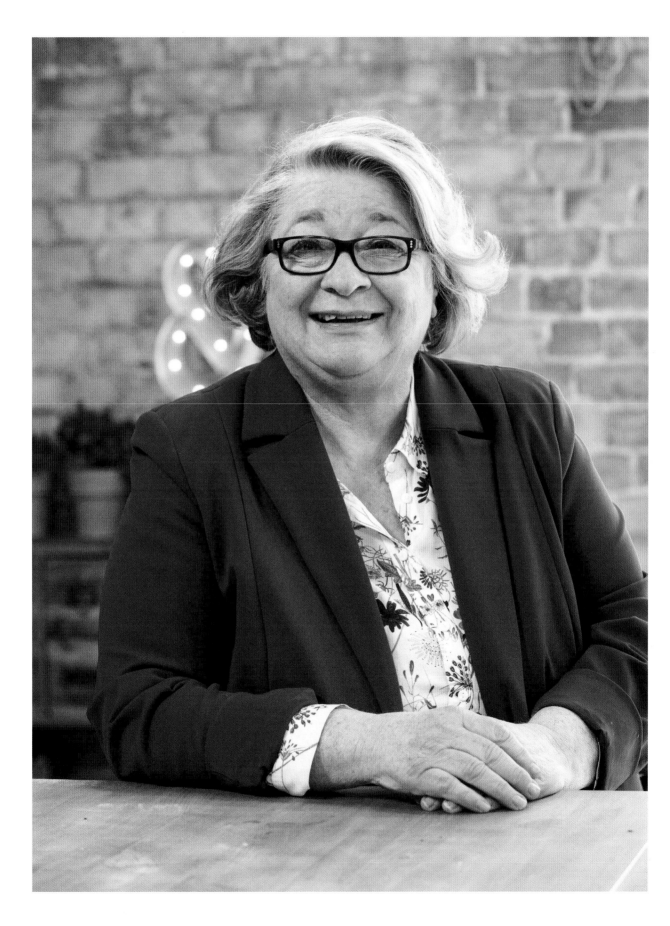

FOREWORD

'The Big Family Cooking Showdown' is a competition with a difference. The show celebrates families enjoying themselves as they work together to create wonderful dishes – and, my goodness, they were incredible!

The programme centres on families cooking and eating together, which is so important. We often hear such negative reports about people not cooking from scratch or not eating as a family around the kitchen table, but this show proves that they do! I got such a buzz out of seeing a 16-year old just wanting to spend time with her parent – absolutely wonderful. Every family was delightful. I wanted them all to win!

My hope is that 'The Big Family Cooking Showdown', and this book, will encourage more people to take up cooking as a fantastic hobby that everyone can take part in. It is a great way to get families communicating, both during the process of preparing and making food, but also from being together in one place sharing something they can all enjoy: discussing the flavours and textures, and wondering whether they'd make it again. And these conversations can lead to all manner of important discussions that go beyond food.

There is a huge emphasis on learning in the show, as the competing teams progress through the qualifying rounds. They were encouraged to listen to Giorgio's and my constructive criticism. Some of them found it easy to follow recipes, others found the rigidity of a written recipe a hindrance, and preferred a more intuitive approach. This isn't so different to developing your confidence at home. I always recommend you read the whole recipe first, before you pick up a knife or reach for the chopping board. And then read it again. When you've made a recipe once, you can add your own ideas and variations when you cook it again, if you wish. This is when the fun really begins.

I absolutely *loved* judging this show and the most exciting thing of all was tasting the diverse range of cuisines that the families cooked. Giorgio and I learned so much. This book features many of the different dishes in the show – from Syrian and Italian, to Indian and British – all simplified down. Whether you're inspired to start cooking for the first time or are already a practiced cook looking for new recipes, you'll find lots of fresh ideas for wonderful meals. I hope you'll enjoy making and eating the dishes as much as we enjoyed judging them.

Rosemary

THE MARKS

THE AYOUBIS

THE BOYES

THE GANGOTRAS

THE RIGNALLS

THE DAWES

THE KARIMS

THE KINGS

THE BELLAMYS

THE HERBERTS

THE PIGOTTS

THE BELLAMORES

THE CHARLESES

THE HILLIARDS

THE MASSACCESIS

THE CODOUGANS

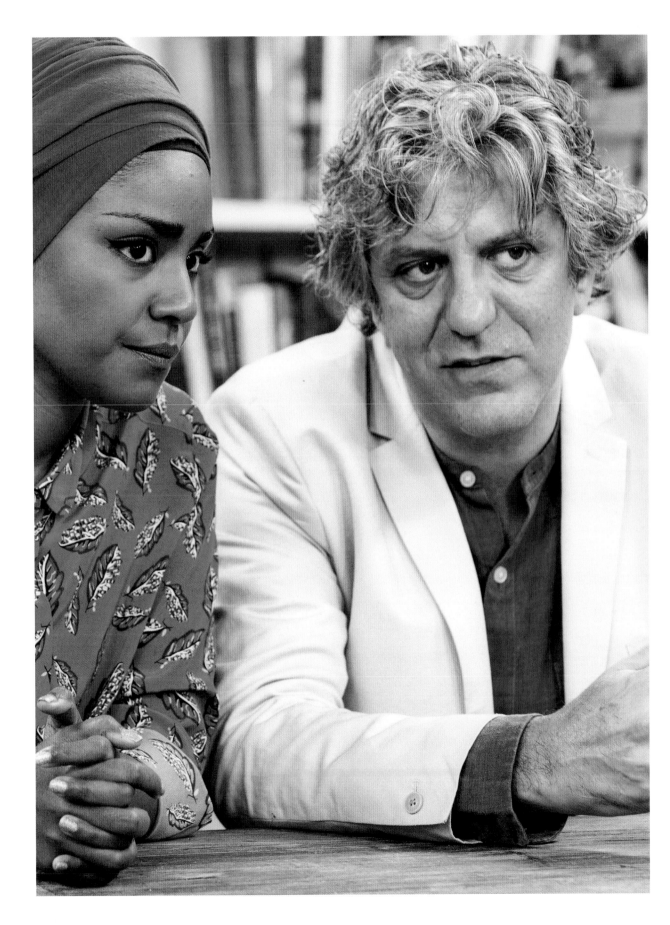

STORE CUPBOARD

What you keep in your store cupboard will depend on your family's likes and dislikes, but the following list is a good place to start. It will not only ensure you are well stocked for making many of the recipes in this book, but it will also mean you're never far from rustling up a satisfying meal, such as the simple recipe ideas. We recommend you look online or in larger supermarkets for unfamiliar ingredients.

BAKING SUPPLIES

Flour is the backbone of countless recipes and, even if baking isn't your forte, it's invaluable for making white sauces, crumbles, Yorkshire puddings, fritters, pancakes and much more.

- Plain flour
- Strong bread flour
- Instant yeast
- Suet (for dumplings)
- Baking powder
- Bicarbonate of soda
- Caster sugar
- Granulated sugar
- Light brown sugar
- Oats
- Dried fruit and nuts
- Vanilla extract and / or vanilla pods
- Cooking chocolate

DRIED GRAINS AND PULSES

Inexpensive and filling, whole and refined grains and dried legumes are the building block of many meals.

- Dried pasta (a variety of shapes)
- Dried noodles
- Basmati and / or long grain rice
- Risotto rice
- Couscous
- Dried lentils, beans and chickpeas

JARS AND TINS

These are the kinds of ingredients that deliver and build flavour. They can also be a real help when you don't have time to soak and boil dried beans or chickpeas, make pesto or roast peppers.

- Tinned and / or jarred anchovies
- Tinned tuna
- Jarred capers
- Black and / or green olives
- Roasted red peppers
- Jarred pesto
- Tinned or jarred beans and chickpeas
- Tinned tomatoes
- Tomato purée
- Coconut milk
- Tahini

OILS, VINEGARS, SAUCES AND CONDIMENTS

Everyone has a favourite condiment that they can't imagine eating chips or a bacon sandwich without and, with the ingredients below to hand, you should always be able to whip up a salad dressing or a marinade, too.

- Olive oil
- Neutral cooking oil such as vegetable or sunflower
- Red and white wine vinegar
- Balsamic vinegar
- Soy sauce
- Fish sauce
- Ketchup and / or brown sauce
- Chilli sauce
- Dijon, wholegrain and English mustard
- Mayonnaise
- Honey
- Golden syrup

SEASONING, HERBS & SPICES

Whole spices last longer but often require toasting and grinding. Keep dried herbs and spices away from light to maximise their lifespan, and sort through your drawers every six months or so to root out anything that's past its best.

- Sea salt
- Table salt
- Black pepper

- Whole and ground spices (a selection of whatever you use most: cinnamon, cumin, coriander, chilli flakes, fennel seeds, garam masala, sumac, turmeric etc.)
- Dried herbs (a selection of whatever you use most: bay leaves, oregano, mint, parsley etc.)
- Good-quality stock cubes or pots (vegetable, chicken, fish and beef)

FRIDGE AND FRESH

Most cuisines have a few fresh ingredients that form the basis of many of its recipes, from the onion, celery and carrot that make up a soffritto or mirepoix, to the garlic, ginger and chilli that are the foundation of much Asian cooking. This is by no means a definitive list but, depending on what you like to cook, it provides a starting point.

- Milk
- Butter
- Cheese
- Crème fraîche and / or yoghurt
- Onions
- Garlic
- Ginger
- Fresh chillies
- Fresh herbs
- Carrots
- Celery
- Potatoes
- Eggs
- Bread and / or tortilla wraps and pitta bread

FREEZER

A freezer really comes into its own for batch cooking and preparing ahead, but there are a few basic items that it is helpful to have always tucked away, too.

- Ready-made puff pastry
- Frozen peas or petit pois
- Frozen berries
- Ice cream

ESSENTIAL KITCHEN KIT

What equipment we keep in our kitchens often depends largely on the space we have available. The following is a comprehensive list of 'basics' that covers most bases – we haven't included gadgets (handy though these can undeniably be). If you have room on the worktop then a food-processor can be wonderfully efficient at whizzing things up; similarly, if you make a lot of cakes, then a stand mixer will prove to be an invaluable investment.

- All-purpose chef's knife
- Serrated or bread knife
- Paring or small knife
- Knife sharpener
- Vegetable peeler
- Sturdy kitchen scissors (use for snipping herbs but good for cutting pizza into slices, too)
- Box grater and fine grater for cheese and zest
- Wooden spoons

- Long tongs
- Silicon spatula
- Metal fish slice
- Balloon whisk
- Ladle
- Slotted spoon
- Measuring spoons
- Tin opener
- Corkscrew or bottle opener
- Sieve and / or colander
- Salad spinner
- Chopping boards (wood is kindest to knives; different coloured plastic boards are good to use for different foods, such as meat, fish, vegetables etc.)
- Baking sheets – a range of sizes
- Roasting tins – a range of sizes
- Cake tins – loose-bottomed and non-stick
- Electronic scales (so much more accurate than the old-fashioned kind, and a must for baking)
- Mixing bowls – a range of sizes
- Rolling pin (it is tricky to make pastry without one of these, although a long, thin glass bottle can substitute if necessary)
- Pestle and mortar
- Good-quality non-stick frying pan and sauté pan
- Saucepans with lids – a range of sizes
- Wok (great for stir fries – or use a frying or sauté pan)
- Ovenproof flameproof casserole dish

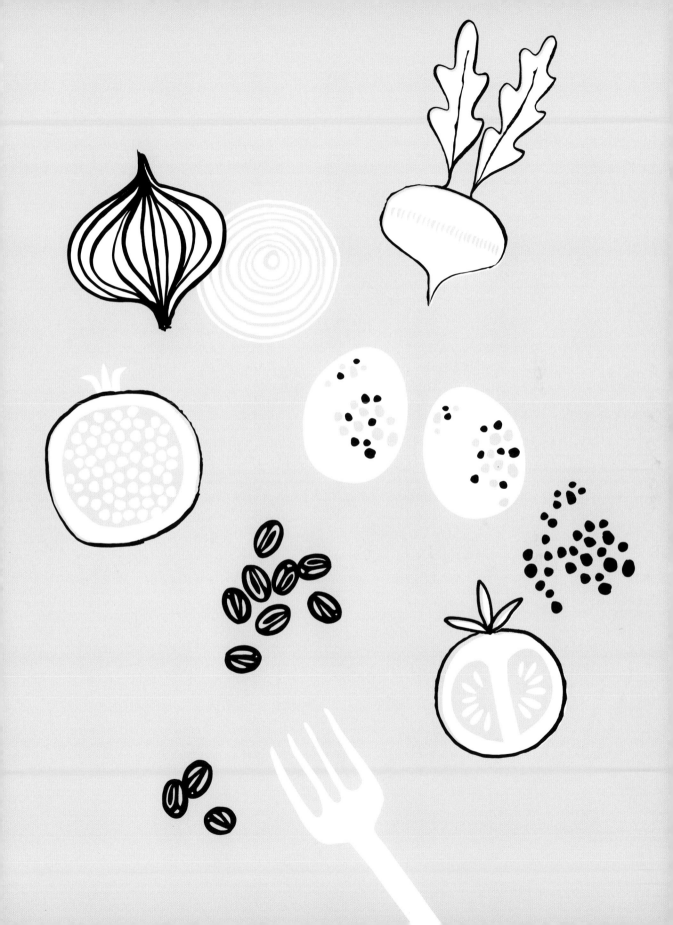

BRUNCH LUNCH
AND
SNACKS

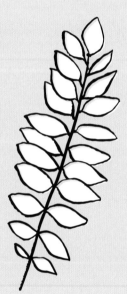

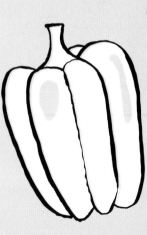

BABA GANOUSH & MOUHAMMARA
AUBERGINE & RED PEPPER DIPS

For the baba ghanoush
2 large aubergines
2 large vine tomatoes, chopped
1 roasted red pepper, chopped
    (from a jar is fine)
1 small bunch flat-leaf parsley,
    chopped, reserving a few
    leaves for garnish
1 garlic clove, peeled and
    crushed
1 tbsp pomegranate molasses
2 tbsp extra-virgin olive oil
seeds of 1 pomegranate
salt and pepper

For the mouhammara
2 roasted red peppers
    (from a jar is fine)
75g walnuts
75g white breadcrumbs
1 tbsp tahini
1 tbsp pomegranate molasses
4 tbsp extra-virgin olive oil
fresh mint, to garnish
salt and pepper

1. Preheat the oven to 200°C/Fan 180°C.

2. Pierce the aubergines with a knife and then roast in the oven for 45–50 minutes, or until really soft and tender. Set aside to cool.

3. Peel the aubergines and scoop the flesh into a large bowl.

4. Stir in the tomatoes, pepper and parsley and mix well.

5. Finally add the garlic, pomegranate molasses, extra-virgin olive oil and season well, stirring to combine.

6. Whizz the red peppers for the mouhammara in a food-processor. Remove to a large bowl and then use the food-processor to whizz the walnuts, keeping a few aside for garnish.

7. Add the ground walnuts to the bowl of peppers, mix in the breadcrumbs and season well.

8. Stir in the tahini and pomegranate molasses and loosen with the olive oil, and a splash of water, if necessary.

9. Arrange both dips in serving dishes. Garnish the mouhammara with fresh mint and the whole walnuts, and the baba ghanoush with a drizzle of olive oil, the reserved parsley leaves and some pomegranate seeds.

TIP For a Syrian mezze serve with Fatoush Salad (see page 252) and toasted pitta.

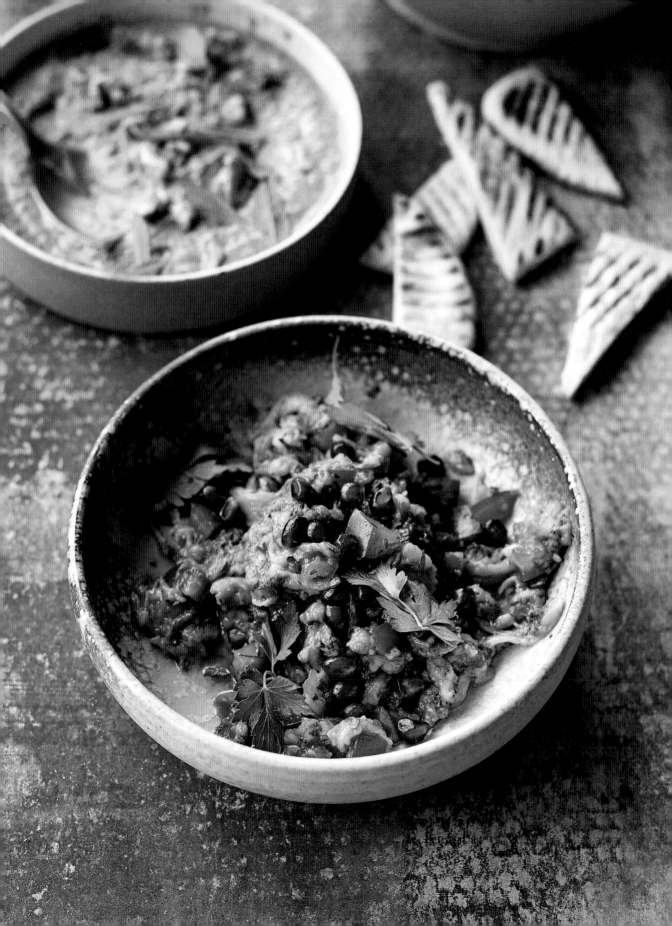

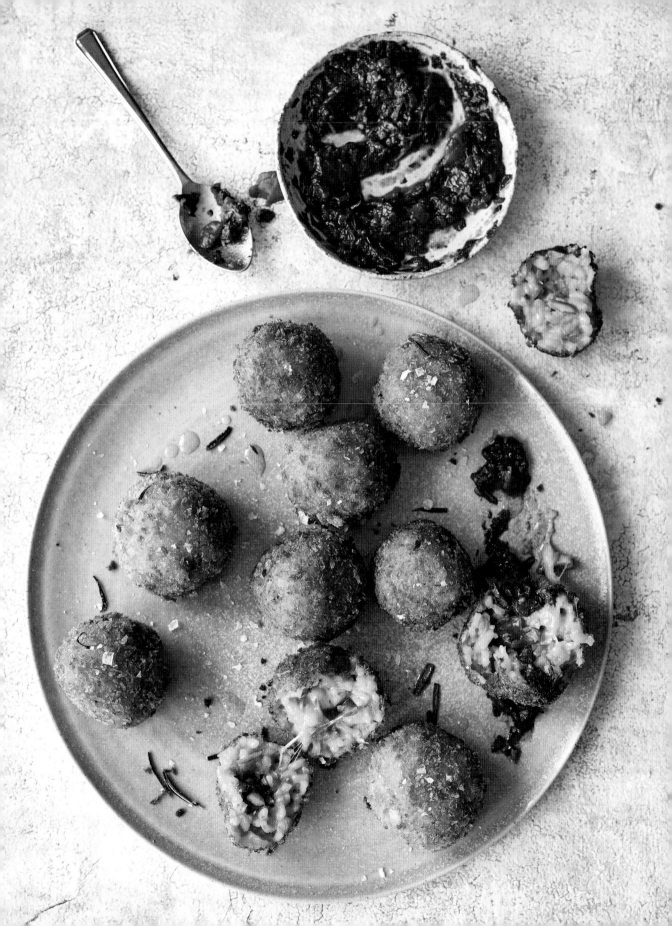

MINI ARANCINI WITH ARRABIATA SAUCE

For the risotto
2 tbsp olive oil
1 onion, peeled and finely
    chopped
1 garlic clove, peeled and
    crushed
250g arborio rice
125ml dry white wine
700ml fresh chicken
    stock, hot
good pinch of saffron
2 tbsp butter
30g Parmesan, grated

For coating and frying
2 rashers pancetta
1 fresh rosemary sprig,
    leaves stripped
150g stale ciabatta,
    cut into pieces
1 egg, beaten
vegetable oil, for deep frying

For the arrabiata sauce
½ tbsp olive oil
2 garlic cloves, peeled and
    bashed
1 red chilli, finely chopped
25g fresh basil, leaves picked
    and stalks finely chopped
1 x 400g tin plum tomatoes

For the filling
30g unsalted pistachios,
    shelled and finely chopped
50g ball buffalo mozzarella,
    finely chopped
25g fontina cheese, grated
30g sun-dried tomatoes in oil,
    finely chopped

1. Heat the oil in a heavy-based pan over a medium heat and add the onion. Cook for 10 minutes, or until translucent. Stir in the garlic and rice and toast for a few minutes. Pour in the wine and cook, stirring, until evaporated.

2. Add a ladleful of hot stock and stir into the rice until it has been absorbed. Keep adding the stock, a ladleful at a time, until the rice is nearly cooked. Add the saffron halfway through cooking.

3. Remove the rice from the heat, stir in the butter and leave covered for 4 minutes.

4. Finally, stir in the Parmesan and spread the mixture onto a baking sheet to cool quickly.

5. Make the breadcrumbs Fry the rashers of pancetta until crisp in a pan with the rosemary. Tip into a food-processor with the ciabatta and whizz into breadcrumbs. Set aside until ready to use.

6. Make the arrabiata sauce Heat the oil in a pan over a medium heat and fry the garlic, chilli and basil stalks lightly for 5 minutes. Stir in the tomatoes and simmer for 20 minutes. Remove from the heat and blitz with a hand blender. Stir in the basil leaves and put to one side until ready to serve.

7. Make the arancini Combine all the filling ingredients and mix well. Form into 16 balls and surround with the cooled rice. Roll each of them in the beaten egg and then through the breadcrumb mixture.

8. Heat a pan of vegetable oil to 180°C, or until a cube of bread browns in 20 seconds. Deep-fry the arancini in batches for 2–3 minutes until golden. Remove from the oil with a slotted spoon and drain on kitchen paper.

9. Serve with the arrabiata sauce.

SPICED POTATO DUMPLINGS
BATATA VADA WITH TAMARIND SAUCE

MAKES 16

4 medium floury potatoes
1 tbsp vegetable oil
100g urid dal
1 tsp black mustard seeds
8–10 curry leaves
pinch of turmeric
1 tbsp grated fresh root ginger
2 garlic cloves, peeled
    and crushed
1 green chilli, finely chopped
good pinch of salt
squeeze of fresh lemon juice

For the batter
100g gram flour
pinch of salt
¼ tsp turmeric
1 tsp baking powder
½ tsp chilli powder
110ml water
sunflower oil, for deep-frying

For the tamarind sauce
50g tamarind purée
pinch of salt
1 tsp ground cumin, roasted
½ tsp hot chilli powder
pinch of ground ginger
4–5 tbsp jaggery

1 : Bring a large pan of water to the boil and cook the potatoes for 20 minutes, or until tender to the point of a knife. Allow to cool. Remove the skin from the potatoes and mash.

2 : Add the vegetable oil to a large pan over a low heat and stir in the urid dal to toast.

3 : Add the mustard seeds, curry leaves, tumeric and ginger, garlic and chill and cook for 30 seconds.

4 : Add the mashed potatoes to the pan, mix thoroughly and season with salt and lemon juice.

5 : Remove from the heat and make into 12–16 balls using a mini ice-cream scoop. Chill in the fridge to firm up.

6 : Make the batter Mix everything together in a bowl, expect the oil. Chill until ready to use.

7 : Make the tamarind sauce Put all the ingredients except the jaggery into a large pan with 100ml water. Place over a high heat and bring to the boil. Simmer for 1 minute, then add the jaggery and bubble until thickened.

8 : Heat the oil in a deep pan to 170°C or until a cube of bread browns in 30 seconds.

9 : Dip each ball into the batter, shake off any excess and then deep-fry the balls in batches for 4–5 minutes, or until golden.

10 : Serve with the tamarind sauce.

ACHARI PRAWN & COCONUT & SWEETCORN MOMOS (DUMPLINGS)

MAKES 32

For the wrappers
250g plain flour, plus
    extra for dusting
¾ tsp salt
¾ tsp baking powder
150ml lukewarm water
1 tsp vegetable oil

For the roasted tomato sauce
6 plum tomatoes
6 Kashmiri chillies, dried
pinch of coriander salt
2 tbsp Chinese vinegar
½ tsp salt
1 tbsp sugar

For the prawn filling
1 tsp vegetable oil
¼ tsp black mustard seeds
pinch of fenugreek seeds
¼ tsp fennel seeds
¼ tsp cumin seeds
¼ tsp chilli powder
¼ tsp onion seeds
¼ tsp turmeric
¼ tsp ground coriander
¼ tsp salt
20g unsalted butter
1.5cm piece fresh root ginger,
    peeled and grated
2 garlic cloves, peeled and
    crushed
½ green chilli, finely sliced
200g raw peeled prawns,
    deveined, washed, dried
    and diced

1 : Preheat the oven to 190°C/Fan 170°C.

2 : **Make the wrappers** Sift the flour, salt and baking powder into a large bowl. Slowly add the water, 50ml to begin with and then tablespoon by tablespoon until you have a medium-stiff dough. Coat with the oil and allow to rest for 30 minutes with a damp tea towel over the top of the bowl.

3 : **Make the roasted tomato sauce** Cook the tomatoes in the oven for 20 minutes and soak the chillies in boiling water. Once the tomatoes are roasted, drain the chillies, reserving the water. Remove the skins from the tomatoes and blend them with the chillies in a food-processor, along with the coriander salt and Chinese vinegar. If it is too thick, add some of the reserved chilli water. Stir in the salt and sugar and then leave to cool.

4 : **Make the prawn filling** Heat the oil in a pan over a medium heat and fry all the spices and salt for 1 minute until fragrant. Add the butter, ginger, garlic and chilli and then take off the heat and leave to cool. Mix in the prawns and set aside.

5 : **Make the coconut and sweetcorn filling** Heat the oil in a pan over a low heat and fry the cumin seeds for 30 seconds. Add the onion and fry until softened. Stir in the ginger and garlic paste and cook for another minute, before adding the chilli, thyme, turmeric, garam masala, salt, sugar, lemon juice and sweetcorn and cooking for a further 2–3 minutes. Finally add the butter until it melts and then take off the heat and leave to cool. Once cool, roughly blend half of the sweetcorn mixture with a hand

Recipe continues

2 tbsp vegetable oil
½ tsp cumin seeds
½ red onion, peeled and diced
1 tbsp ginger and garlic paste
1 green rocket chilli,
    finely sliced
½ tsp dried thyme
½ tsp tumeric
½ tsp garam masala
½ tsp salt
¼ tsp sugar
4 tbsp fresh lemon juice
200g frozen sweetcorn,
    defrosted
25g butter
1 tbsp roughly chopped
    fresh coriander
4 tbsp desiccated coconut

blender and stir into the unblended half. Add the fresh coriander and stir. Finally, stir in the coconut – it should have a thick consistency. Leave to one side.

6 : Create loosely bound rounds of each filling the size of a cherry tomato and place in the fridge to chill.

7 : **Make the momos** Divide the dough into four pieces. Take one piece of dough, returning the other quarters back to the bowl and keeping them under the damp towel.

8 : Roll the dough to an oval shape. Use extra flour on the work surface if it's sticking. Roll the dough through a pasta maker until it is on the second thinnest setting.

9 : Lay the dough on the work surface and, using an 8–9cm plain cutter, cut rounds from the sheet of dough. Remove the excess dough and pop back into the bowl.

10 : Place a small round of filling in the centre of the dough and lift opposing sides of the dough circle and pinch together. Repeat with the other sides to close any gaps, and twist.

11 : Once all the momos in this batch are formed, place onto a lightly oiled plate with a second damp tea towel over the top.

12 : Repeat the process with the other quarters of dough until all the filling has been used.

13 : Bring a large pan of water to the boil and place a steamer over the top, or use a steamer, and oil the base. Place the momos 1cm apart in the steamer and steam for 15 minutes, or until the wrappers turn a glossy yellowish colour. Continue until all the momos have been cooked.

14 : Serve with the roasted tomato sauce.

> **TIP** If you don't have a pasta maker, you can break off small rounds of the dough and roll circles by hand.

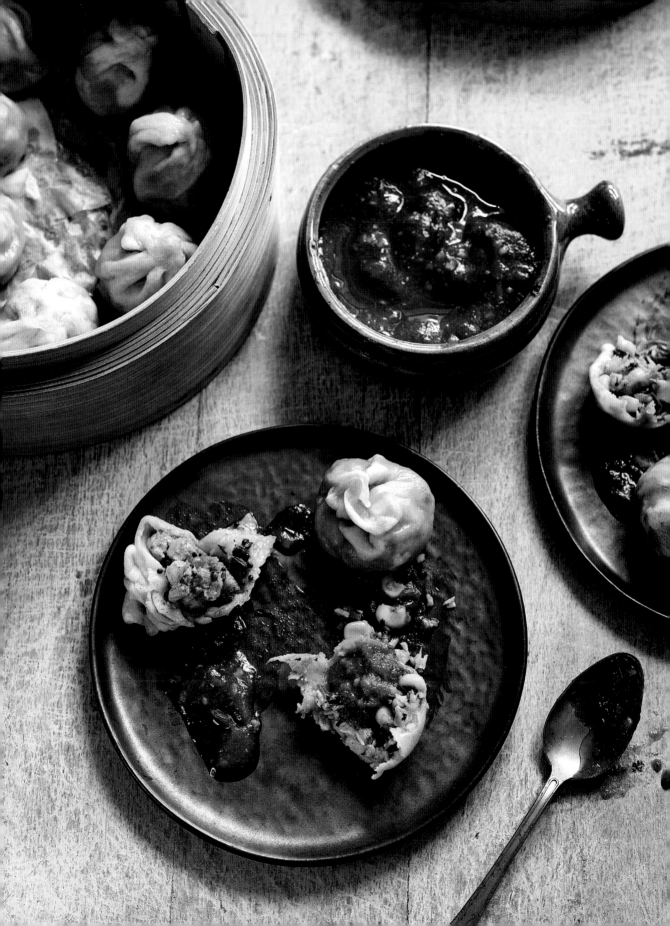

VIETNAMESE SPRING ROLLS & DIPPING SAUCE
CHA GIO & NUOC MAM CHAM

MAKES 12-14

For the spring rolls
25g dried shredded Chinese
    wood ear mushrooms
1 x small packet dried glass
    vermicelli noodles
    (about 30g)
250g minced pork
½ onion, peeled and
    finely chopped
1 garlic clove, peeled and
    crushed
1 medium carrot, peeled
    and finely sliced into
    matchsticks
½ tbsp caster sugar
1½ tbsp fish sauce
½ tsp ground black pepper
¼ tsp sea salt
12–14 spring roll pastry sheets
    (about 15 x 15cm)
1 banana, to make a banana
    glue stick (see tip)
vegetable oil, for deep-frying

For the dipping sauce
juice of 2 large limes
    (3–4 tbsp)
1 garlic clove, peeled and
    crushed
2 tbsp sugar
3 tbsp fish sauce
2 tbsp rice wine vinegar
½–1 whole small fresh birds
    eye chilli, finely sliced

1. Place the mushrooms and noodles in 2 separate bowls, cover with boiling water and let them stand for 5 minutes.

2. Drain both well and then chop everything up with a pair of scissors.

3. Add them to a large mixing bowl and combine with the minced pork, onion, garlic, carrot, sugar, fish sauce, pepper and salt. Mix well.

4. Make the spring rolls Place a spring roll wrapper with one corner pointing towards you and place 1 tablespoon of the mixture just above the centre of the wrap. Fold the top corner over the mixture and then fold the 2 sides in. Roll from top to bottom, making sure it's quite tight, stopping before you get to the triangle at the end. Use the banana to glue the end triangle and carry on rolling to the end. Repeat until all the mixture has been used up.

5. Make the dipping sauce Combine all the ingredients in a bowl. Stir and leave for 15 minutes.

6. Heat a good amount of oil in a high-sided pan or wok to 160°C, or until a cube of bread browns in 1 minute. Cook the spring rolls in batches for 4–5 minutes and then drain on kitchen paper.

7. Serve the spring rolls with the dipping sauce.

FAMILY TIP 'Cut a banana in half and remove 1–2cm of the peel from the cut end. The exposed banana makes a great natural glue.'

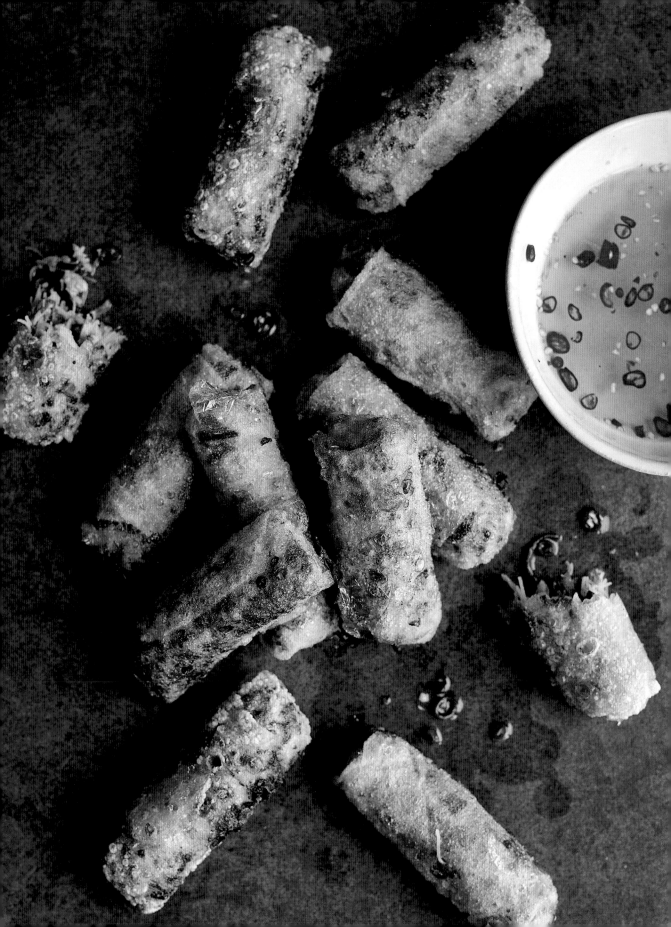

PORK BELLY CROQUETTES

500g skinless and
boneless pork belly
1 litre chicken stock
4 fresh bay leaves
1 tbsp black peppercorns
75g butter
1 tsp paprika
2 tbsp clear honey
2 tbsp light soy sauce
3 large baking potatoes
(about 800g), peeled
50ml double cream
2 garlic cloves, peeled and
crushed
100g Manchego cheese,
grated
a large handful of flat-leaf
parsley, chopped
50g plain flour, for dusting
3 eggs, beaten
500g panko breadcrumbs
1.5 litre vegetable oil,
for deep-frying
sea salt

1 : Preheat the oven to 170°C/Fan 150°C.

2 : **Cook the pork** Place the pork in an ovenproof dish with the stock, bay and peppercorns and cook in the oven for 2–3 hours, or until very tender. Strain and shred the meat with two forks, discarding any large bits of fat.

3 : Put the shredded pork in a pan with 25g of the butter, the paprika, honey and soy.

4 : **Cook the potatoes** Bring a large pan of salted water to the boil and cook the potatoes for 10–12 minutes, or until tender. Drain and then return to the pan.

5 : **Make the croquettes** Mash the potatoes with the remaining butter, the cream, garlic, cheese and parsley. Add the pork mixture to the pan and mix to combine. Season to taste and spoon into a bowl. Chill for at least 1 hour.

6 : Use your hands to shape into barrel-shaped croquettes.

7 : Tip the flour into a shallow bowl, the egg into another and the breadcrumbs into a third. Roll each croquette in the flour to cover with a light dusting and then dip into the beaten egg. Finally, cover in the breadcrumbs and put to one side on greaseproof paper until ready to fry.

8 : Heat a deep pan with oil until 180°C, or a cube of bread browns in 20 seconds.

9 : Fry the croquettes in batches for 2–3 minutes, or until golden brown.

10 : Serve immediately with a sprinkling of sea salt.

PORK WITH SAGE & ONION MARMALADE & CRACKLING

SERVES 4

300g high-quality pork rind, cut into thin strips
150ml white wine vinegar
vegetable oil, for deep-frying
1 tbsp sunflower oil
20g unsalted butter
4 x pork chops (about 125g each), cut into strips
salt and pepper

For the onion marmalade
30g unsalted butter
2 onions, peeled and finely sliced
2 garlic cloves, peeled and crushed
75ml balsamic vinegar
2 tbsp soft brown sugar
2 tbsp freshly chopped sage

1 Preheat the oven to 220˚C/Fan 200˚C.

2 Make the crackling Soak the rind in the white wine vinegar and a good pinch of salt for 2–3 minutes. Drain and transfer to a wire rack set over a roasting tray. Cook in the oven for approximately 15 minutes, or until starting to become crispy. Finally, heat a small deep pan with vegetable oil to 180˚C, or until a cube of bread browns in 20 seconds. Deep-fry the crackling for a few seconds until crispy. Remove to kitchen paper to drain and then season.

3 Make the marmalade Melt the butter in a pan over a very gentle heat and fry the onions and garlic until soft and caramelised; this will take at least 30 minutes.

4 Turn the onions up to a moderately high heat and add the balsamic vinegar. Cook for 2–3 minutes and then add the sugar and the chopped sage, and reduce to a jam-like consistency.

5 Heat the sunflower oil and butter in a pan over a high heat and fry the pork chop strips on one side for 2–3 minutes. Turn the strips and add a few spoonfuls of the marmalade. Continue to fry until the pork is cooked through.

6 Serve as a starter or snack with the crackling.

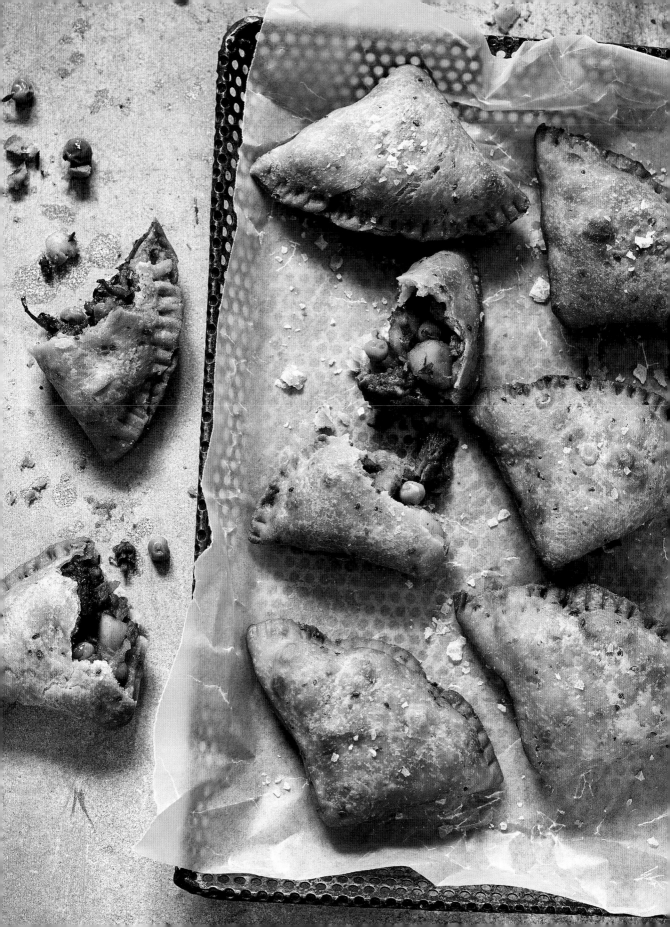

VENISON SAMOSAS

vegetable oil, for deep-frying

For the filling
35g oil
250g venison shoulder,
    cut into pieces
1 small red onion, peeled
    and finely diced
1 whole dried red chilli
1 fresh green chilli, finely
    chopped
2cm piece fresh root ginger,
    peeled and grated
1–2 garlic cloves, peeled
    and crushed
1 tsp cumin seeds
1 tsp coriander seeds
1 tsp black mustard seeds
3 cardamom pods
1 cinnamon stick
8 curry leaves
1 tbsp tamarind paste
1 tbsp tomato purée
100ml red wine
50ml Marsala wine
50ml beef stock
175g floury potatoes –
    King Edward, Desiree etc.,
    peeled and cubed
50g peas (frozen or fresh)
1 small bunch coriander,
    roughly chopped
1 small bunch fenugreek,
    roughly chopped

For the pastry
240g plain flour
2 tsp ajwain seeds,
    or nigella seeds
pinch of salt
4 tbsp vegetable oil
5–6 tbsp cold water

1. Make the filling Melt half the oil in a large pan over a low heat. Season the venison and brown in batches. Set aside.

2. Add the remainder of the oil to the pan and fry the onion over a medium heat for 10 minutes, or until softened. Add both the chillies, the ginger and garlic and fry for 1 minute more.

3. Add the whole spices and curry leaves and fry for 1 minute and then return the meat to the pan.

4. Add the tamarind, tomato purée, wine and Marsala and bubble for 1–2 minutes, then pour in the stock and season. Bring to a simmer, cover and cook for 2 hours, or until the meat is very tender.

5. Add the potatoes and peas and continue to cook until the mixture is dry but not sticking and the potato is tender. Ensure all the meat is shredded into the sauce.

6. Stir in the chopped herbs and set aside to cool.

7. Make the pastry Mix the flour with the ajwain or nigella seeds and salt in a bowl. Add the oil and water and bring together to a pliable but firm dough. Knead until smooth. Divide into 8 pieces (about 50g each).

8. Roll out the pieces of pastry into approximately 15cm circles. Cut each one in half. Brush the straight side with water and then fold and bring the sides together to form a cone and press to seal. Fill the with the venison mixture and then seal the top edge to form a samosa parcel. Repeat until you have 16 samosas.

9. Bring a deep pan of vegetable oil up to 180°C, or until a cube of bread browns in 20 seconds, and deep-fry the samosas in batches for 3–4 minutes, or until golden brown. Remove with a slotted spoon and drain on kitchen paper. Sprinkle with salt and serve.

LAAB IN LETTUCE CUPS
WITH PICKLED CARROTS

1–2 Little Gem lettuces
1 lime, cut into wedges, to serve
a handful of salted peanuts,
   toasted and chopped
1 spring onion, finely sliced
1 Thai red chilli, finely sliced

For the laab
1 small bunch coriander with
   roots, leaves chopped
2 Thai red chillies, seeded
1 small piece fresh root
   ginger, peeled
1 stick lemon grass, outer leaves
   peeled and core chopped
2 banana shallots, peeled
   and finely diced
1 tbsp vegetable oil
300g minced pork
1–2 tbsp fish sauce
2 tbsp fresh lime juice
a handful of fresh mint
   leaves, chopped

For the pickled carrots
5 tbsp rice vinegar
1 tbsp caster sugar
pinch of salt
2 carrots, peeled and shredded

For the naam prik sauce
1 tbsp vegetable oil
1 tsp shrimp paste
2 garlic cloves, peeled and
   crushed
2.5cm piece fresh root ginger,
   peeled and grated
1 tbsp freshly chopped coriander
2 small red Thai chillies, seeded
   and finely chopped
4 tsp caster sugar
3 tbsp light soy sauce
juice of 1 lime

1. **Make the laab** Whizz the roots of the coriander, the chillies, ginger and lemon grass to a paste in a mini food-processor.

2. Fry the shallots in the oil in a pan over a medium heat for 4–5 minutes, or until they just start to catch.

3. Add the minced pork and brown.

4. Stir in the paste from the food-processor and cook for another 10 minutes.

5. Measure in the fish sauce and lime juice, and add the coriander leaves and the mint. Stir and taste for seasoning.

6. **Make the pickled carrots** Combine all the ingredients and leave to pickle for 15 minutes. Once they have had their time, leave to drain in a sieve for 5 minutes.

7. **Make the naam prik sauce** Heat the oil in a pan over a low heat and gently fry the shrimp paste, garlic and ginger for 3–4 minutes. Add all the other ingredients, stir well to combine and dissolve the sugar. Pour into a container to cool.

8. Separate the lettuce into individual leaves and serve the laab in the lettuce cups with the pickled carrot, naam prik, lime wedges, and garnished with the peanuts and a little sliced spring onion and/or chilli sprinkled on top.

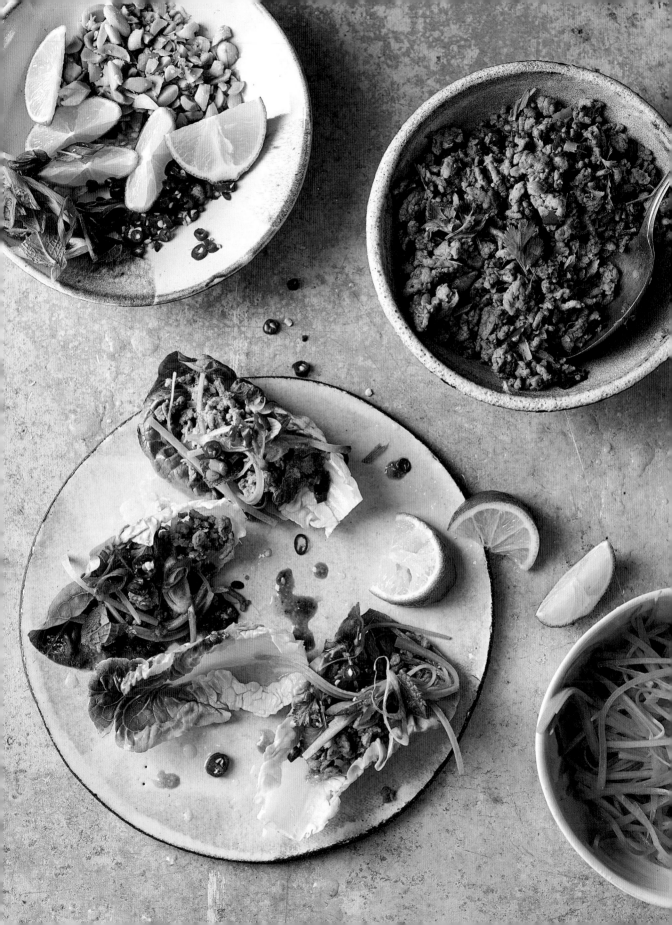

LAMB SPRING ROLLS WITH MINT & YOGHURT SAUCE

MAKES 12

For the spring rolls

3 tbsp olive oil
2 tsp cumin seeds
2 large onions, peeled and
    finely chopped
½ tsp turmeric
1 tsp garam masala
1 tbsp grated fresh root ginger
2 garlic cloves, peeled
    and crushed
½ tsp salt
2 green chillies, finely chopped
450g minced lamb
100g frozen petit pois,
    defrosted
a handful of freshly chopped
    coriander
12 spring roll pastry sheets
    (about 15 x 15cm)
1 tbsp cornflour, mixed with
    enough water to make
    a thin paste
1.5 litres vegetable oil,
    for deep-frying

For the mint and yoghurt sauce

300ml full-fat yoghurt
a handful of freshly
    chopped mint
1 tsp salt (or to taste)
2 tsp sugar
1 tsp ground cumin, toasted
½ tsp paprika
squeeze of fresh lemon juice
    (to taste)

1 : Make the filling Heat the olive oil in a pan over a low heat, add the cumin seeds and fry for 30 seconds. Add the onion and fry for 5 minutes until softened and then add the remainder of the spices, ginger, garlic, salt and chillies and fry for 2–3 minutes more.

2 : Add the minced lamb and cook for 4–5 minutes until browned all over.

3 : Stir in the peas and then take off the heat and leave to cool. Stir the coriander into the cooled lamb mixture.

4 : Make the mint and yoghurt sauce Mix all the ingredients together and chill until ready to serve.

5 : Make the spring rolls Put 2 tablespoons of the lamb mixture into the centre of each spring roll wrapper and lightly brush the edges of the wrapper with the cornflour paste. Turn the wrapper so one corner points towards you. Fold the top corner over the mixture and then fold the 2 sides in. Roll from top to bottom, making sure it's quite tight until you have a spring roll shape.

6 : Heat the oil in a deep frying pan to 180°C, or until a cube of bread browns in 20 seconds.

7 : Deep-fry the spring rolls in batches for 2–3 minutes, or until golden brown. Drain on kitchen paper.

8 : Serve piled on a plate with the yoghurt sauce on the side.

GLAMORGAN SAUSAGES

MAKES 12

25g unsalted butter
100g leek (about 1 leek), finely chopped
¼ tsp freshly grated nutmeg
200g wholemeal breadcrumbs, plus an extra 75g to coat the sausages
2 tsp fresh thyme leaves
2 heaped tsp fresh laverbread
175g strong Cheddar, grated
1½ tsp English mustard
2 eggs, 1 beaten
splash of milk (if required)
50g plain flour
1 tbsp vegetable oil
salt and pepper

1 : Melt half the butter in a pan over a medium heat. Add the leek and season with salt, pepper and nutmeg. Cover and cook for 10–12 minutes, or until soft, stirring occasionally. Allow to cool.

2 : In a bowl, combine the 200g breadcrumbs, thyme, laverbread and Cheddar. Stir in the cooled leek mixture, the mustard and the whole egg. Season well, adding a splash of milk, if necessary, to bring together into a dough.

3 : Shape into 12 small sausages and chill in the fridge for about 20 minutes.

4 : Preheat the oven to 200°C/Fan 180°C and line a baking tray with greasproof paper.

5 : Place the beaten egg, flour and the 75g breadcrumbs in individual shallow bowls. Once the sausages are chilled, roll them in the flour, then the beaten egg and then the breadcrumbs.

6 : Melt the remaining butter and the vegetable oil in a frying pan over a medium heat and fry the sausages for 2–3 minutes, or until golden all over.

7 : Place on the prepared baking tray and cook in the oven for 12–15 minutes, or until dark golden brown.

TIP Serve with Welsh Rarebit and Laverbread Cakes (see page 35).

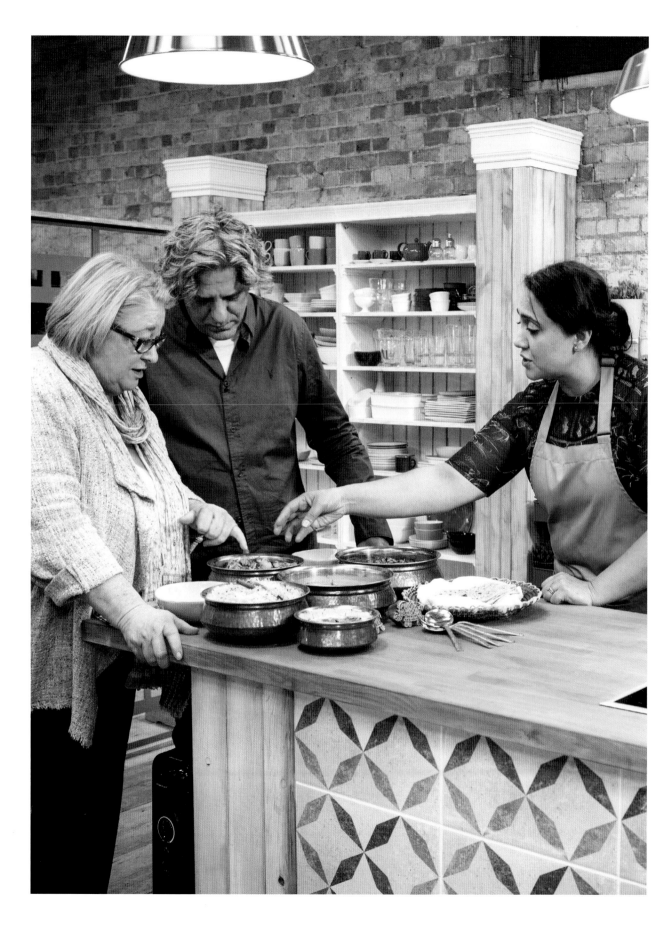

LAVERBREAD CAKES

MAKES 8

4 tbsp laverbread
4 tbsp rolled oats
2 tsp olive oil
8 thin rashers streaky bacon

1. In a small bowl, mix the laverbread and oats together. Form into 8 small balls and flatten into 8 small patties, about 4cm diameter.

2. Place a large pan with the olive oil over a medium heat and fry the bacon until crispy and it has released its fat. Remove from the pan with a slotted spoon.

3. Add the cakes to the pan and fry on each side for 2–3 minutes, or until golden brown.

4. Serve the laverbread cakes with the crispy bacon on top.

WELSH RAREBIT

SERVES 4

30g unsalted butter
20g plain flour
80ml stout
225g strong Cheddar, grated
1½ tsp English mustard
   powder
2 tsp Worcestershire sauce
4 thick slices sourdough,
   or other bread
salt and pepper

1. Preheat the grill to high.

2. Melt the butter in a small pan over a medium heat, then add the flour and stir together, cooking for 1 minute.

3. Whisk in the stout, then add the cheese, a little at a time, stirring until it has all come together. Add the mustard powder and Worcestershire sauce and season to taste.

4. Toast the bread and then place on a baking tray. Top each slice with a thick layer of the cheese mixture, ensuring it goes right to the edges. Place the toast under the grill and cook until bubbling and golden.

BRUNCH, LUNCH AND SNACKS

You could buy 1 x 500g packet ready-to-use pastry and skip step 2

CARAMELISED RED ONION & GOATS' CHEESE TARTLETS

SERVES 4

For the pastry
300g plain flour
70g salted butter
70g lard

For the filling
1 tbsp olive oil
3 red onions, peeled and
    finely sliced
1 tbsp brown sugar
2 tbsp balsamic vinegar
100g goats' cheese or feta
2 eggs
200ml double cream
salt and pepper

1 . Butter 4 x 10cm loose-bottomed tartlet tins.

2 . Make the pastry Rub the flour, butter and lard in a large bowl until it resembles fine breadcrumbs. Add approximately 2–3 tablespoons of cold water to bring it together.

3 . Split the pastry into 4 and roll out each quarter to line each prepared tin, ensuring there are no holes in the pastry. Chill for 10–20 minutes.

4 . Preheat the oven to 200°C/Fan 180°C.

5 . Make the filling Heat the oil in a large pan and add the onions and cook for 10 minutes. Add the sugar, vinegar and some seasoning, cover and cook over a low heat for 20–30 minutes, until really soft and sticky. Set aside.

6 . Meanwhile, line the chilled pastry cases with greaseproof paper and add ceramic baking beans or rice, and bake for 12–15 minutes.

7 . Remove the paper and beans and return to the oven and bake for a further 5 minutes, until lightly golden. Set aside to cool slightly.

8 . Reduce the oven temperature to 160°C/Fan 140°C.

9 . Divide the onion mix between the pastry cases. Crumble 25g of the goats' cheese or feta into each case.

10 . Mix the eggs and cream and then season well. Pour the egg mixture in equal quantities into each tin and then cook in the oven for approximately 30 minutes, or until the egg mixture is cooked and golden.

11 . Cool the tartlets in their tins and then remove from the tins to serve.

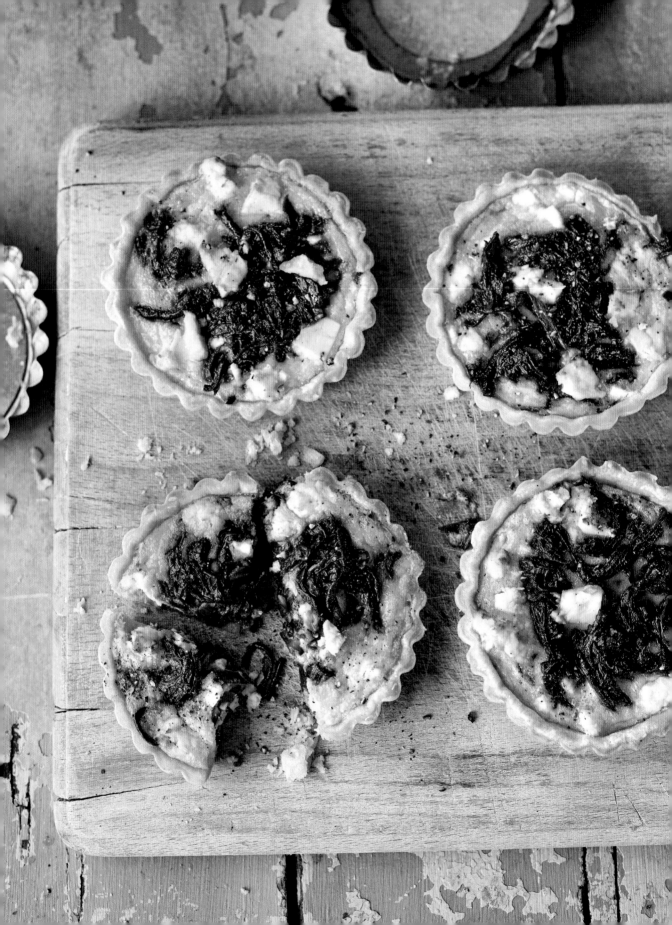

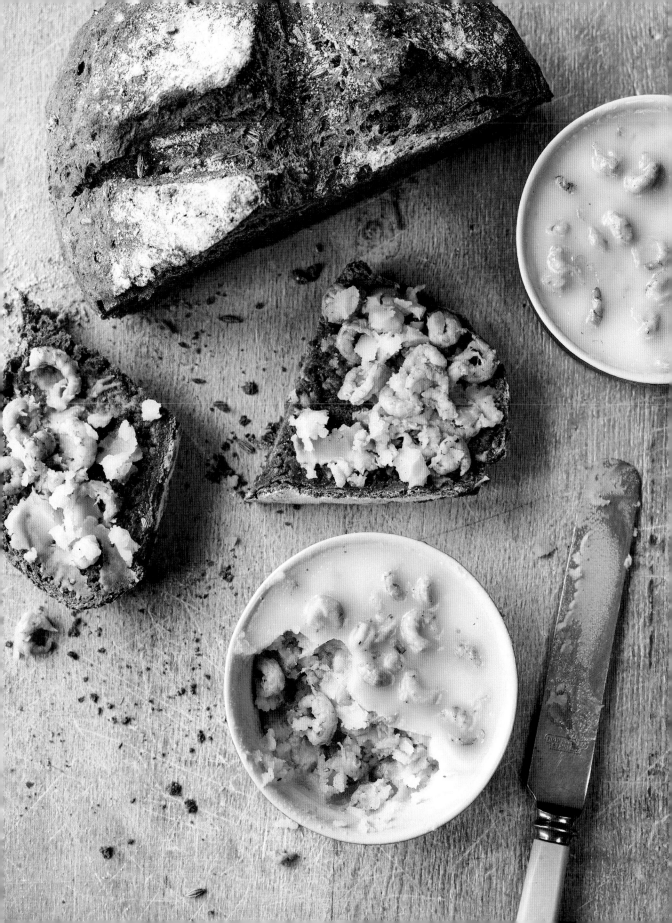

POTTED BROWN SHRIMP WITH BEETROOT SODA BREAD

For the potted shrimp
1 anchovy fillet in oil
250g unsalted butter
1–2 blades mace
1 bay leaf
pared rind and juice of
　½ lemon
200g brown shrimps
pinch of grated nutmeg
salt and white pepper
sprinkle of cayenne pepper,
　to garnish

For the beetroot soda bread
300g cooked beetroot
100ml buttermilk
1 tsp fennel seeds
500g wholemeal spelt flour
1 tsp salt
2 tsp baking powder
1 tsp cream of tartar

1. Preheat the oven to 200°C/Fan 180°C.

2. Make the potted shrimp Melt the anchovy in a large pan over a low heat and then add the butter, mace, bay leaf and lemon rind. Once the butter separates, remove the scum from the top and leave to stand for a few minutes to allow the remaining clarified butter to infuse.

3. Tip the butter into a bowl, leaving behind any milk solids from the bottom of the pan, and mix with the shrimps, lemon juice, nutmeg and season with salt and white pepper to taste. Mix well. Divide into 4 ramekins and leave to set in the fridge.

4. Make the soda bread Place the beetroot in a food-processor with the buttermilk.

5. Dry-fry the fennel seeds over a low heat and then mix with the beetroot in a large bowl, along with all the remainder of the bread ingredients, until combined.

6. Knead and shape into a round. Place on a floured baking sheet and make a large cross in the top with a sharp knife.

7. Bake in the centre of the oven for 25–30 minutes.

8. Cool on a wire rack and serve with the potted shrimp.

TIP Serve with blanched, buttered samphire.

SMOKED TROUT, SALMON & AVOCADO TERRINE

SERVES 4

500g sushi-grade salmon fillet,
   skinned, pin boned and diced
200g smoked trout fillet,
   skinned and flaked
1 banana shallot, peeled
   and finely chopped
juice of 1 lemon
splash of Worcestershire sauce
pinch of cayenne pepper
50g pea shoots, plus extra
   to garnish
200g crème fraîche
1 tsp horseradish cream
2 tbsp finely snipped
   fresh chives
2 avocados, peeled and sliced
extra-virgin olive oil, to drizzle
salt and pepper

1 . Place the salmon and trout in a bowl with the banana shallot. Stir in the lemon juice and season with salt and pepper. Add the Worcestershire sauce and cayenne pepper and mix well.

2 . Mix the crème fraîche, horseradish and chives together in a small bowl.

3 . Assemble the terrine in 4 rings – place a layer of salmon and trout on the bottom, top with a layer of pea shoots, then the crème fraîche mixture and finally the avocado slices.

4 . Gently lift off the rings, garnish with pea shoots and a drizzle of extra-virgin olive oil to serve.

> **FAMILY TIP** 'We use loads of fresh vegetables, love fish and venison and our family motto is "Families that cook together stay together."'

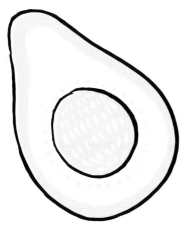

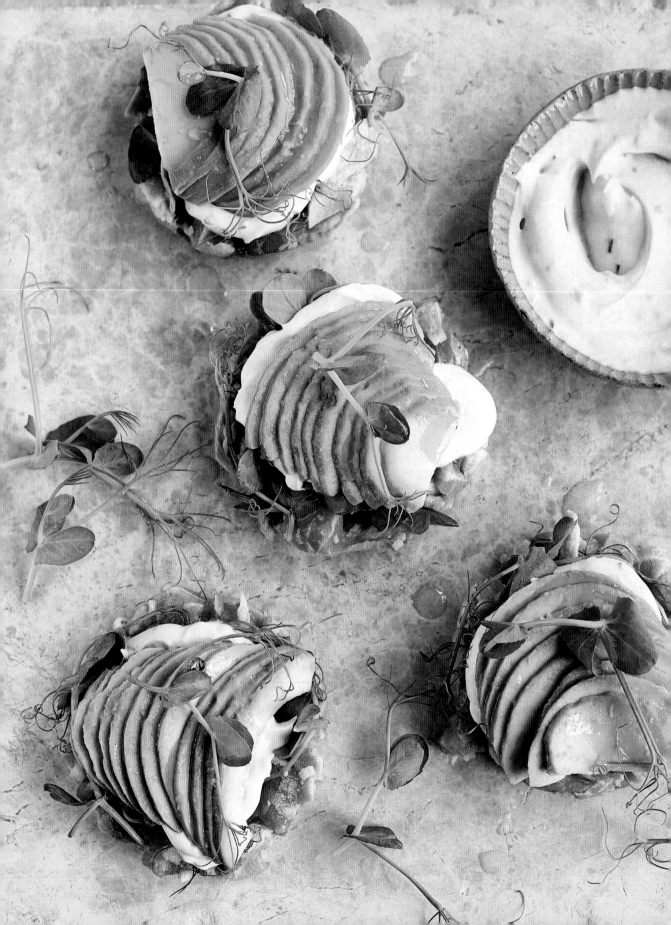

BUTTERNUT SQUASH SOUP

SERVES 4

2 tbsp sunflower oil
2 shallots, peeled and
    finely chopped
1 butternut squash, peeled,
    seeded and diced
500ml fresh vegetable stock,
    plus extra to thin if
    necessary
30g unsalted butter
4 fresh sage sprigs, leaves
    picked
salt and pepper

To finish
extra-virgin olive oil, to drizzle
1 x 200ml pot goats' yoghurt
good-quality balsamic vinegar,
    to drizzle

1. Put the sunflower oil in a deep pan over a medium heat and fry the shallots for 2–3 minutes, or until starting to brown.

2. Add the butternut squash and cook for 5–6 minutes until a touch coloured.

3. Pour in the stock and season well. Bring to the boil and then turn down the heat and simmer for 20–25 minutes, or until the squash is nice and tender.

4. Using a hand blender, blitz the mixture until smooth, adding a little more stock if the soup is too thick.

5. Meanwhile, melt the butter in a separate pan over a medium heat until foaming and fry the sage leaves. Drain on kitchen paper and sprinkle with salt.

6. To serve, pour the soup into bowls and drizzle with extra-virgin olive oil. Add a swirl of goats' yoghurt and a dash of balsamic vinegar. Garnish with the fried sage.

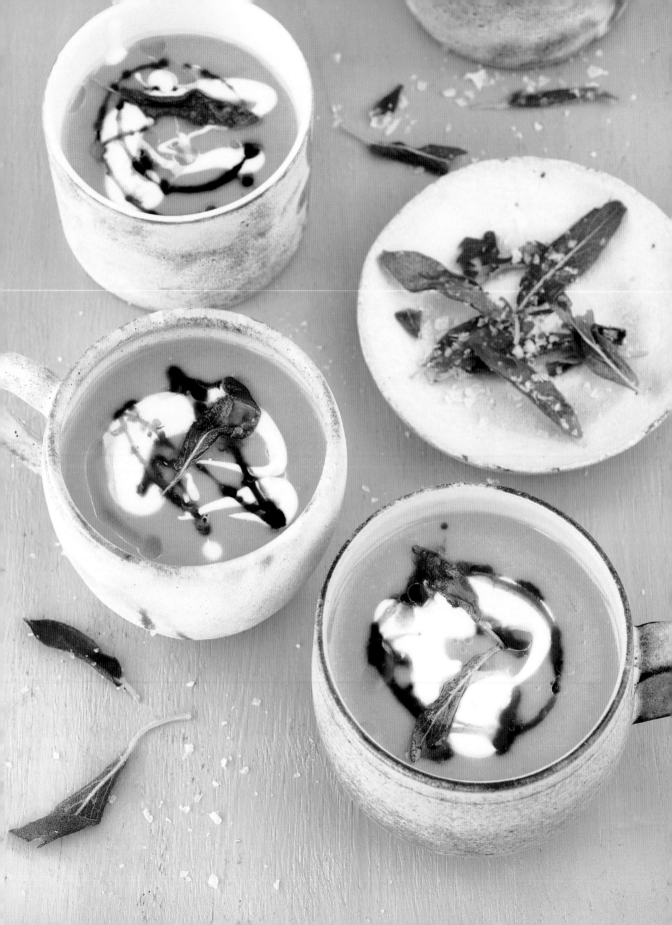

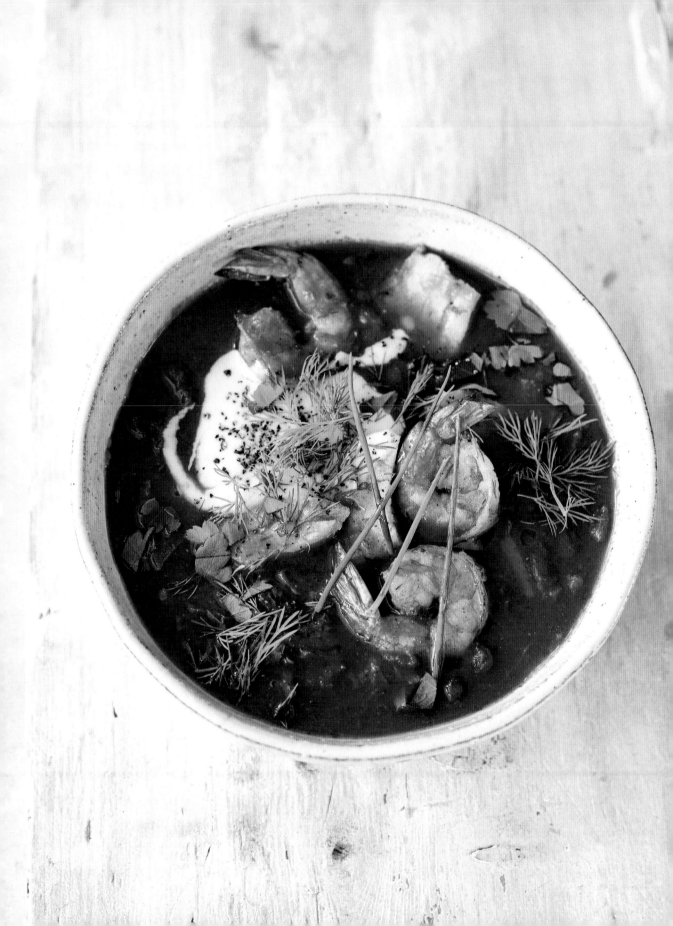

FISH SOUP WITH AÏOLI

SERVES 4

400g cod loin, cut into
   1.5cm chunks
1 tsp lemon pepper
1½ tbsp olive oil
1 garlic clove, peeled and
   finely sliced
1 large red onion, peeled
   and finely sliced
1 fennel bulb, finely sliced
1 medium carrot, peeled
   and finely diced
1 tsp mild curry powder
½ tsp paprika
1 small bunch dill, chopped
1 x 400g tin tomatoes, drained
400ml white wine
2 tsp sugar
250ml fish stock
200g king prawns, deveined
20g butter
15g fresh flat-leaf parsley,
   chopped
1 small bunch chives, snipped
salt and pepper

For the aïoli
2 egg yolks
1 tbsp fresh lemon juice
250ml sunflower oil
100ml crème fraîche
1 garlic clove, peeled
   and crushed

1. **Prepare the soup** Toss the cod in the lemon pepper and set aside.

2. Heat the olive oil in a large pan over a medium heat. Sweat the garlic and onion, fennel and carrot for 10 minutes, until soft. Add the curry powder and paprika, and fry for a further minute.

3. Add 2 tablespoons of the dill, the tomatoes, white wine and sugar. Add the stock and bring to the boil, then simmer for 25 minutes.

4. **Make the aïoli** Place the egg yolks in a mini food-processor. Add the lemon juice and blend together. Gradually add the oil, drop by drop while blending, for about 5 minutes or until it thickens. Season to taste. Mix the mayonnaise with the crème fraîche and crushed garlic and keep to one side.

5. **Finish the soup** When the soup has been cooking for 25 minutes, add the cod, season to taste and simmer for 3 minutes.

6. Meanwhile, fry the prawns in the butter for 3 minutes, or until cooked through.

7. Stir the prawns into the soup and serve the soup in bowls garnished with parsley, chives and dill, a dollop of the aïoli and plenty of pepper.

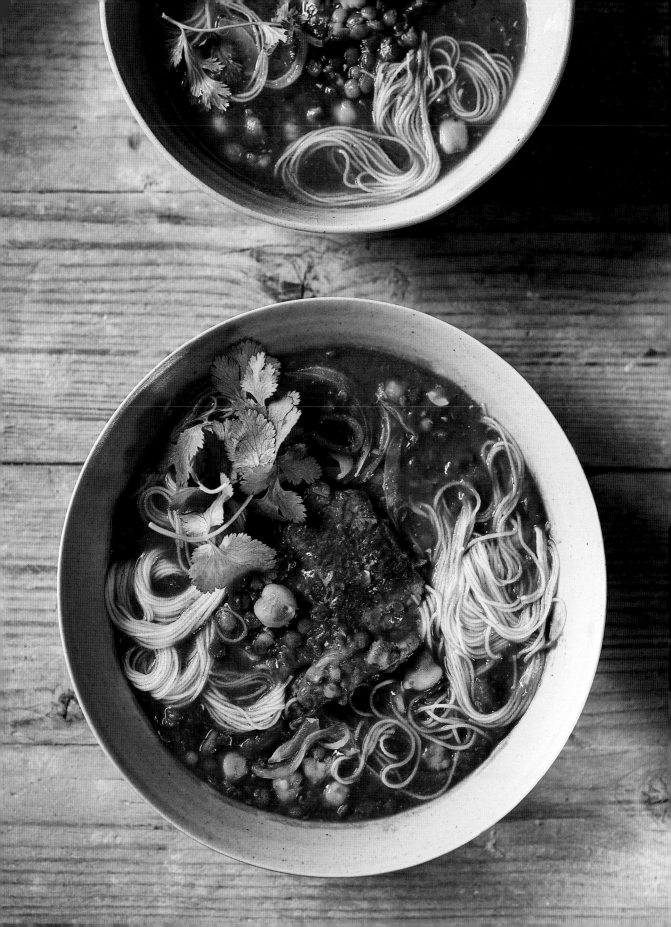

HARIRA LENTIL & LAMB SOUP

3 tbsp vegetable oil
1 onion, peeled and diced
500g spring lamb chops,
   fat removed
100g brown lentils
1 beef stock cube
good pinch of salt
½ tsp ground white pepper
½ tsp ground black pepper
good pinch of saffron
½ tsp ground ginger
1 bunch flat-leaf parsley,
   leaves roughly chopped
1 litre boiling water
1 x 400g tin chopped tomatoes
2 tbsp tomato purée
1 x 400g tin chickpeas
2 tbsp cornflour
85g vermicelli noodles
1 bunch coriander, leaves
   roughly chopped

1 . Heat the oil in a large pan over a medium heat and gently fry the onion for 10 minutes. Add the lamb chops, lentils, stock cube, salt, peppers, saffron, ground ginger and parsley and then pour in 600ml of the boiling water and cover with a lid. Leave to simmer over a low heat for 30 minutes.

2 . Remove the pan from the heat and add the tomatoes and tomato purée. Stir in the chickpeas and another 400ml of water and leave to simmer gently for a further 30 minutes.

3 . Finally, whisk a little of the sauce with the cornflour to form a paste and whisk this into the pan. Add the vermicelli noodles and leave to cook for a further 15 minutes.

4 . Stir in the fresh coriander and serve.

HAM, EGG & CHIPS

MAKES 12

6–8 slices Parma ham
1 tbsp vegetable oil
12 quail's eggs

For the mayonnaise
1 egg yolk
1 tsp white wine vinegar
1 tsp Dijon mustard
75ml sunflower oil
75ml rapeseed oil
1 small bunch fresh
   chives, snipped
fresh lemon juice, to taste
salt and pepper

For the fries
4 large Maris Piper potatoes,
   peeled
a few fresh thyme sprigs,
   leaves picked and chopped
1.5 litre vegetable oil, for
   deep-frying

1. Preheat the oven to 200°C/Fan 180°C.

2. Make the mayonnaise Whisk the egg yolk, vinegar and mustard with some seasoning, and then very gradually adding in the oils, whisking slowly all the time. When emulsified and thickened, add the chopped chives and lemon juice to taste.

3. Make ham cups Tear the ham a little and use to line a 12-hole mini muffin tin so it forms little cups. Cook in the oven for 12–15 minutes or until they are crispy but not too dark. Cool in the tins and then remove and put on a wire rack.

4. Make the chips Slice the potatoes with the julienne attachment of a mandolin and put into a bowl of salted water.

5. Heat the oil in a deep pan to 180°C, or until a cube of bread browns in 20 seconds.

6. Drain the chips and pat dry on kitchen paper. Deep-fry in batches for 2–3 minutes in the hot oil, or until golden and really crisp. Drain on kitchen paper. Mix the thyme with some salt and sprinkle over the fries.

7. Meanwhile, heat the oil in a large non-stick pan and fry the quail's eggs until just cooked.

8. To assemble, spoon a dollop of mayo into the base of each ham cup. Top with some fries and a fried egg and serve immediately.

> **TIP** Keep any leftover mayonnaise in the fridge for another day. Make sure you use it within a week.

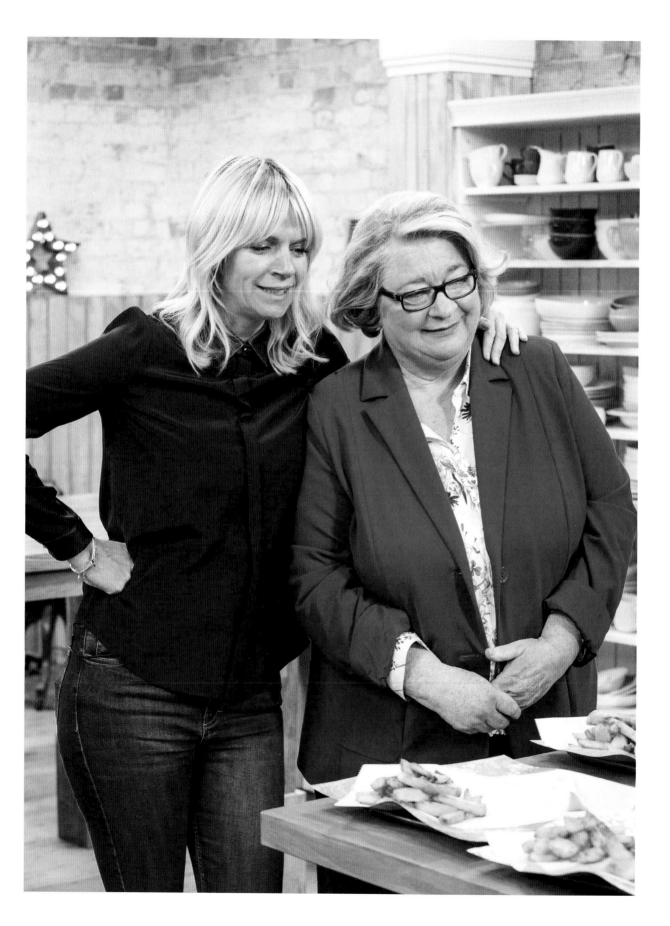

BAKED BEANS & BUBBLE & SQUEAK HASH BROWNS

SERVES 4

For the hash browns
600g floury potatoes
2–3 tbsp double cream
200g pancetta, cubed
1 large bunch thyme
30g unsalted butter
300g Savoy cabbage,
    finely shredded
1 large bunch flat-leaf
    parsley, choppped
3–4 fresh oregano sprigs,
    leaves picked
1 tbsp wholegrain mustard
2 tbsp sunflower oil
salt and pepper

For the beans
2 tbsp unsalted butter
1 tbsp sunflower oil
400g smoked pancetta, cubed
10 fresh thyme sprigs
2 fresh bay leaves
3 fresh rosemary sprigs
1 large white onion, peeled
    and finely chopped
1 carrot, peeled and finely chopped
2 celery sticks, finely chopped
30g dried porcini, soaked in
    boiling water
3 garlic cloves, peeled and crushed
1 cinnamon stick
300ml red wine
2 tbsp tomato purée
50g light brown sugar
500ml fresh beef stock
200ml passata
1 tbsp smoked paprika
1 x 400g tin pinto beans
1 x 400g tin haricot beans
a large handful of flat-leaf
    parsley, chopped
3 fresh oregano sprigs,
    leaves picked

1. **Prepare the hash browns** Bring a large pan of water to the boil and cook the potatoes for 15–20 minutes, or until tender. Drain and roughly mash with the cream, season then set aside to cool.

2. Fry the pancetta and thyme in the butter until the pancetta is crispy. Remove with a slotted spoon and add to the mash. Using the same unwashed pan, add the cabbage and a splash of water, cover and cook for 2–3 minutes, or until the cabbage is just tender. Scoop out with a slotted spoon and add to the mash. Mix everything together with the herbs and mustard and season well. Cool completely and then chill.

3. **Make the beans** Melt the butter and oil in a large pan over a medium heat and fry the pancetta and the thyme, bay leaves and rosemary until the pancetta is brown and starting to crisp. Remove with a slotted spoon.

4. Add the onion, carrot and celery to the pan with the pancetta fat and fry for 10 minutes, or until softened.

5. Drain the porcini and finely chop them. Add to the pan with the garlic and cinnamon stick and fry for 1 minute. Pour in the red wine and bubble to reduce by half.

6. Add the tomato purée, sugar, stock and passata, bring to the boil and cook until reduced by approximately half.

7. Stir in the paprika and the drained beans and heat through.

8. **Make the hash browns** Divide the mixture into 8 and shape each one into a cake. Heat the oil in a pan over a high heat and fry the hash browns for 2–3 minutes on each side, or until golden and piping hot.

9. Stir the fresh herbs through the beans and check the seasoning before serving with the hash browns.

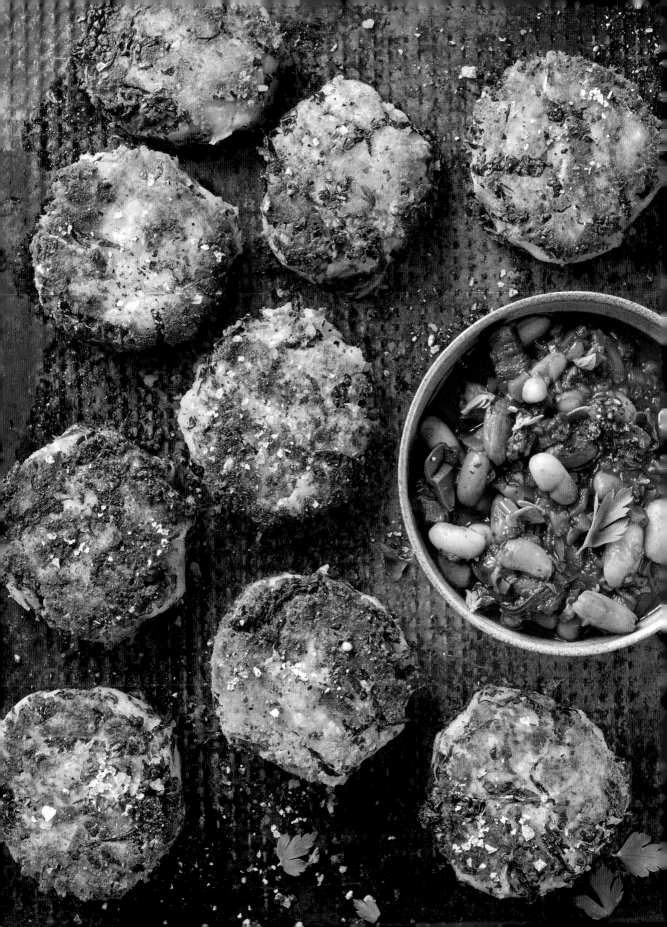

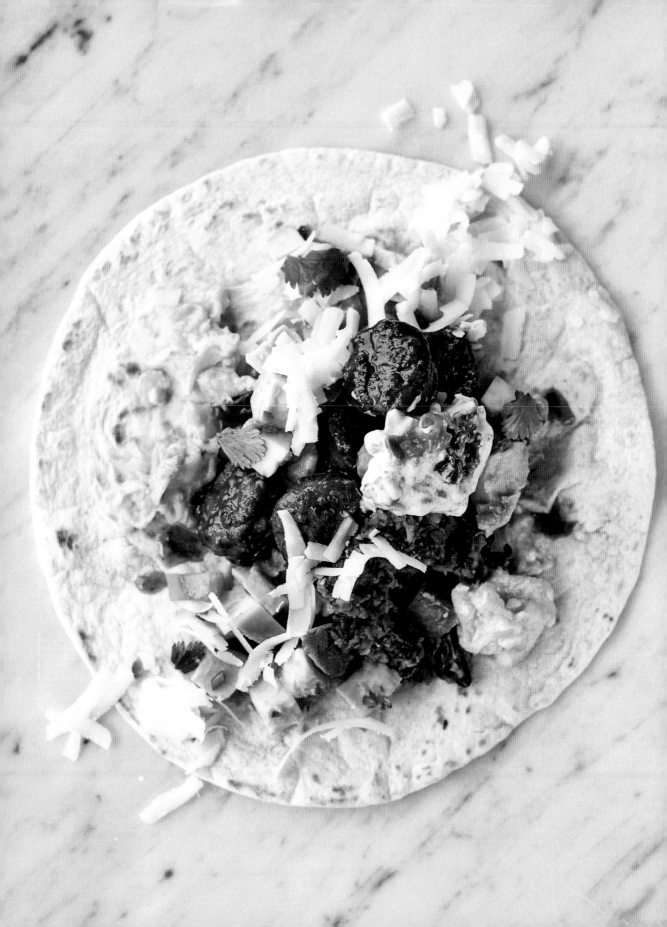

Buy ready-made refried beans and guacamole and skip steps 1, 2 and 4

BRUNCH BURRITOS

SERVES 4–6

For the refried beans
100g dried black beans,
    washed and soaked
    overnight in cold water
1 onion, peeled and halved
1 dried ancho chilli
2 garlic cloves, peeled
    and chopped
3 tbsp lard
salt and pepper

For the sour cream sauce
2 sun-dried tomatoes,
    finely chopped
1 jalapeño, finely chopped
100g sour cream

For the guacamole
1½ large avocados, peeled
    and diced
1 large hot red chilli,
    finely diced
2 tsp freshly chopped coriander
juice of ½ lime
1 tsp olive oil

For the chorizo filling
½ tbsp olive oil
200g spicy cooking chorizo,
    sliced
5 chestnut mushrooms,
    chopped
2–3 tbsp chipotle sauce

For the scrambled eggs
40g butter
4 large eggs

To assemble
60g strong Cheddar, grated
2 large tomatoes, chopped and
    drained of excess liquid
4–6 large flour tortillas

1 . Make the refried beans Drain the beans, put them in a pan and cover with water. Add the halved onion and dried ancho chilli and simmer for 45–50 minutes, or until tender. Alternatively, use a pressure cooker and leave to cook for 20 minutes.

2 . Drain the cooked beans, reserving the liquid, and mash in the pan with the garlic. Melt the lard in a large frying pan over a medium heat and fry the beans for 4–5 minutes. Mix some of the reserved cooking liquid into the beans until it reaches a thick spreadable consistency. Season to taste.

3 . Make the sour cream sauce Combine the sun-dried tomatoes and jalapeño with the sour cream in a bowl and mix into a paste.

4 . Make the guacamole Measure all the ingredients into a bowl and mix well.

5 . Make the chorizo filling Heat the oil in a frying pan over a high heat and fry the chorizo for 2–3 minutes. Add the mushrooms and continue to fry until both are cooked through. Add enough chipotle paste to cover the ingredients.

6 . Make the scrambled eggs Just before serving, melt the butter in a small pan over a medium heat. Crack in the eggs and stir continuously. After 1–2 minutes, when the eggs are still slightly runny, remove from the heat. Season with salt and pepper and then transfer to a serving dish to finish cooking in their own heat.

7 . Serve the chorizo alongside the scrambled eggs, refried beans, sour cream sauce, guacamole, Cheddar, tomatoes and tortillas and let everyone build their own burrito.

BRUNCH, LUNCH AND SNACKS

FRESH BREAD ROLLS &
HOME-MADE BUTTER

MAKES 8

For the bread rolls
500g strong white bread flour
50g butter
10g sugar
10g salt
150ml milk
1 tbsp vegetable oil
1 x 7g sachet fast-action yeast

For the home-made butter
300ml double cream
salt flakes, to taste

1 . Make the bread rolls Combine all the ingredients in a bowl with 150ml water (making sure the salt and yeast do not come together before mixing) to form a dough.

2 . Knead for 10 minutes and then leave to rest for 45–60 minutes, or until the dough has doubled in size.

3 . Knock back the dough and divide into 8 pieces. On a lightly floured surface, roll each piece into a long sausage shape. Take the ends and knot them together and then tuck the ends under to form a pretty knot shape. Put onto a lightly greased baking sheet, cover with oiled clingfilm and leave to prove for 45 minutes.

4 . Preheat the oven to 220°C/Fan 200°C.

5 . Bake the rolls for 5 minutes and then turn the heat down to 190°C/Fan 170°C and bake for a further 20–25 minutes, or until golden and sounding hollow when tapped. Leave to cool on a wire rack.

6 . Make the butter Whizz the cream in a food-processor until it forms curds and whey; this will only take 2–3 minutes – you will see the solids come together and the water separate from the curds. Remove the curds and squeeze out the excess fluid using a muslin cloth.

7 . Mix salt flakes into the solid butter to taste and then place in the fridge to chill.

8 . Serve the bread warm with the salty butter.

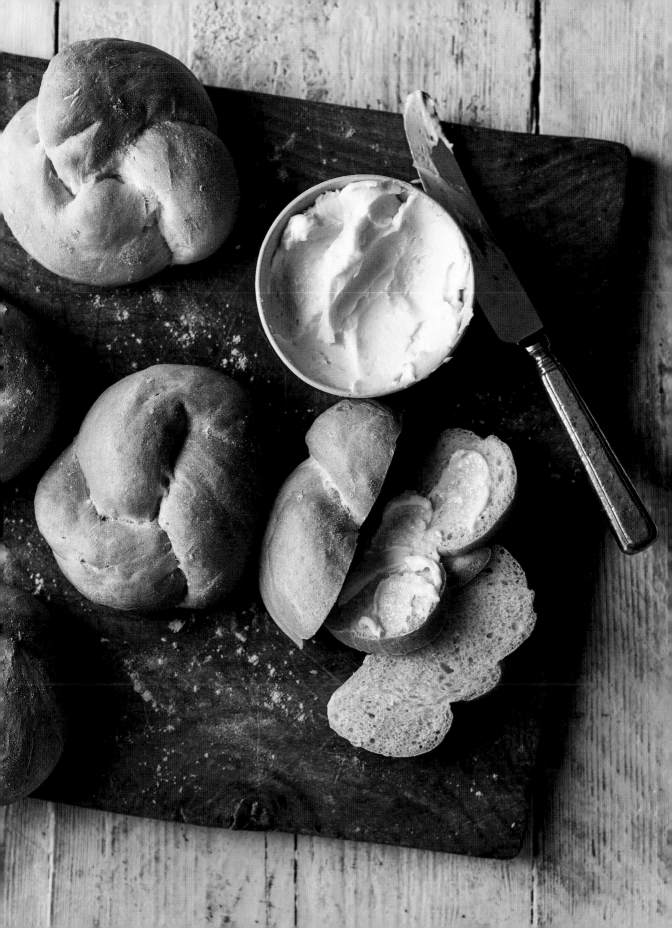

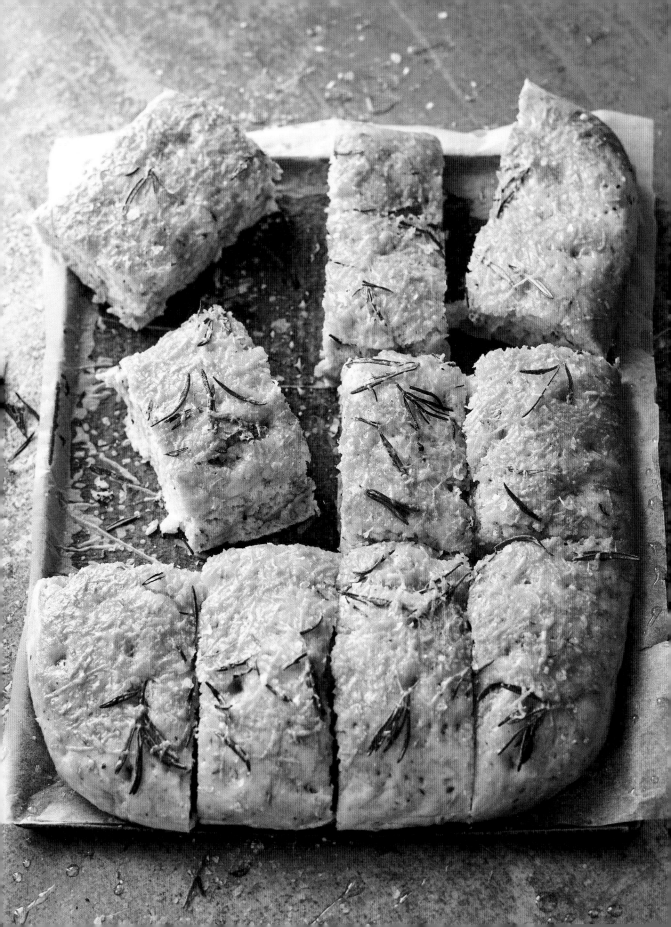

ROSEMARY & SEA SALT FOCACCIA

MAKES 1 LOAF

1 x 7g sachet fast-action yeast
250ml warm water
300g plain flour
1 tsp fine salt
1 tsp caster sugar
1 tsp dried oregano
½ tsp dried thyme
½ tsp dried basil
¼ tsp freshly ground
    black pepper
1 tbsp vegetable oil
2 tbsp olive oil
50g Parmesan, grated
a small handful of fresh
    rosemary leaves
sea salt

1. Mix the yeast and 50ml of the warm water in a small bowl. Let it stand for 10 minutes until it bubbles.

2. Measure the flour, salt, sugar, oregano, thyme, basil and black pepper into a large bowl and stir well.

3. Add the yeast mixture and the vegetable oil to the dry ingredients, along with the remainder of the warm water, and combine with your hands to a soft, slightly wet dough.

4. When the dough has pulled together, turn out onto a lightly floured surface and knead until smooth and elastic – you will need to stretch the dough and fold it as it will be quite sticky. Don't add any more flour.

5. Lightly oil a large bowl, place the dough inside and cover with a damp cloth. Leave to rise in a warm place for 30–45 minutes.

6. Punch down the dough and place on a greased baking sheet. Pat into a 1.25cm-thick rectangle and leave in a warm place to prove for a further 30 minutes, covered with lightly greased clingfilm.

7. Preheat the oven to 230°C/Fan 210°C.

8. Using your fingers, make indentations in the dough about 2.5cm apart. Drizzle with the olive oil and then sprinkle with the Parmesan, rosemary needles and sea salt.

9. Bake for 15–25 minutes, or until golden brown. Cool a little then serve.

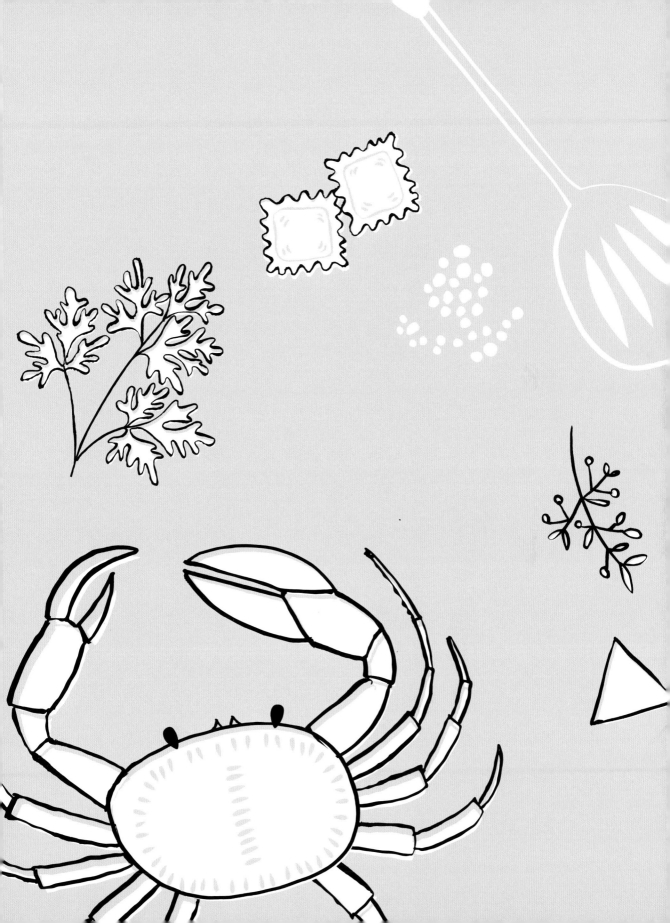

CHAPTER TWO

FISH

SIMPLE RECIPE IDEAS

For a **one-pot pasta**, bring a large pot of salted water to the boil and cook **dried pasta** until al dente. Scoop out a mug of the cooking water, and then drain the pasta and return it to the pan. Add some **crème fraîche**, a squeeze of **lemon juice**, sliced strips of **smoked salmon**, **peas** and combine until the pasta is evenly coated. Season with **salt** and **pepper** and add a tiny splash of the cooking water. Place the pan back over a low heat and stir to amalgamate.

A **niçoise-inspired salad** can make a satisfying pitta bread filling. Top and tail **green beans** and cut into 1cm pieces. Bring a pan of water to the boil and then blanch the beans until just cooked. Drain and leave to cool. Mix with diced **cucumber**, **tomatoes**, quartered **black olives** and drained **tinned tuna**. Make a dressing by mixing together **olive oil**, **red wine vinegar**, **wholegrain mustard** and **salt and pepper** and then stir through the salad, before carefully folding in quartered hard-boiled **eggs**. Toast some **pitta bread** and slice open carefully so you are left with an open pocket. Fill with the salad and serve.

> **FAMILY TIP** 'Eating as a family brings us together and helps us celebrate the simple things in life: good food, good chat and good company!'

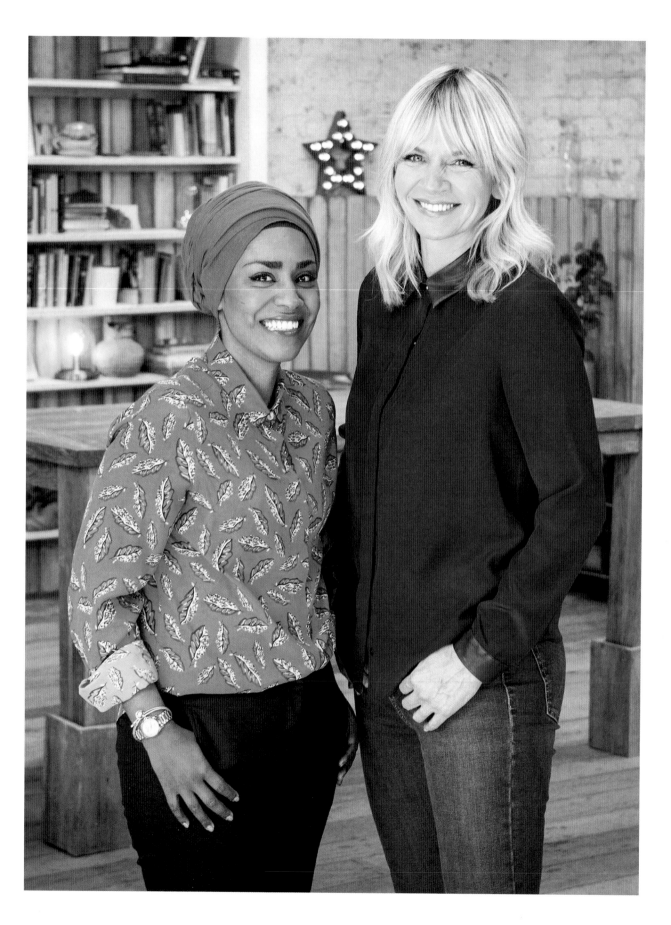

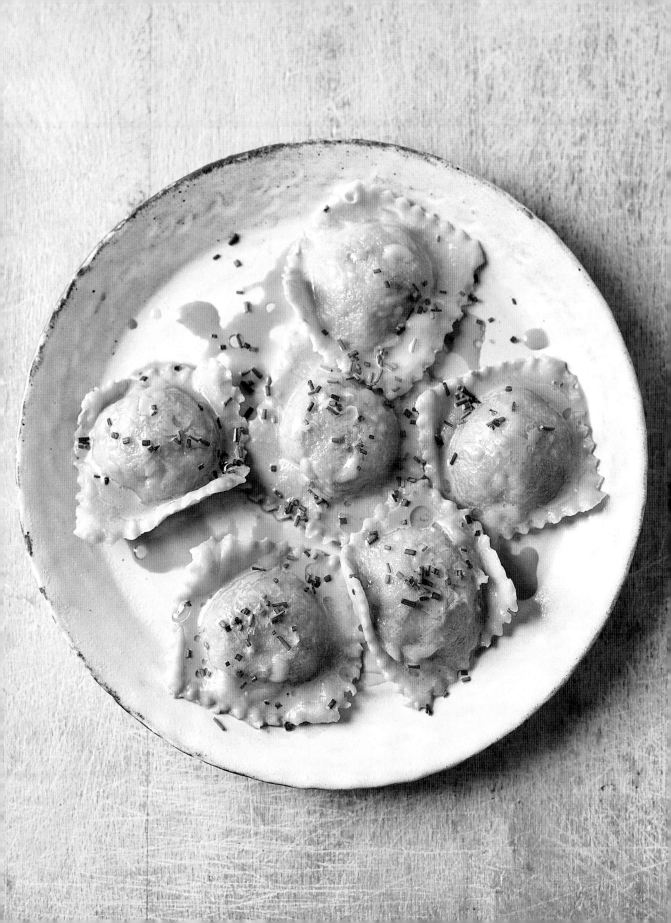

CRAB & PRAWN RAVIOLI WITH SEAFOOD BISQUE

SERVES 4 AS A STARTER

1 egg, beaten
finely snipped chives,
    to garnish
extra-virgin olive oil,
    to garnish
salt and pepper

For the pasta
450g Italian '00' flour
3 large eggs plus 2 yolks,
    whisked
finely grated zest of 1 lemon
pinch of fine salt
semolina flour, for dusting

For the filling
150g fresh prawns with shells
1 tbsp olive oil
squeeze of fresh lemon juice
150g white crab meat
50g brown crab meat
1 egg white
1 tbsp finely snipped chives

For the sauce
1 tbsp vegetable oil
reserved prawn shells
    from filling
1 small onion, peeled and
    roughly chopped
1 garlic clove, peeled and
    crushed
3 tbsp brandy
2 tomatoes, chopped
1 bay leaf
1 tbsp tomato purée
1 star anise
300ml shellfish (or fish) stock
125ml double cream

1 . **Make the pasta** Measure the flour into a large bowl and make a well in the centre. Stir in the whisked eggs, lemon zest and salt, and gradually combine together and work into a dough. Knead for 10 minutes and then wrap in clingfilm and chill for 30 minutes, or until ready to roll.

2 . **Make the filling** Fry the prawns in the olive oil, salt, pepper and lemon juice in a pan over a medium heat.

3 . Remove the prawns from their shells (reserve the shells), place them in a food-processor with the crab meat and whizz until smooth.

4 . Add the egg white, lemon juice, salt and pepper to the food-processor and whizz again until just mixed.

5 . Stir in the chives, cover and set aside.

6 . **Make the sauce** Heat the oil in a heavy pan and fry the reserved prawn shells with the onion until the onion starts to brown.

7 . Add the garlic and cook for another 30 seconds.

8 . Add the brandy, tomatoes, bay leaf, tomato purée and star anise, and stir well.

9 . Finally, stir in the stock and simmer over a medium heat for 20 minutes.

10 . Strain the sauce using a funnel and muslin cloth and then return to the pan.

11 . Stir in the cream and place over a medium heat to reduce until it has the consistency of single cream. Season to taste.

Recipe continues

12 . **Make the ravioli** Cut the pasta into 4 pieces and roll each piece using a pasta machine, working it through the settings until it is on the thinnest setting.

13 . Sprinkle semolina flour onto a work surface and lay a sheet of the pasta on top. Spoon tablespoons of the filling up the centre of the pasta, leaving a 4cm gap between each spoonful. Brush around the filling with beaten egg, lay a second sheet of pasta over the top and seal each one by cupping and expelling any air. Then use a cutter to cut out the individual ravioli. Repeat with the last two sheets of pasta until you have 12–16 individual ravioli.

14 . Bring a large pan of water to the boil and cook the ravioli for 3–4 minutes.

15 . Transfer to the pan of bisque to coat and then plate up, spooning over the sauce and garnishing with chives and a small drizzle of extra-virgin olive oil.

FAMILY TIP 'Make sure you've got a well-worked, smooth dough so that when you pass it through the pasta machine it'll be a breeze.'

SCALLOPS WITH LEMON & PARSLEY BUTTER & CAPERS

SERVES 4 AS A STARTER

zest and juice of 1 lemon
a small handful of finely
    chopped flat-leaf parsley
75g unsalted butter
16 large, fresh, dry scallops
2 tsp vegetable oil
2 tbsp capers, rinsed
salt and pepper

1 : Combine the lemon zest in a bowl with the parsley and beat in the butter until thoroughly mixed.

2 : Season the scallops and coat in the oil.

3 : Heat a heavy-based pan over a very high heat. Just as it is beginning to smoke, sear the scallops for 30 seconds on each side until golden.

4 : Place four dots of the butter on each plate and sit a scallop on top of each one to melt it. Add the capers to the buttery juices and serve with a squeeze of lemon and crusty bread.

FISH

SEARED SCALLOPS ON A PEA & MINT PURÉE WITH PANCETTA CRUMBS

SERVES 4 AS A STARTER

200g thinly sliced pancetta
300g frozen petits pois
1–2 fresh mint sprigs,
   leaves picked
4 tbsp double cream
12 large scallops with roe
rapeseed oil, to coat
salt and pepper

1. Preheat the oven to 200°C/Fan 180°C.

2. Make the pancetta crumbs Place the pancetta on a lined baking sheet and crisp in the oven until golden. Remove and drain on kitchen paper. Once cool, break into crumbs.

3. Make the pea and mint purée Bring a small pan of water to the boil and cook the peas with a few mint leaves for 2–3 minutes. Drain and cool under cold running water.

4. Purée the peas and the mint leaves with the cream to thicken. Season with salt and pepper.

5. Cook the scallops Toss the scallops in rapeseed oil and place a griddle pan over a high heat. Chargrill for 30 seconds on each side.

6. Warm the pea purée through and season to taste.

7. Serve the scallops on a bed of pea purée, sprinkled with the pancetta crumbs.

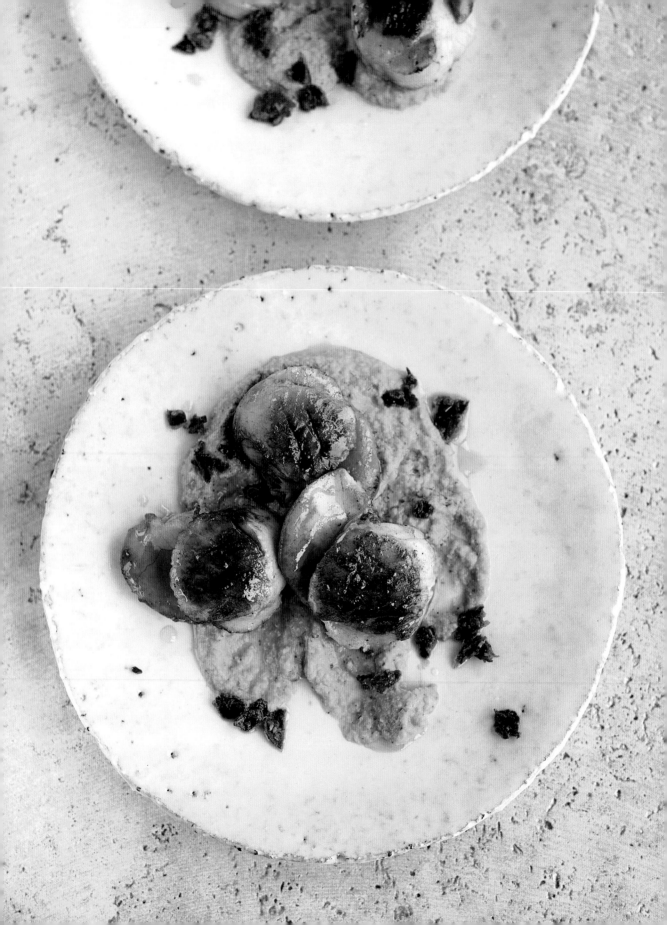

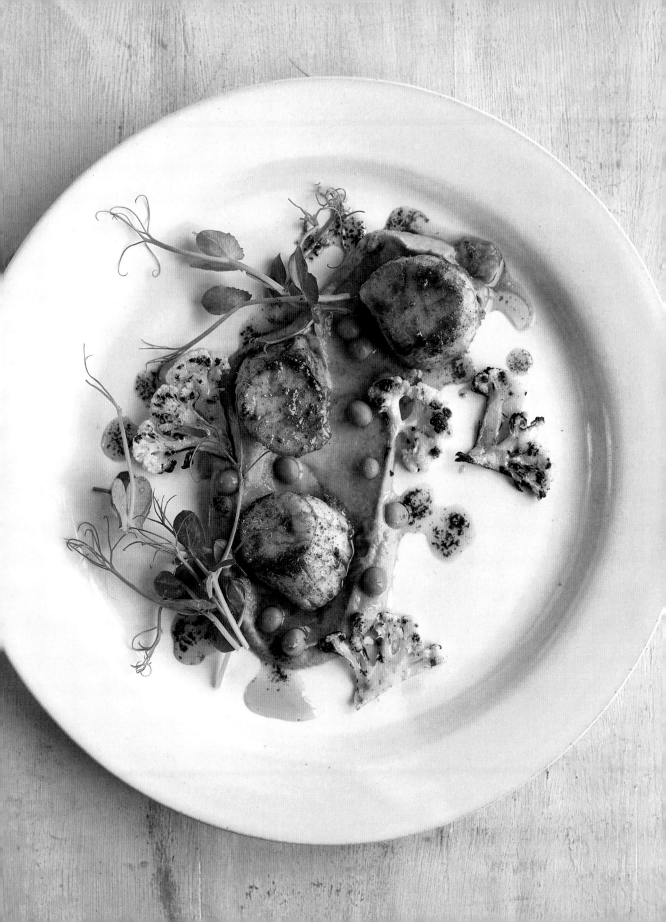

CURRIED SCALLOPS WITH CAULIFLOWER PURÉE

12 scallops (prepared,
    roe removed)
2 tbsp olive oil
1 tbsp tandoori masala
40g butter
100g fresh shelled peas
4 small handfuls of pea shoots
squeeze of fresh lemon juice
extra-virgin olive oil, to serve

For the cauliflower
1 tbsp vegetable oil
3 onions, peeled and chopped
4cm piece fresh root ginger,
    peeled and grated
1 tsp turmeric
2 tsp ground ginger
2 tsp ground coriander
1 tsp chilli powder
1 tsp cumin seeds
1 large cauliflower, cut
    into florets
200ml double cream
50g butter
squeeze of fresh lemon juice
olive oil, for brushing
salt and pepper

1 Make the cauliflower purée Heat the oil in a pan over a medium heat and fry the onions for 10 minutes, or until softened. Add the ginger and spices and cook for a further 2 minutes. Add all but a few florets of the cauliflower and a small amount of water, cover and cook until the cauliflower is tender.

2 Tip everything into a food-processor with the cream, butter and lemon juice and whizz. Pass through a fine sieve and then spoon back into the pan. Season to taste and keep warm.

3 Make the charred cauliflower Slice the reserved cauliflower florets and brush with oil and seasoning. Char in a griddle pan over a high heat and then set aside and keep warm.

4 Cook the scallops Marinate the scallops in a little of the olive oil and the tandoori masala for at least 10 minutes.

5 Heat the remaining oil in a pan over a high heat and fry the scallops for 20–30 seconds on each side to brown before adding the butter, basting, and then removing from the heat.

6 Meanwhile, bring a pan of water to the boil, cook the peas for 1 minute, then drain.

7 When the scallops are cooked, place a dollop of the purée on each plate and top with the scallops. Place the charred cauliflower alongside and dot with peas and pea shoots. Add a squeeze of lemon juice and drizzle with extra-virgin olive oil to serve.

RED PRAWN CURRY

2 tbsp vegetable oil
1 garlic clove, peeled and
   chopped
2 tbsp Red Curry Paste
   (see page 278 or use
   shop-bought)
2 kaffir lime leaves
400ml coconut milk
2 tbsp fish sauce
1 tbsp palm sugar
400g raw king prawns,
   deveined
a handful of sweet Thai basil
   leaves, or ordinary basil
a small handful of fresh
   coriander, roughly chopped

1 . Heat the oil in a large non-stick pan over a medium heat. Add the garlic and curry paste, as well as the kaffir lime leaves, and fry for 1 minute.

2 . Stir in coconut milk and cook for 5 minutes. Season with fish sauce and palm sugar and stir well. Add 50ml water and cook for a further 5 minutes.

3 . Stir in the prawns and cook for 3–5 minutes, or until cooked through.

4 . Finally, add half the basil leaves and serve over jasmine rice, sprinkled with the remaining basil leaves and the coriander.

TIP Serve with Aubergines with Chilli (Ca Tim Nuong) on page 192.

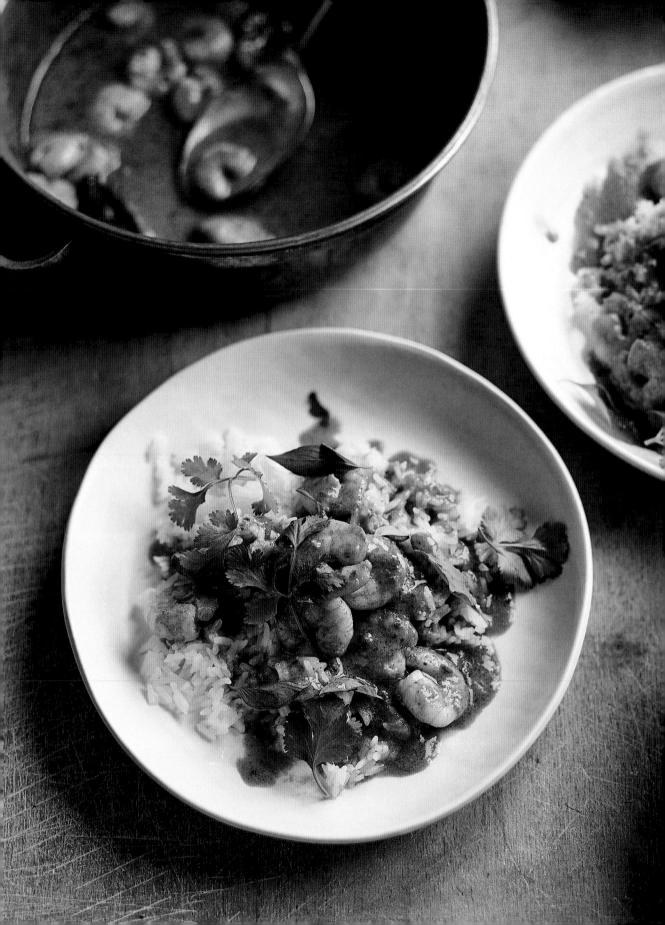

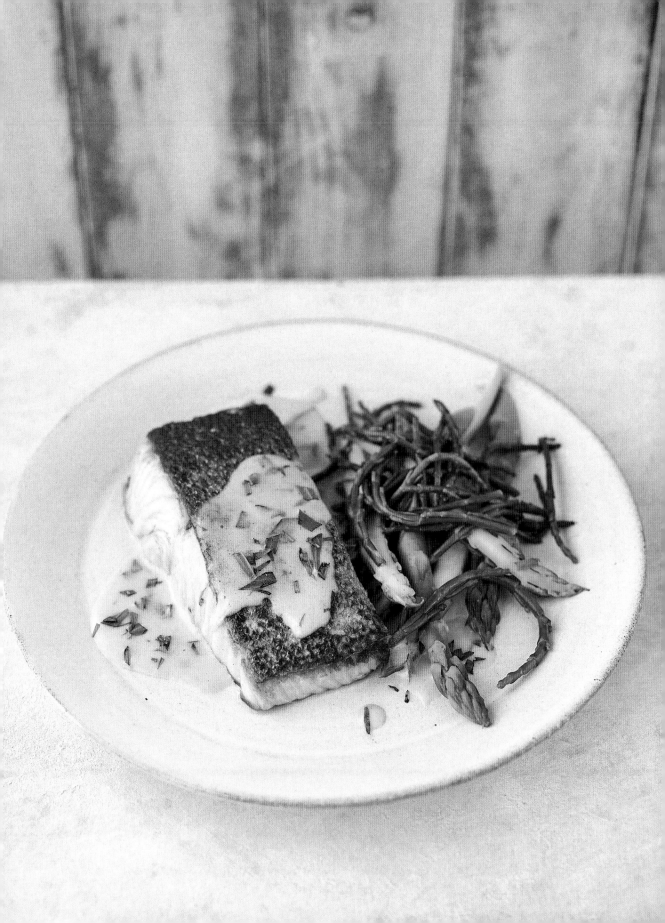

Use shop-bought hollandaise, add chopped fresh tarragon and skip steps 1 and 2

SALMON WITH TARRAGON HOLLANDAISE

SERVES 4

1 tbsp white wine vinegar
1 bunch tarragon, leaves finely chopped, stalks reserved
4 black peppercorns
2 egg yolks
110g unsalted butter
juice of 1 lemon (to taste)
250g asparagus
100g samphire
4 salmon fillets, skin on
1 tbsp olive oil
salt and pepper

1. **Make the tarragon hollandaise** Heat the white wine vinegar and 1 tablespoon of water with the stalks from the tarragon and the peppercorns in a small pan, and reduce to 1 tablespoon. Remove the stalks and peppercorns from the pan and discard.

2. Whisk the egg yolks in a bowl with an electric whisk. Slowly, while whisking, pour in the hot vinegar. When it has all been incorporated, use the now-empty pan to melt the butter. When it starts frothing, pour it very slowly into the egg mixture, whisking all the time. Mix in lemon juice to taste, and the chopped tarragon leaves, and season with salt and pepper.

3. **Cook the asparagus and samphire** Bring a large pan of water to the boil over a high heat. Add the asparagus, boil for 1 minute, and then add the samphire. Boil for 1 minute more. Drain and drizzle with some of the remaining lemon juice, and season with salt and pepper.

4. **Cook the salmon** Pat the salmon fillets dry with kitchen paper. Heat the oil in a large frying pan over a high heat. Put the fillets in the pan, skin side down, and immediately turn the heat down low. Use a fish spatula to press down on the fillets for the first minute so the skin doesn't curl up. Cook for 3–4 minutes, then flip over and cook on the other side for about 1 minute, until the salmon is just cooked.

5. Serve the salmon with the warm asparagus and samphire and the tarragon hollandaise.

SEA BASS BAKED IN SALT

SERVES 2-4

1–1.5kg whole sea bass,
    gutted with fins and
    scales removed
1.5kg coarse sea salt
2 large egg whites
1 lemon, sliced
1 bunch thyme
pepper
½ lemon, to serve
1 bunch parsley, to serve

1. Preheat the oven to 220°C/Fan 200°C and line
a baking sheet, large enough to hold the whole fish,
with greaseproof paper.

2. In a large bowl, mix the salt and egg whites together.
Spread half the salt mixture onto the lined baking sheet
to allow the fish to be placed on top. Fill the fish cavity with
the lemon slices and the thyme and season with the pepper.
Place the fish on the salt mixture on the baking sheet and
cover with the remaining salt, ensuring the fish is totally
sealed in the salt mixture.

3. Place in the oven and cook for approximately 8 minutes,
to crust the salt, and then turn the oven down to 190°C/
Fan 170°C.

4. Continue to cook for a further 25–30 minutes, or
until the salt around the fish is hard and starting to turn
golden. To test the fish is cooked, insert a skewer into the
thickest part of the fish and test on your upper lip. If
the skewer is hot, the fish is cooked.

5. Lift the greaseproof paper with the fish off the baking
sheet straight onto a serving plate. Garnish with half
a lemon and a bunch of parsley placed by the tail.

TIP Serve with new potatoes, spinach,
Green Beans and Almonds (see page 256)
and Hollandaise Sauce (see page 280).

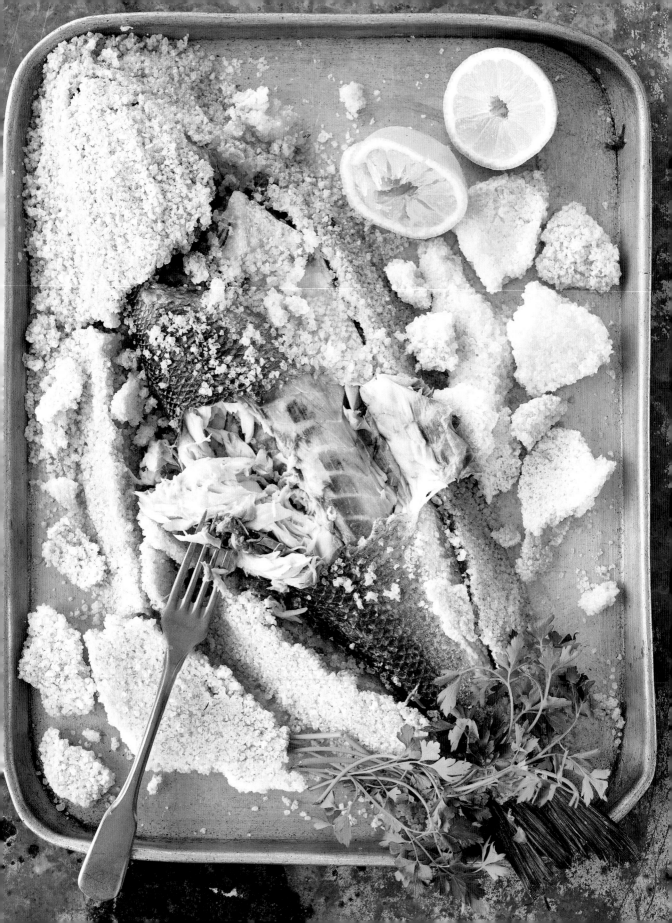

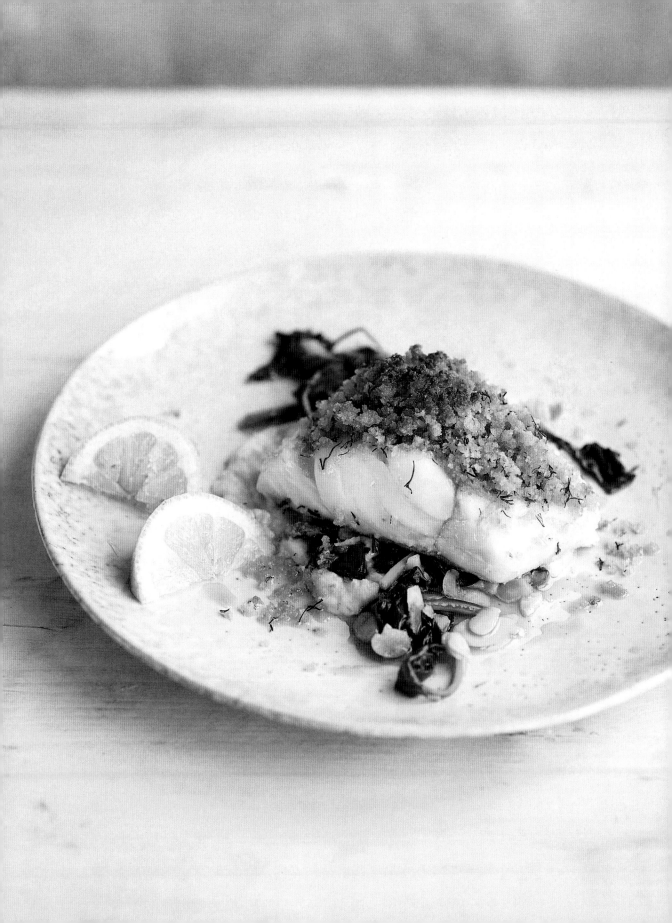

HERB CRUSTED COD WITH ARTICHOKE & SPINACH

SERVES 4

4 x 200g cod loin fillets
125g butter
100g panko breadcrumbs
1 small bunch dill,
    finely snipped
1 onion, peeled and sliced
1 celery stick, sliced but leaves
    kept whole and to one side
1 litre whole milk
500ml fresh beef stock
600g Jerusalem artichokes,
    peeled and chopped
250g potatoes, peeled and
    chopped
200ml double cream
4 garlic cloves, peeled and
    diced
2 tbsp olive oil
600g spinach leaves
50g almonds, crushed
juice of 1 lemon
salt and pepper

1. **Brine the fish** Submerge the cod pieces in a bowl of water with 2 tablespoons of salt added and leave to brine for 20 minutes.

2. Remove the cod and pat dry with kitchen paper. Cover with clingfilm and set aside in the fridge.

3. **Make the breadcrumb topping** Melt 50g of the butter in a pan over a medium heat, add the breadcrumbs and fry for 1 minute, or until golden.

4. Remove from the heat and leave to cool, then stir through the dill and a good pinch of salt and set aside.

5. **Poach the fish** Place the sliced onion and celery in a large pan with a big pinch of sea salt and some freshly cracked black pepper. Add 600ml of the milk with 500ml of water and place over a low heat. Bring to 55°C and then add the fish. Keeping the temperature at 55°C, allow the fish to sit submerged for 30–40 minutes, or until just cooked. Add more milk if the fish is not completely covered.

6. **Make the Jerusalem artichoke mash** Meanwhile, reduce the beef stock in another pan over a medium heat until it has halved in volume.

7. Place the Jerusalem artichokes and potatoes in a pan with the cream, the remaining 400ml of milk, the reduced beef stock and a couple of pinches of salt. Simmer for 20 minutes, or until the vegetables are soft and breaking up.

8. Strain away most of the liquid (leaving 2 tablespoons in the pan with the vegetables) and add 50g of the butter and some salt, and mash with a ricer.

Recipe continues

9 . **Cook the spinach** Fry the garlic in the remainder of the butter and the olive oil for 1 minute. Add the spinach and cook for a further 3 minutes. Finally stir in the almonds.

10 . Preheat the grill to high.

11 . Remove the fish from the poaching milk and place on a baking sheet. Sprinkle the fish with the breadcrumb mixture and place under the grill for about 2 minutes, or until the topping goes crispy and brown.

12 . To serve, spoon a dollop of the Jerusalem artichoke and potato mash into the middle of the plate and press down into a rough circle. Top with some spinach and then place a piece of fish on top. Season with freshly ground black pepper, a pinch of sea salt and a dash of freshly squeezed lemon.

FAMILY TIP 'Our top tip for home cooking is to plan ahead and cook healthy, simple but delicious meals using seasonal ingredients and lots of fresh herbs.'

MOROCCAN-SPICED SALMON & RICE

SERVES 4

For the salmon
1 tsp paprika
½ tsp ground cumin
pinch of cayenne pepper
finely grated zest of 1 lemon,
    plus a squeeze of juice
2 tbsp olive oil
4 x 200g salmon fillets
a handful of freshly chopped
    flat-leaf parsley
salt and pepper

For the rice
3 tbsp sunflower oil
1 small onion, peeled and
    finely sliced
1 tsp cumin seeds
250g rice
1 small head broccoli,
    broken into florets

1 : Preheat the oven to 200°C/Fan 180°C.

2 : Marinate the fish Mix all the spices for the salmon with the lemon zest and oil and then coat the fish with the mixture and leave to marinate for 10–15 minutes.

3 : Cook the fish Place on a baking sheet, season and cook in the oven for 20 minutes.

4 : Make the rice Heat the oil in a pan over a medium heat and gently fry the onion and cumin seeds for 5 minutes.

5 : Add the rice and broccoli and stir to coat. Pour in 500ml water and season well. Cover and bring to the boil and simmer for 8 minutes.

6 : Remove from the heat and leave covered for a further 3–5 minutes to steam until the rice is cooked. Fluff up with a fork.

7 : Scatter the salmon with parsley and serve with the rice and a squeeze of lemon juice.

> **FAMILY TIP** 'This dish is simple, tasty and yet affordable.'

MASALA FISH & CHIPS WITH CORIANDER CHUTNEY

SERVES 4

sunflower oil, for deep-frying
squeeze of lemon juice

For the beer-battered fish
1 tsp turmeric
1 tsp ground cumin
1 tsp ground coriander
¼ tsp chilli powder
juice of 2 lemons
4 haddock fillets (about
    175g each), skinned
200g self-raising flour
65g gram/chickpea flour
¼ tsp carom seeds
1 tsp crushed peppercorns
300ml cold lager

For the chips
10 medium floury potatoes,
    peeled and sliced into
    thick chips
½ tsp ground cumin
¼ tsp chilli powder
½ tsp chaat masala

For the coriander chutney
1 large bunch coriander,
    roughly chopped
    (including stalks)
pinch of sea salt (to taste)
1 tsp caster sugar
juice of 1 lemon
1 tsp cumin seeds, dry roasted
4 garlic cloves, peeled
250g Greek yoghurt

1. **Make the chutney** Place the coriander, salt, sugar, lemon juice, cumin seeds and garlic in a food-processor and whizz. Add the yoghurt and whizz again until you have a smooth green sauce. Adjust the seasoning to taste.

2. **Prepare the chips** Place the potatoes in a pan of cold, salted water and bring to the boil. Simmer for 8–12 minutes, or until al-dente but firm. Drain and cool under cold running water. Drain again, place them on kitchen paper and pat dry.

3. **Marinate the fish** Combine the spices with the lemon juice in a bowl and add the fish. Leave to marinate for at least 5 minutes.

4. **Make the batter** Combine the flours in a clean bowl and add a pinch of salt and the carom seeds and pepper. Add the lager and whisk well until you have a smooth batter that will coat the fish quite thickly.

5. **Cook the chips** Heat a good depth of oil in a high-sided pan to 150°C. Par-fry the chips in the oil for 5–6 minutes, or until yellow tinged, and then remove with a slotted spoon. Increase the heat and, when the temperature of the oil reaches 180°C, re-fry the chips for 5 minutes, or until golden brown. Remove with a slotted spoon and sprinkle with the spices. Keep warm whilst you fry the fish.

6. **Cook the fish** Coat each piece of fish in batter and then deep-fry in the oil for 5–6 minutes, turning half way, or until golden brown. Drain on kitchen paper.

7. Serve the fish and chips with a squeeze of lemon and the coriander chutney.

> **TIP** Serve with Curried Mushy Peas
> (see page 257).

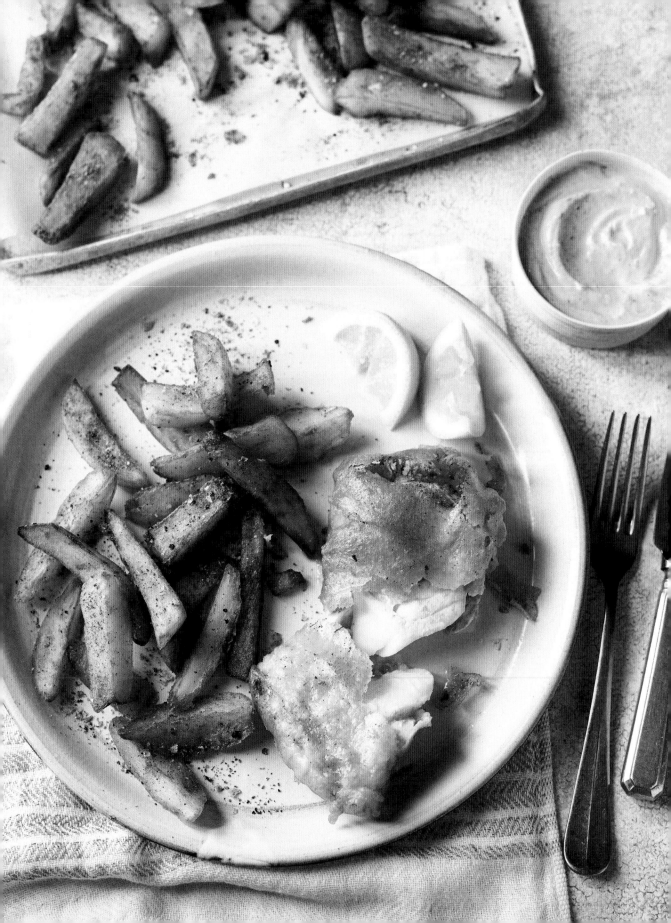

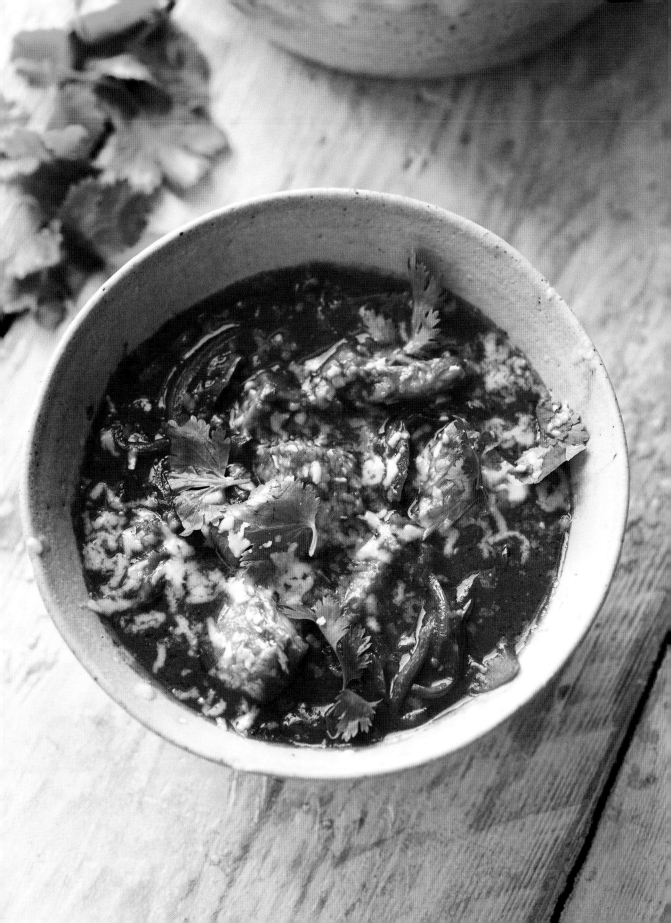

SALMON CURRY

3 tbsp sunflower oil

2 large onions, peeled and finely chopped

4 garlic cloves, peeled and crushed

4cm piece fresh root ginger, peeled and grated

1 tsp ground coriander

2 tsp garam masala

10 curry leaves

2–3 tbsp palm sugar

1 x 400g tin coconut milk

juice of 3 limes

5 vine-ripened tomatoes, whizzed in a food-processor

700g salmon fillet, skinless, cut into finger-length pieces about 2cm wide

3 tbsp grated creamed coconut, to garnish

a handful of freshly chopped coriander, to garnish

1 . Heat the oil in a pan over a low heat and fry the onions for 15 minutes, or until really soft and starting to turn golden. Add the garlic, ginger, ground spices and curry leaves and cook for 1 minute.

2 . Add the palm sugar, coconut milk, lime juice and vine-ripened tomatoes, and cook for 10–15 minutes, or until slightly reduced.

3 . Add the fish and gently poach for 5–6 minutes.

4 . Serve garnished with the creamed coconut and fresh coriander, alongside some steamed rice.

> **TIP** Serve with Yoghurt Curry & Fritters (see page 189), Roasted Aubergine (see page 185) and Missi Roti (see page 274).

ROSEMARY'S LUXURY FISH PIE

150g smoked haddock
500g white fish fillets
   (cod, haddock, sole)
100g unsalted butter
400ml whole milk
50g plain flour
75ml dry white wine
50ml double cream
1 tsp English mustard powder
100g smoked salmon, torn
200g raw king prawns,
   deveined
2 tbsp freshly chopped
   flat-leaf parsley
salt and pepper

For the topping
700g Maris Piper potatoes,
   peeled and quartered
40g unsalted butter
3 tbsp double cream
1 tbsp finely grated Parmesan
50g panko breadcrumbs

1. Preheat the oven to 180°C/Fan 160°C.

2. **Poach the fish** Place all the fish, except the smoked salmon and prawns, in a large ovenproof dish with half the butter, and pour over the milk. Bake for 8–10 minutes, or until the fish is just cooked – this is to release the juices.

3. Remove the fish with a slotted spoon, reserving the milk and butter, and leave until cool enough to handle. Once cooled, carefully remove the skin and any bones from the fish and flake into chunks into a large bowl.

4. **Make the sauce** Melt the remaining butter in a small pan and add the flour, cooking for 1 minute, being careful not to brown. Add the white wine and bubble away for 1 minute, stirring. Now slowly add the reserved milk and butter, stirring all the time, and continue cooking until it thickens. Add the cream and mustard powder and season well. Leave to cool a little.

5. Place the smoked salmon, prawns, parsley and cooked fish into a deep pie dish and pour over the sauce. Mix carefully, trying not to break the fish up too much. Ensure everything is well coated. Leave to cool completely.

6. **Make the topping** Bring a large pan of salted water to the boil and cook the potatoes for 15 minutes, or until tender. Drain well and mash, with a ricer if you have one.

7. Warm the butter and cream together in a small pan and add this to the potatoes, mashing until smooth. Mix in the Parmesan and season to taste.

8. **Cook the pie** Top the fish with the mashed potato and smooth with a fork. Sprinkle with the breadcrumbs and then bake for 30–40 minutes, or until the potato is golden and the pie is piping hot and bubbling.

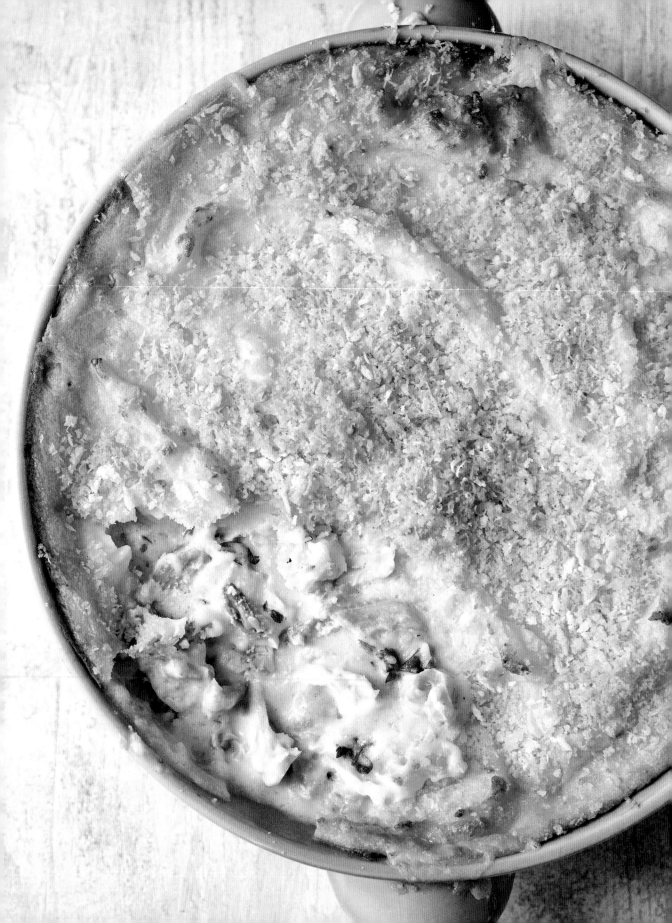

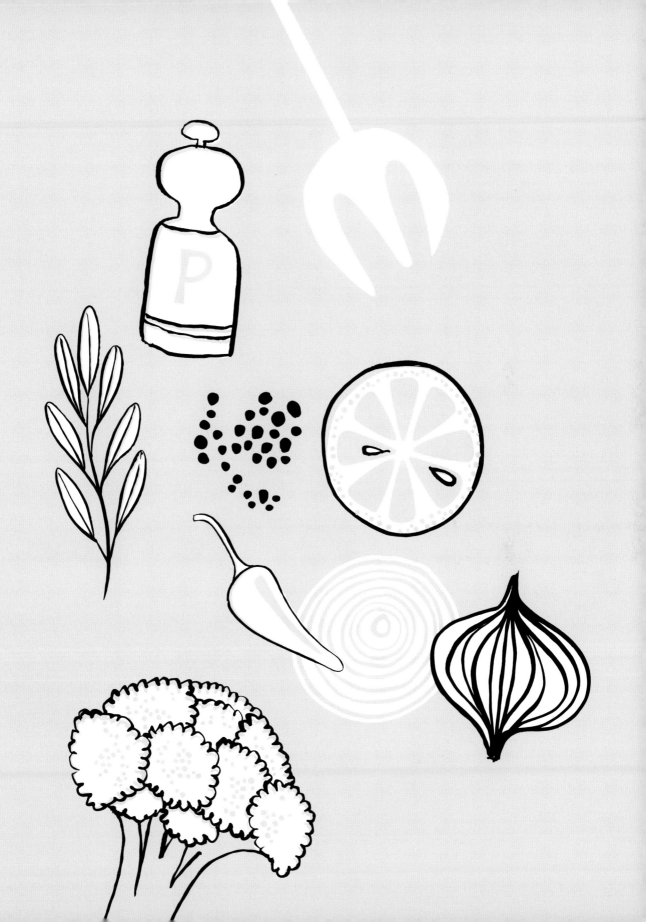

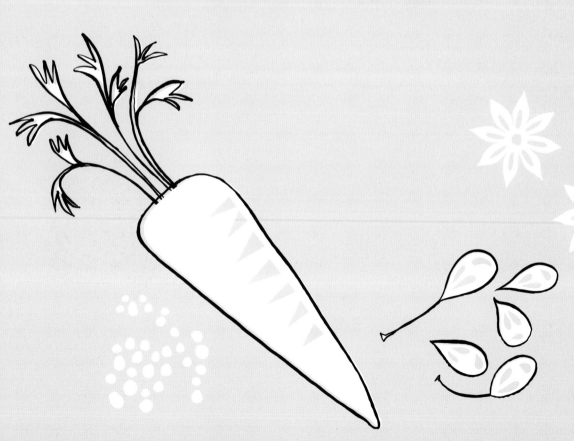

CHAPTER THREE

POULTRY

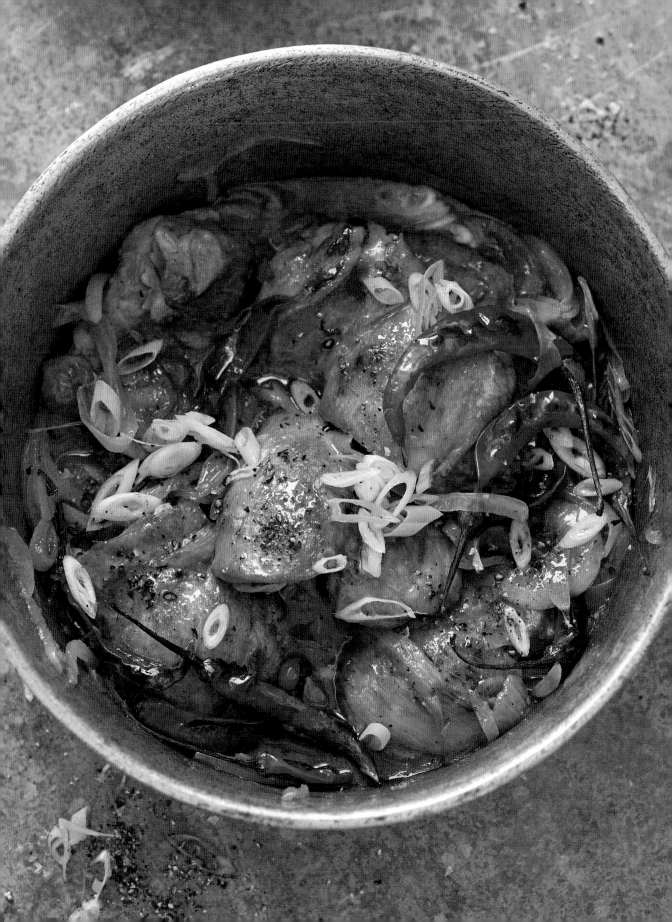

CHILLI CHICKEN

SERVES 4

4 tbsp vegetable oil
8–10 whole bird's-eye chillies
2 tbsp freshly grated root
    ginger
2 garlic cloves, peeled and
    finely chopped
2 onions, peeled and finely
    chopped
6 chicken thighs, boneless
    and skinless
2–3 tbsp dark soy sauce
2–3 tbsp white vinegar
pinch of salt
spring onions, finely sliced,
    to garnish

1 : Heat the oil in a large pan over a medium heat and add the chillies. Cover and cook for 3–4 minutes until they are blackened.

2 : Stir in the ginger, garlic and onions and cook uncovered for 10 minutes, or until really softened.

3 : Add the chicken and cook for 8–10 minutes, or until just cooked through.

4 : Stir in the soy sauce and white vinegar and a pinch of salt, if needed, and leave to bubble for 1 minute.

5 : Serve sprinkled with the spring onion.

FAMILY TIP 'There's nothing more satisfying than seeing someone eating and enjoying your food.'

BONELESS CHICKEN CURRY WITH RAITA

SERVES 4

5 tbsp vegetable oil
3 medium onions, peeled and
    finely chopped
1 garlic clove, peeled and
    finely sliced
5cm piece fresh root ginger,
    peeled and grated
1 medium tomato, chopped
1½ tsp each dried chilli flakes,
    turmeric, garam masala,
    ground ginger, garlic powder,
    ground cumin, ground
    coriander and dried
    fenugreek (methi) leaves
4 boneless skinless chicken
    breasts (about 125g each),
    cut into cubes
2 fresh green chillies
1 tbsp freshly chopped
    coriander
salt and pepper

For the raita
300g natural yoghurt
1 tsp cumin seeds
½ cucumber, peeled
    and grated

1. **Make the curry** Heat a little of the oil in a pan over a medium heat and fry the onions until medium brown. Add the garlic, ginger and tomato, and stir. Add the spices and season with salt before adding a splash of water. Cover with a lid and leave to cook for 20 minutes.

2. Take the pan off the heat and whizz with a hand blender to make a smooth masala paste.

3. Stir in the chicken pieces, pierce the green chillies and add these, too. If the sauce needs loosening, add a little more water. Return to the heat and cook for a further 15–20 minutes.

4. **Make the raita** Whisk the yoghurt with a fork to make a smooth paste. Dry fry the cumin seeds over a low heat and then add them to the yoghurt with the grated cucumber. Season to taste.

5. Garnish the chicken curry with coriander before serving with the raita and rice.

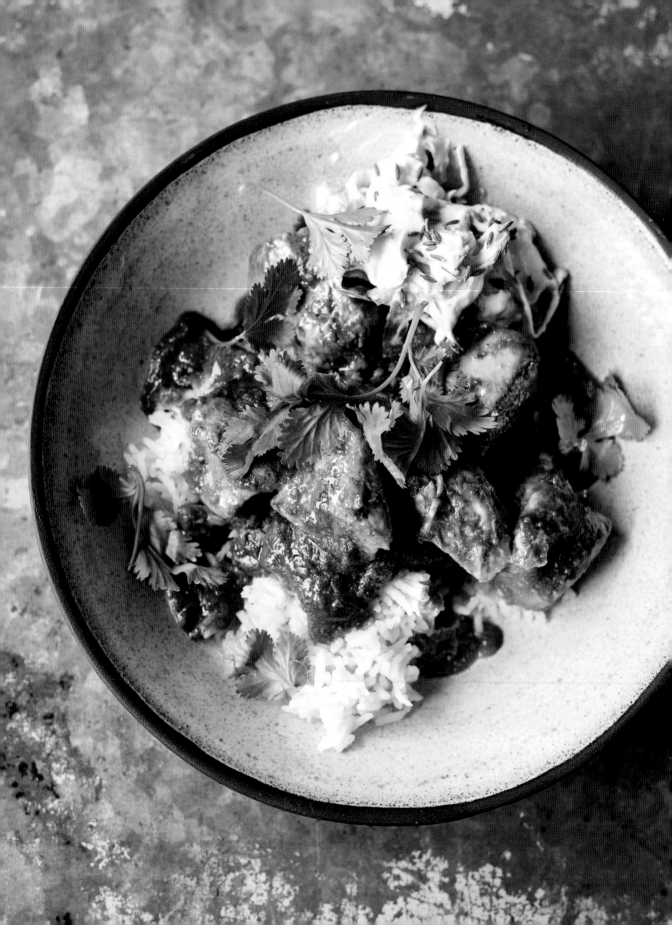

CHICKEN CACCIATORE WITH WHITE BEAN MASH & GARLIC GREEN BEANS

4 chicken legs (or 4 thighs
  and 4 drumsticks)
15g plain flour
2 tbsp olive oil
70g pancetta, diced
1 carrot, peeled and finely
  diced
1 onion, peeled and finely diced
1 celery stick, finely diced
2 garlic cloves, peeled and
  finely chopped
2 fresh rosemary sprigs
200g mixed wild mushrooms,
  sliced
200ml Chianti
2 tbsp tomato purée
400–500ml fresh chicken stock
2 dried chillies
1 tbsp baby capers
100g black olives, pitted
salt and pepper

For the white bean mash
60ml olive oil
2 garlic cloves, peeled
  and crushed
1 fresh rosemary sprig
grated zest of 1 lemon
2 x 400g tins white beans
  (butter, cannellini, haricot),
  drained and rinsed
extra-virgin olive oil, to drizzle

For the garlic green beans
300g green beans
30g butter
1 garlic clove, peeled and
  thinly sliced
pinch of dried chilli flakes

1. Preheat the oven to 200°C/Fan 180°C.

2. Make the cacciatore Season the chicken and dust with the flour. Heat the oil in a large flameproof casserole over a medium heat and colour the chicken on all sides. Remove from the pan and set aside.

3. Add the pancetta, carrot, onion, celery, garlic and rosemary to the pan. Gently fry, allowing the vegetables to soften in the fat released from the pancetta. Stir in the mushrooms and fry for a further 5 minutes, until brown and softened. Pour in the wine and bubble until reduced by two thirds.

4. Add the tomato purée and stock, then return the chicken to the pan, along with the dried chillies, capers and olives. Season and bring to the boil. Cover with a lid and transfer to the oven for 45–50 minutes. Remove the lid for last 10 minutes, if it is too saucy.

5. Make the white bean mash Put the olive oil in a pan over a low heat and add the garlic, rosemary and lemon zest and warm through gently for 2–3 minutes. Remove the rosemary and place on one side. Add the beans and warm through, stirring and squishing with a wide, flat spoon so that the beans become a nobbly mush. Season to taste.

6. Make the garlic green beans Bring a large pan of salted water to the boil and blanch the green beans for 3 minutes. Drain and steam dry. Melt the butter for the beans in a pan over a low heat and add the garlic. Tip in the green beans and toss together with salt and a pinch of chilli flakes.

7. Serve the chicken alongside the garlic green beans and the white bean mash garnished with the saved rosemary and drizzled with extra-virgin olive oil.

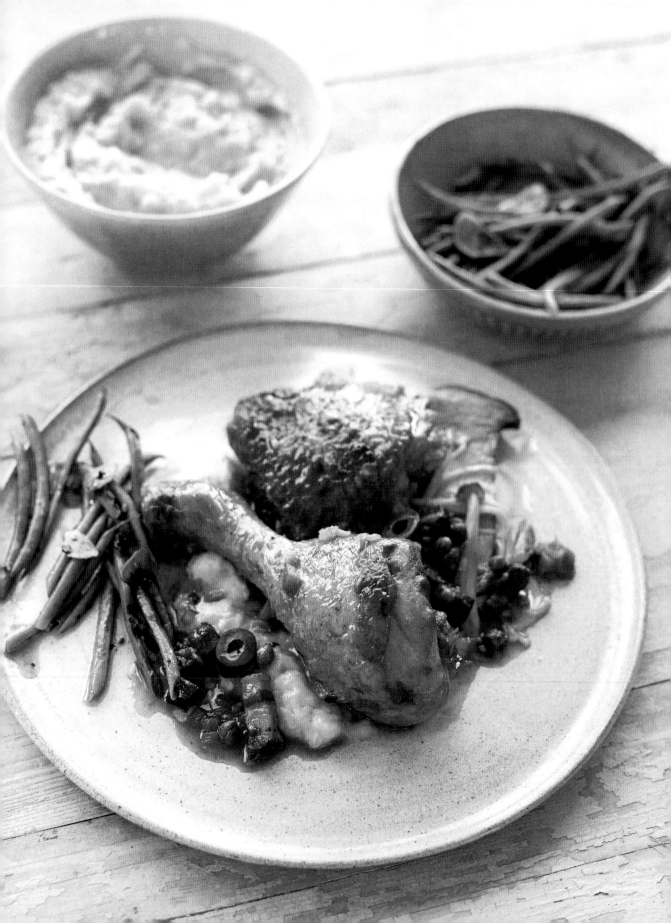

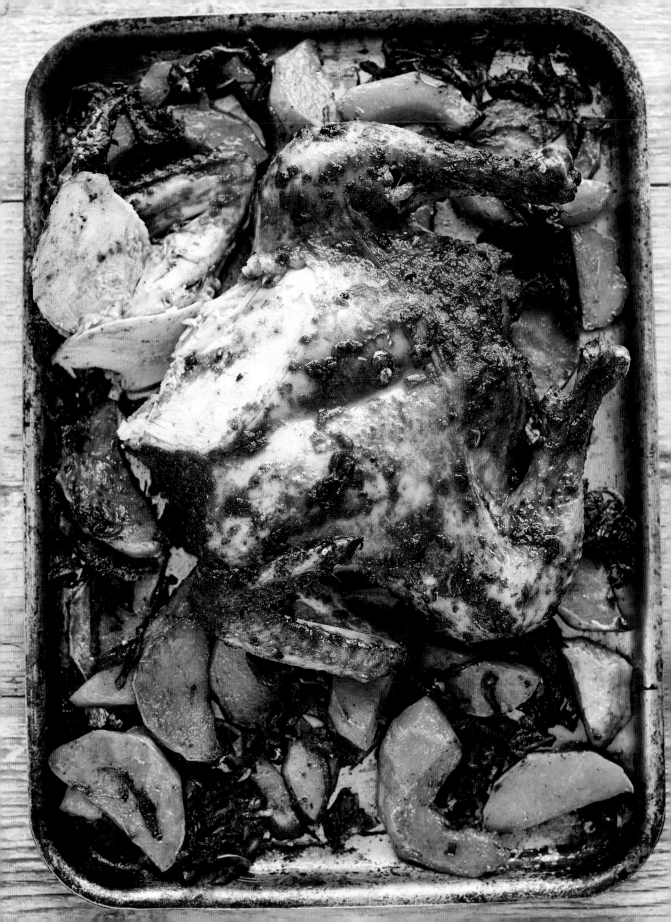

SPATCHCOCKED GINGER CHICKEN WITH BENGAL-SPICED SQUASH

1 whole chicken (about 1.5kg)
zest and juice of 1 lemon
½ tsp chilli powder
1 tsp sweet smoked paprika
2 garlic cloves, peeled and
 crushed
4cm piece fresh root ginger,
 peeled and grated
2 tbsp olive oil

**For the Bengal-spiced
 squash**
4 tbsp olive oil
1 large onion, peeled and
 thinly sliced
2 garlic cloves, peeled and
 finely sliced
1 red chilli, finely chopped
2cm piece fresh root ginger,
 peeled and cut into
 matchsticks
1 tsp ground cumin
1 tsp sweet paprika
8 cardamom pods, cracked
1 tsp garam masala
1 butternut squash, peeled,
 seeded and cut into wedges

1. Preheat the oven to 200°C/Fan 180°C.

2. Remove the backbone and flatten the chicken (or ask your butcher to do this).

3. Marinate the chicken Make a rub by combining the lemon zest, chilli powder, paprika, garlic, ginger and olive oil in a small bowl. Rub all over chicken.

4. Place the chicken skin side up in a large roasting tin and squeeze over the lemon juice.

5. Make the squash Heat the oil in a pan and gently fry the onion in a pan over a medium heat with the garlic, chilli and ginger until tender. Add all the spices and cook for a few minutes more.

6. Arrange the squash around the chicken, spread the spice mixture over the squash and toss gently.

7. Cook the chicken and squash in the oven for 50 minutes, basting the chicken at 10-minute intervals, until the chicken is cooked and the squash sticky.

8. Serve the chicken with the squash wedges on the side.

> **TIP** Serve with Raita (see page 90) and Flatbreads (see page 99).

CHICKEN CURRY, JEERA RICE & SPICED YOGHURT

SERVES 4

For the chicken curry
2–3 tbsp sunflower oil
2½ tsp cumin seeds
2 tsp black mustard seeds
6 garlic cloves, peeled and finely diced
4cm piece fresh root ginger, peeled and grated
3 large onions, peeled and chopped
2–3 tsp turmeric
2 tsp freshly chopped green bird's-eye chillies (to taste)
1 x 400g tin plum tomatoes, chopped
8 skinless chicken thighs, bone in
2 tsp garam masala
fresh coriander, to garnish

For the jeera rice
350g Basmati rice
2 tbsp sunflower oil
1 large onion, peeled and thinly sliced
2 tsp cumin seeds
1 bay leaf
1 cinnamon stick
3 green cardamom pods

For the spiced yoghurt
2½ tsp chaat masala
500g natural yoghurt
1 tbsp sunflower oil
1 tsp cumin seeds
½ tsp chilli powder
¾ tsp black mustard seeds
8–10 curry leaves

1. **Make the curry** Heat the oil in a large pan over a medium heat and add the cumin seeds, black mustard seeds, garlic, ginger, onions, turmeric and green chillies. Fry for 1–2 minutes before adding the tomatoes. Cook for a further 10–12 minutes then add the chicken to the pan. Continue to cook for a further 20–30 minutes, or until the chicken is cooked through. Stir in the garam masala and season with salt to taste.

2. **Make the jeera rice** Wash and soak the rice while you prepare the spices. Place the oil in a large pan over a medium heat. Add the onion, cumin seeds, bay leaf, cinnamon stick and cardamom pods and gently fry for 1–2 minutes. Add the rice to the pan and pour over 800ml water. Bring up to the boil, cover, reduce the heat and leave to simmer for 15–20 minutes.

3. **Make the spiced yoghurt** Mix the chaat masala into the yoghurt and put in a serving dish. Heat the oil in a small pan over a medium heat and add the cumin seeds, chilli powder and black mustard seeds, to temper. After a few minutes, pour the spices over the yoghurt and garnish with curry leaves.

4. Garnish the curry with coriander and serve alongside the spiced yoghurt and jeera rice.

> **TIP** Serve with Tarka Dal (see page 190) and Chapattis (see page 144).

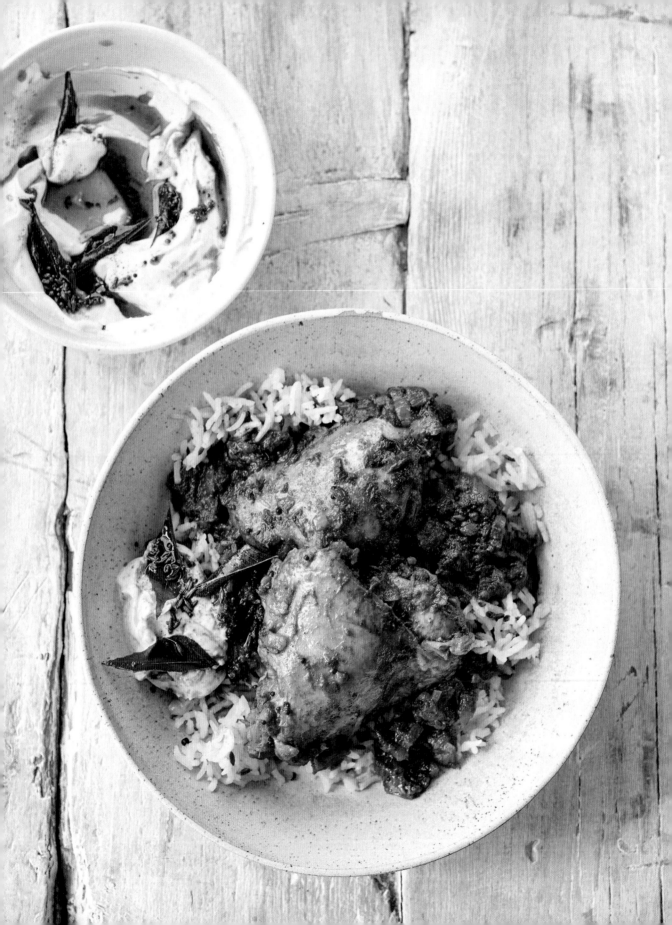

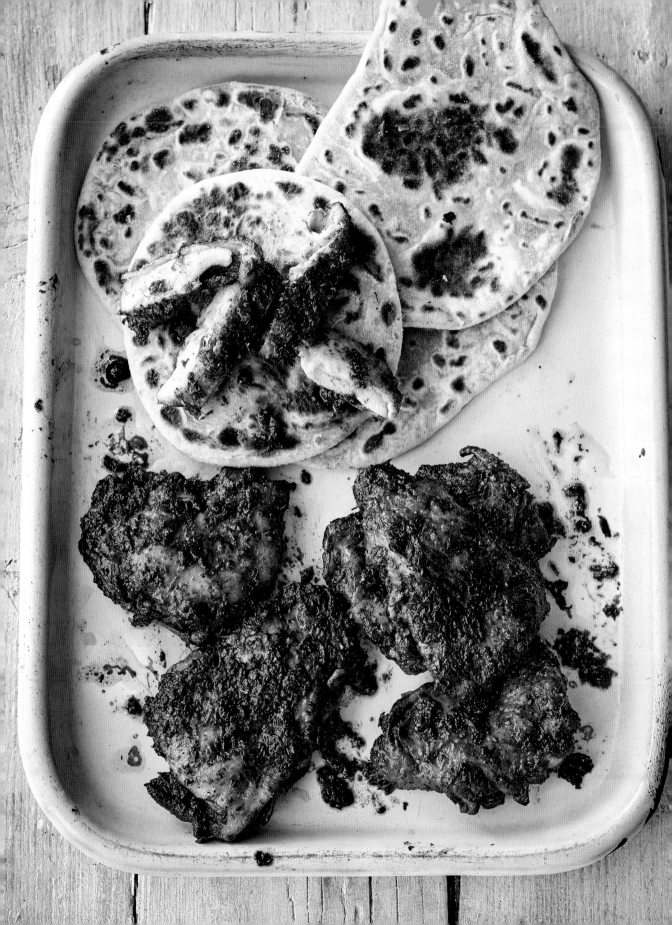

JERK CHICKEN & FLATBREADS

SERVES 4

8 boneless chicken thighs, skin on (if possible)

For the jerk paste
5 Scotch bonnet chillies, stalks removed
1 bunch spring onions, trimmed
50g fresh coriander
juice of 1 lime
2 tbsp palm sugar, or soft light brown sugar
1 tbsp soy sauce
1 tbsp ground allspice
5 garlic cloves, peeled
1 tbsp dark rum
10–12 fresh thyme sprigs, leaves stripped
½ tbsp ground cinnamon
2cm piece fresh root ginger, peeled
splash of fresh orange juice
3 tbsp vegetable oil (or enough to create smooth paste)
salt and pepper

For the flatbreads
50g butter, melted
180ml whole milk
½ tsp salt
300g plain flour
vegetable oil, for cooking

1. **Make the jerk paste** Combine the ingredients in a food-processor and blend until smooth, adding enough oil to create a thick but smooth paste. Cover the chicken in the paste and leave for at least 2 hours or preferably overnight.

2. Preheat the oven to 180°C/Fan 160°C.

3. **Make the flatbread dough** Combine the butter, milk and salt in a bowl, before adding the flour slowly until you reach a standard dough consistency.

4. Knead the dough on a lightly floured work surface for a short period of time until smooth. Wrap in clingfilm and leave to rest in the fridge for around 30 minutes.

5. **Cook the chicken** Place a ovenproof griddle pan over a high heat and add the chicken, turning until brown on both sides, and then transfer to the oven and bake for 40 minutes.

6. Place the rested dough on a lightly floured work surface and divide into quarters. Roll each one out to 3mm thick.

7. **Cook the flatbreads** Using a heavy-based pan, or metal skillet, heat a little oil over a medium heat and cook the flatbreads one at a time for 1–2 minutes on each side.

8. Serve the chicken with the warm flatbreads.

> **TIP** Serve with rice, pickled onion and charred pineapple.

CHICKEN BASTILLA
MOROCCAN CHICKEN PIE

6 skinless chicken legs
2 onions, peeled and
   roughly diced
1 large bunch parsley,
   leaves roughly chopped
1 large bunch coriander,
   leaves roughly chopped
2 tsp salt
3 tsp ground ginger
2 tbsp sugar
2 cinnamon sticks
   (10cm in total)
good pinch of saffron
2 tsp white peppercorns
1 tsp black peppercorns
225g unsalted butter
200g blanched almonds
1 tbsp vegetable oil
3 tbsp icing sugar, plus
   extra for dusting
1 tsp ground cinnamon
6 large eggs
1 x packet filo pastry

1 . **Prepare the chicken** Place the chicken in a large pot along with the onions, parsley, coriander, salt, ground ginger, sugar, cinnamon, saffron and peppercorns with 50g of the butter. Bring to the boil, then reduce the heat and gently simmer for 45–50 minutes. Set aside.

2 . **Prepare the almonds** Lightly toast the almonds in the oil in a pan over a low heat. Remove from the heat, cool and then whizz in a small food-processor or crush in a large pestle and mortar. Place the ground almonds in a bowl with the icing sugar and ground cinnamon.

3 . Remove the chicken legs from the pot and place in a large bowl to cool. Once cooled, shred the meat from the bones.

4 . **Prepare the eggs** Strain the chicken cooking liquid to remove the solids and return 500ml of the liquid to the pan. Put over a medium-high heat and whisk in the eggs. Cook, whisking, until they have thickened and strain them thorough a sieve lined with muslin and keep to one side.

5 . Preheat the oven to 200°C/Fan 180°C.

6 . **Assemble the bastilla** Melt the remaining butter in a small pan and use some to grease a 23cm loose-bottomed cake tin. Line the tin with 4 layers of the filo pastry, buttering each layer as it goes in.

7 . Spread the almond mixture on the base, top with the egg and finally add the shredded chicken. Fold the edges of the filo over the top and cover with more buttered filo pastry.

8 . Bake in the oven for 30–40 minutes, or until golden and crisp. Cool for 5 minutes and then remove from the tin and allow to cool a little more.

9 . Dust with icing sugar to serve.

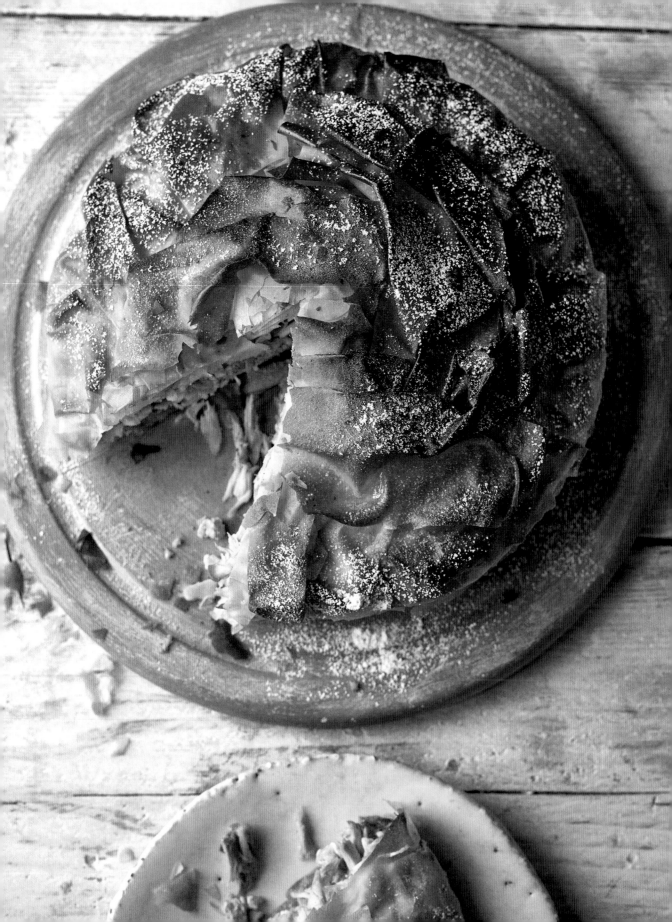

CHICKEN IN PANDAN LEAVES

SERVES 4

4 skinless boneless
   chicken thighs
2 tbsp Red Curry Paste
   (see page 278 or use
   shop-bought)
1 tbsp palm sugar
3 tbsp fish sauce
1 tbsp vegetable oil
½ tsp turmeric
2 tbsp coconut milk
8 pandan leaves
   (approximately 2 per
   chicken thigh)

1. Combine all the ingredients (except the pandan leaves) and leave to marinate in the fridge for 1 hour.

2. Either dip the leaves in boiling water or ping them in the microwave for 1 minute to make them more pliable and less likely to tear.

3. Wrap each chicken thigh in the pandan leaves, securing with cocktail sticks.

4. Fry in a large pan or wok over a medium heat for 6–8 minutes on each side, or until cooked.

5. Serve with jasmine rice.

TIP Serve with Aubergine with Chilli (Ca Tim Nurong) on page 192.

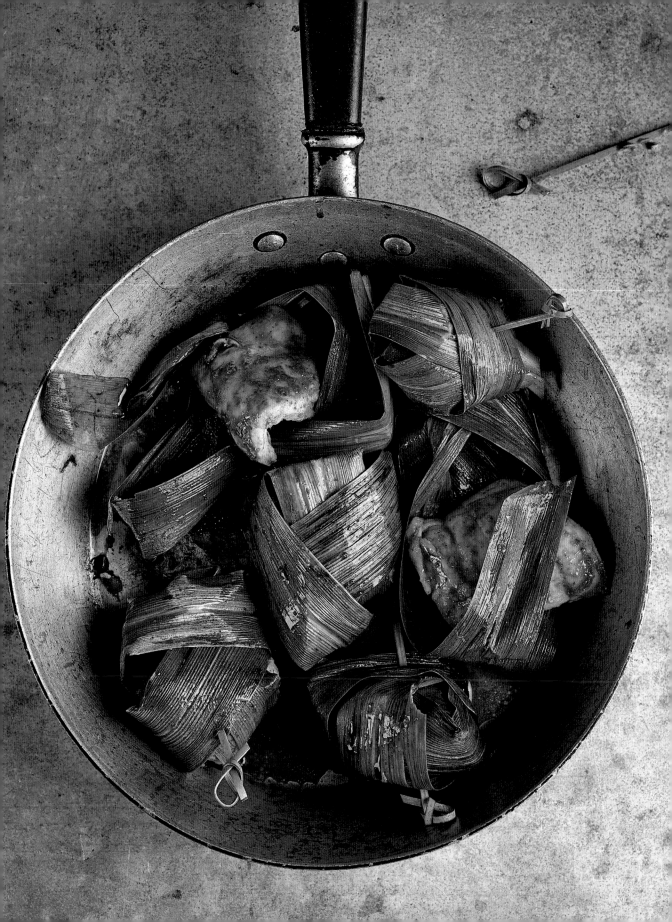

CHICKEN CASSEROLE & COUSCOUS SALAD

SERVES 4

For the chicken

2 tbsp olive oil
6 boneless chicken thighs,
    chopped
1 onion, peeled and finely sliced
1 red chilli, finely sliced
zest of 1 lemon
2cm piece fresh root ginger,
    peeled and grated
2 garlic cloves, peeled
    and bashed
175ml white wine
450ml vegetable stock
150g spinach leaves
salt and pepper

For the couscous

200g couscous
300ml chicken or vegetable
    stock, hot
good glug of extra-virgin
    olive oil
100g cherry tomatoes,
    quartered
5 spring onions, sliced
a handful of chopped
    flat-leaf parsley
a small of handful of
    snipped chives
finely grated zest and juice
    of 1 lemon

1 : **Cook the chicken** Place the oil in a large pan over a high heat and fry the chicken in batches until brown all over. Remove with a slotted spoon and place on one side.

2 : Add the onion, chilli, lemon zest and ginger to the pan and cook for 5 minutes, or until the onion has softened.

3 : Add the garlic and return the chicken to the pan. Pour over the wine and stock, season well, lower the heat and cook for 30–35 minutes.

4 : **Make the couscous** Put the couscous in a bowl and pour over the hot stock and olive oil. Stir, cover with clingfilm and leave to absorb for 5 minutes. Fluff up with a fork, add the remainder of the ingredients and season to taste.

5 : Stir the spinach into the chicken and serve with the couscous.

CHICKEN & BUTTERBEAN CURRY WITH PICKLED RED ONION

SERVES 4

For the curry
2 tbsp vegetable oil
1 onion, peeled and
   finely chopped
5 garlic cloves, peeled
   and crushed
3cm piece fresh root ginger,
   peeled and grated
500g boneless chicken
   thighs, chopped
2 tsp ground cumin
2 tsp ground coriander
1 tsp turmeric
pinch of cayenne pepper
2 long green chillies, sliced
400g cherry tomatoes, blitzed
100–150ml chicken stock
1 x 400g tin butterbeans,
   drained
1 bunch of coriander, chopped
salt and pepper

For the pickled onion
juice of 1 lemon
1 fresh mint sprig, leaves
   picked
1 tsp sugar
1 tsp salt
1 red chilli, sliced
1 large red onion, peeled
   and finely sliced

1 : Make the pickled onion Put all the ingredients except the onion in a mortar and pestle and grind to a coarse paste. Add to the sliced onion and chill until ready to serve.

2 : Make the curry Heat the oil in a large pan over a medium heat and fry the chopped onion for 5 minutes, or until softened. Add the garlic and ginger and cook for 1–2 minutes.

3 : Add the chicken and seal all over and then add the spices and chillies. Cook for 1 minute and then stir in the tomatoes and stock and cook for a further 20–25 minutes.

4 : Add the butterbeans and cook for 5 minutes more.

5 : Stir the chopped coriander into the curry and serve alongside the pickled red onion and some steamed rice.

ROSEMARY'S ROAST CHICKEN
WITH SWEET POTATOES & SPRING GREENS

1 whole chicken (1.8–2kg)
100g butter
4 fresh parsley sprigs,
    leaves picked
6 fresh tarragon sprigs, leaves
    picked
4 rashers streaky pancetta
1 garlic clove, peeled
1 lemon
4 tbsp rapeseed oil
3 fresh lemon thyme sprigs
1.25kg sweet potatoes, washed,
    halved lengthways and
    cut into half moons
2 tbsp za'atar
85g pancetta, diced
400g spring greens,
    washed and sliced
30g pine nuts, toasted
salt and pepper

1. Preheat the oven to 200°C/Fan 180°C.

2. Prepare the chicken Trim the excess fat off
the chicken.

3. Place the butter, parsley, tarragon, rashers of pancetta,
garlic and the juice of ½ the lemon in a food-processor
and whizz until smooth.

4. Using your fingers and starting at the neck end, ease
the skin away from the breast, push in half the butter
mixture between the flesh and the skin, and spread evenly.
Rub the remainder over the top of skin then drizzle with
2 tablespoons of the rapeseed oil. Season with salt. Using
the other ½ lemon, squeeze the juice into the cavity and
place both squeezed lemon halves inside the bird with
the lemon thyme.

5. Cook the chicken Place in a roasting tin and cook in
the oven for approximately 1–1½ hours, or until the juices
run clear. Allow to rest for 10 minutes before slicing.

6. Make the sweet potatoes Place the sweet potatoes
in another roasting tin, toss with the remaining oil and
season with salt. Roast in the oven for 15 minutes. Remove
from the oven and sprinkle with the za'atar. Toss to coat
and return to the oven for a further 10–15 minutes.

7. Make the spring greens Place the diced pancetta
in a pan over a medium heat and fry until golden in colour
and the fat is rendered. Remove from the pan with a slotted
spoon and turn down the heat. Stir in the spring greens
and sauté until starting to wilt. Return the pancetta to
the pan with the toasted pine nuts, saving some to garnish.

8. Serve slices of roast chicken with the spiced sweet
potatoes and spring greens.

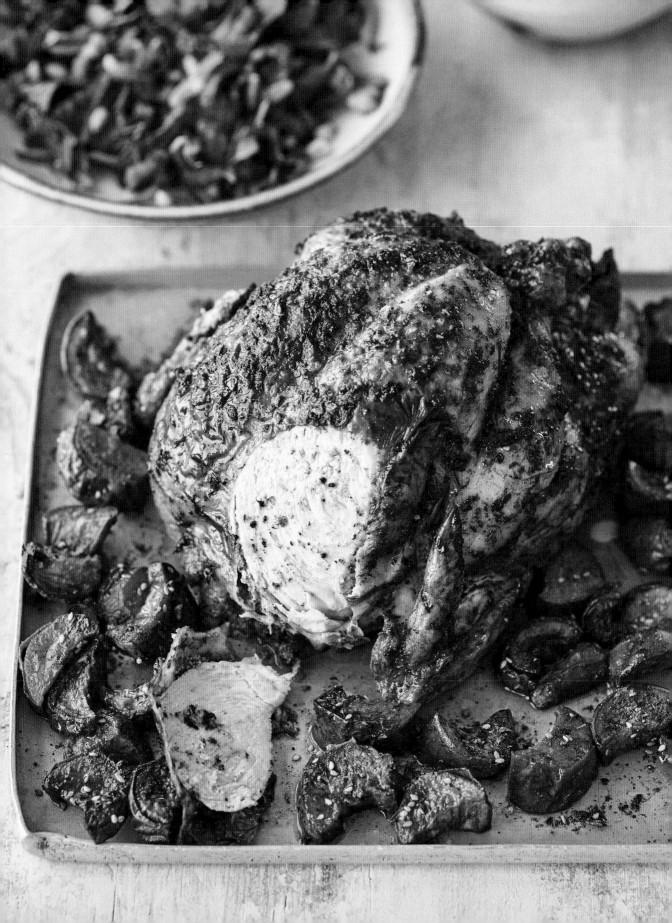

GUINEA FOWL SUPREMES WITH TRUFFLE MASH & WHITE WINE SAUCE

SERVES 4

2 tbsp rapeseed oil
2 guinea fowl legs and
    4 guinea fowl supremes
2 banana shallots, peeled
    and diced
2 celery sticks, diced
1 bay leaf
1 bunch tarragon, leaves
    roughly chopped
6 white peppercorns
1 garlic clove, peeled and
    very finely chopped
50g chestnut mushrooms,
    sliced
15g dried porcini or morel
    mushrooms, soaked in water
500ml chicken stock
150ml Pinot Blanc, preferably
    from the Alsace region
125ml double cream
juice of 1 lemon
1 bunch chives, snipped
salt and pepper

For the mash
600g potatoes, peeled
a good knob of butter
50ml double cream
2 tbsp truffle oil

1 . Preheat the oven to 200°C/Fan 180°C.

2 . **Prepare the sauce** Heat 1 tablespoon of the oil in a pan over a medium-low heat. Chop up the guinea fowl legs and add to the pan with the shallots, celery, bay leaf, tarragon, peppercorns, garlic and sliced mushrooms and sauté for 5 minutes.

3 . Remove the dried mushrooms from their soaking liquid, chop and add to the pan. Sauté for a further 1–2 minutes.

4 . Pour in the stock, strained mushroom liquid and the wine. Simmer vigorously for 15–20 minutes, or until the liquid has reduced by half.

5 . **Cook the supremes** Heat the remaining oil in a pan. Season the supremes all over and then brown the skin in the pan for a couple of minutes. Transfer to a baking sheet and roast in the oven for 15–20 minutes. Set aside to rest.

6 . **Make the sauce** Strain the sauce, discarding the solids. Return the liquid to the pan and add the double cream. Simmer to thicken, then add lemon juice to taste.

7 . **Make the mash** Put the potatoes in a pan of cold salted water and bring to the boil. Reduce the heat and simmer for 15 minutes, or until tender. Drain well and put through a potato ricer back into the pan. Place over a low heat, add the butter, cream and a tiny drizzle of the truffle oil and mix well. Season.

8 . To serve, place a supreme on top of some mash and drizzle with a little more truffle oil. Pour some of the sauce around the plate and garnish with chives.

TIP A supreme is where the breast fillet is served with the wing still attached.

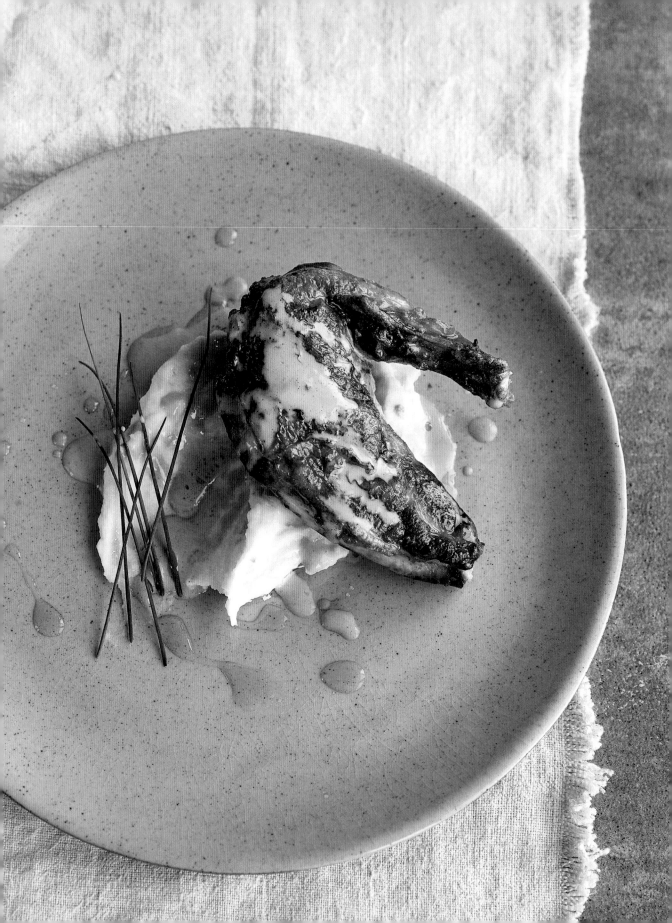

ROSEMARY'S INDIAN-SPICED DUCK BREAST WITH CHILLI PEACH SALSA

4 duck breasts, skin scored
   with a sharp knife
1 tsp ground cumin
1 tsp garam masala
¼ tsp chilli powder
¾ tsp ground coriander
good pinch of salt
1 tbsp rapeseed oil

For the chilli peach salsa
3 fresh peaches, finely diced
1cm fresh root ginger, peeled
   and finely grated
2 garlic cloves, peeled and
   finely diced
2 tbsp honey
1 tbsp Marsala
1 tbsp cider vinegar
½ red chilli, very finely diced
good pinch of salt

For the peaches in Marsala
1 tsp cumin seeds, crushed
250ml Marsala
1 star anise
1 tsp honey
2 peaches, quartered
1 tsp fine sea salt

1. Preheat the oven to 190°C/Fan 170°C.

2. Make the chilli peach salsa Measure the ingredients into a small pan and cook for about 20 minutes on a low simmering heat, or until the liquid has evaporated and thickened. This can be done well in advance.

3. Prepare the peaches in Marsala Add the crushed cumin seeds to a dry pan and toast over a low heat. Pour in the Marsala, add the star anise and honey and cook for 2–3 minutes. Add the peaches and cook for 1 minute and then allow to cool.

4. Prepare the duck Combine the spices for the duck with the salt and oil and rub into the breasts.

5. Cook the duck Place skin side down in a dry pan over a low heat and cook slowly for 8–10 minutes, or until the skin is crispy, draining off the fat that is released. Turn and cook for a further 3–4 minutes.

6. Remove the breasts to a plate and allow to rest skin side up for at least 5 minutes before carving into slices.

7. Serve the duck with the warm salsa and peaches.

TIP Serve with Rosemary's One Large Rösti (see page 272).

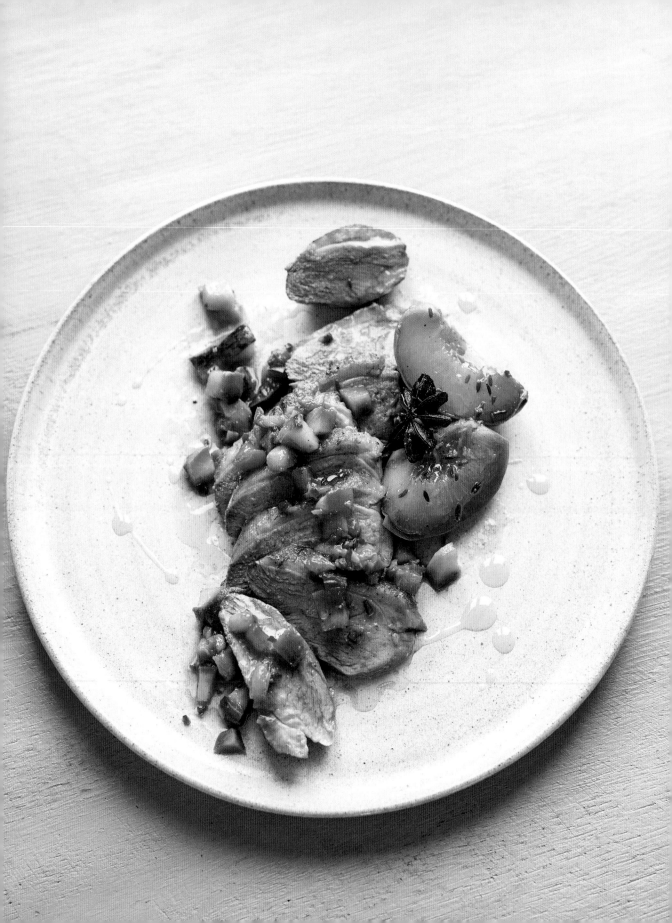

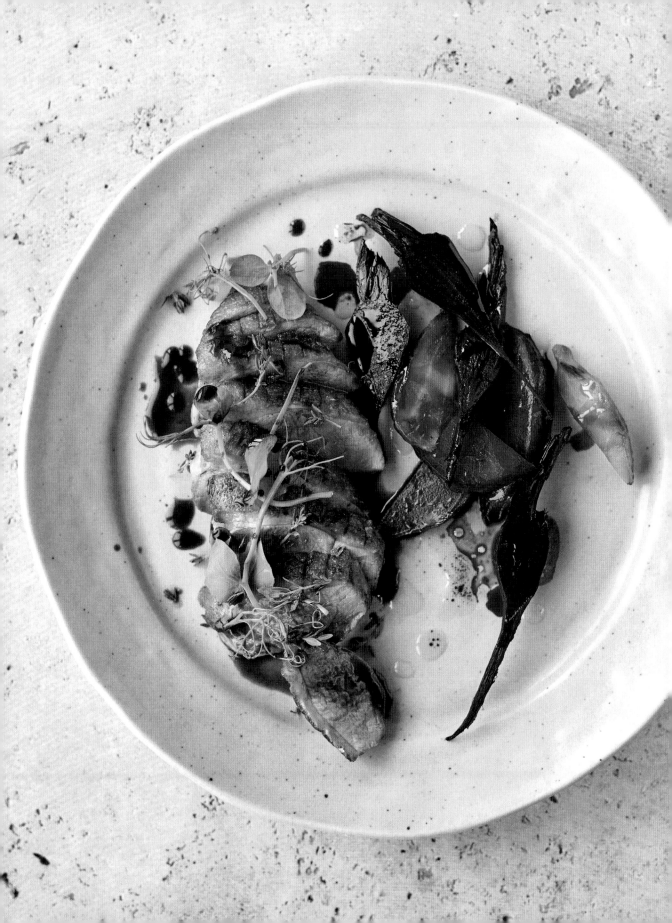

PAN-FRIED DUCK BREASTS WITH BEETROOT

SERVES 4

4 large duck breasts
a few knobs of butter
1–2 fresh thyme sprigs,
    leaves picked, to serve
a handful of pea shoots,
    to serve
salt and pepper

For the sauce
4 large chicken wings
2 large carrots, peeled and
    roughly chopped
2 medium onions, peeled
    and roughly chopped
175ml full-bodied red wine
50ml Port
50ml Madeira (optional)
250ml chicken stock

For the beetroot
4 baby beetroot, washed and
    trimmed but retaining
    some of the stem
2 baby yellow beetroot, washed
    and trimmed but retaining
    some of the stem
1 tbsp rapeseed oil
1 tbsp red wine vinegar
1–2 fresh thyme sprigs,
    leaves picked
2 garlic cloves, peeled and
    very finely chopped
pinch of sea salt

1. Preheat the oven to 200°C/Fan 180°C.

2. Make the sauce Place the chicken wings in a roasting tray with the carrots and onions and cook in the oven for 40–45 minutes. Once golden brown, tip everything into a large pan.

3. Deglaze the roasting tray with the red wine, Port and Madeira, if using, over a high heat and reduce to a sticky syrup. Pour this into the pan with the wings and vegetables, add the stock, cover and gently simmer for about 1 hour.

4. Pass the sauce through a sieve to remove the solids and return the liquid to the pan. Reduce over a high heat to a sauce consistency – check and season, if necessary.

5. Make the beetroot Place two sheets of tin foil on top of each other and put all the beetroot in the centre. Drizzle with the oil, vinegar and 2 tablespoons of water, and season with the thyme, garlic and sea salt. Wrap up the foil like a pasty and place in the oven for 30–45 minutes, or until they are tender – test them with a skewer.

6. Remove the beetroot from the oven, pour any liquid collected in the foil into a pan and put to one side (this will be used to warm the beetroot through later).

7. Remove the skins from the beetroot with kitchen paper and slice each one into half or quarters, depending on size.

8. Cook the duck Score the skin side of the breasts and season. Put the breasts, skin side down, in a cold ovenproof frying pan and place over a medium-low heat. Gently cook

Recipe continues

for 6–7 minutes to render out the fat, pouring out any excess fat as they cook.

9 . Once the skins are golden brown, turn the breasts over, add the butter to the pan and, once melted, spoon over the duck. Transfer to the oven for 6–8 minutes for pink meat.

10 . Remove the duck from the oven and leave to rest on a warm plate (skin side up) for about 10 minutes.

11 . Meanwhile, place the beetroot in the pan with their juices and warm over a medium heat. Reheat the sauce in its pan until steaming.

12 . Carve each breast into slices and serve alongside the beetroot. Place a few pea shoots and thyme leaves on top of the duck and serve with the sauce.

FAMILY TIP 'Home-cooked food always tastes so much better when made together with family and friends while sharing a nice bottle of wine!'

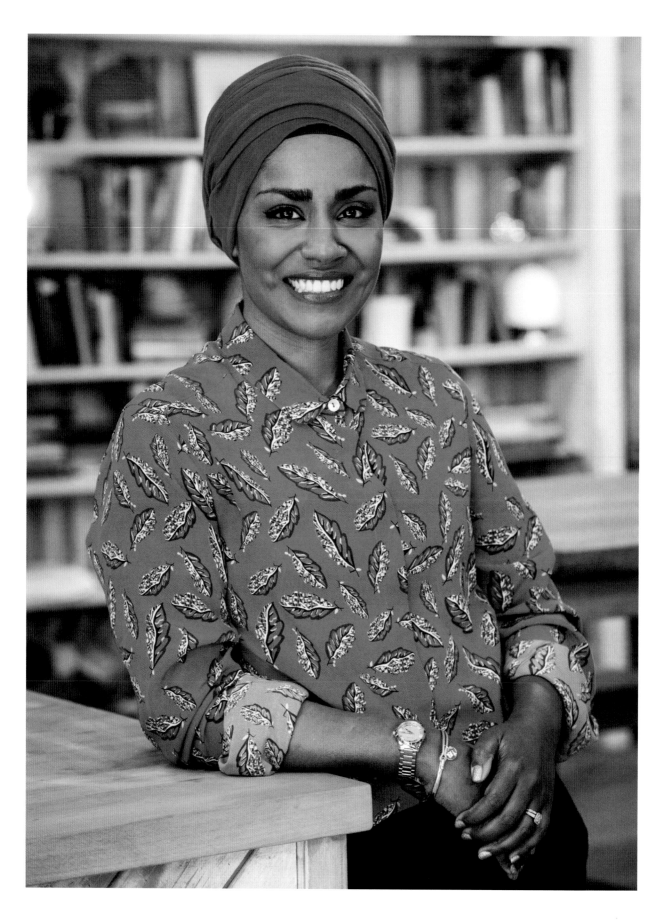

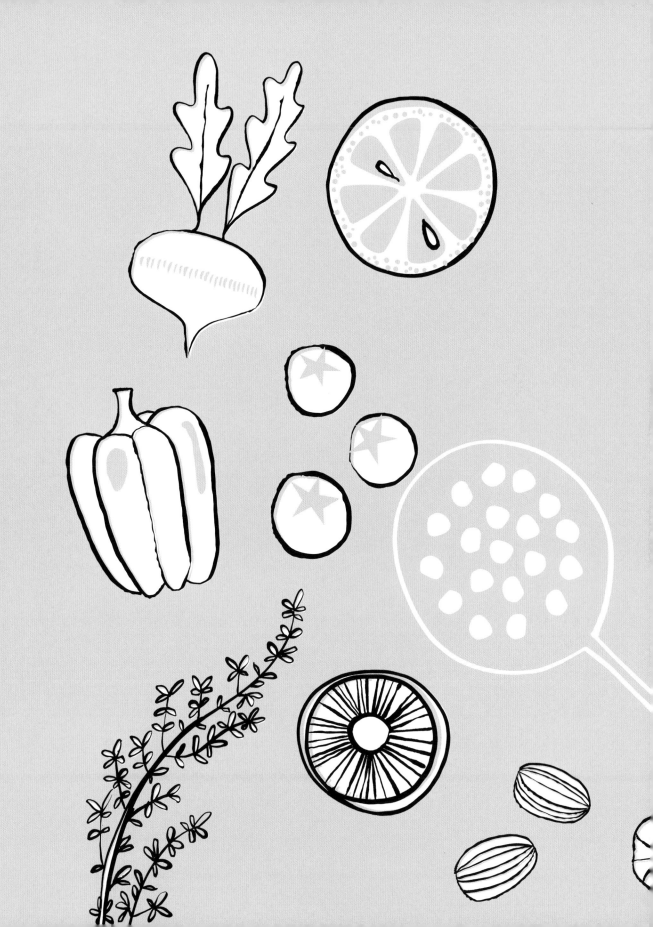

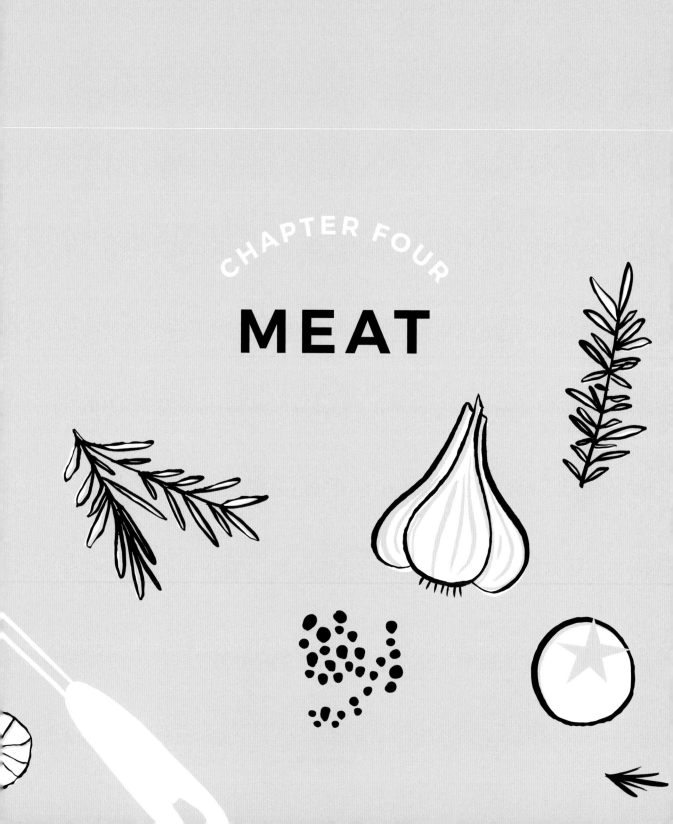

CHAPTER FOUR

MEAT

Sausage and fennel stuffed roast peppers
are a filling treat: slice **red** or **yellow peppers** in half
lengthways, keeping the stalks. Remove the seeds so
you are left with a hollow shell. Stuff each half with some
thinly sliced **fennel**, a couple of halved **cherry tomatoes**
and some **sausage meat** – roughly half a sausage for each
half pepper (remove it from its casing and break up into
small pieces). Drizzle with **olive oil**, season with **salt
and pepper** and roast at 200°C/Fan 180°C for around
40 minutes, or until soft, caramelised and a little charred.
For a vegetarian option, try **fennel**, **goats' cheese** and
black olives.

Pancakes shouldn't be limited to one day of the year –
they make a simple, tasty dinner when filled with savoury
ingredients. To make **ham and cheese crêpes** start
with a classic pancake batter (**120g plain flour**, **245ml
milk**, **1 whole egg** plus **1 egg yolk** and a pinch of **salt**)
and whisk until smooth. Leave in the fridge to rest for 30
minutes. Melt **butter** in a frying pan over a medium heat
then pour in a small ladleful of batter, tilting the pan so
that it swirls out into a circle. When the bottom is cooked,
ease away from the pan with a spatula and flip. Cook the
other side briefly, then sprinkle **grated cheese** on one
half of the pancake and top with **ham**. Leave to cook for
1 minute, then fold the plain half of the pancake over the
filled half so you are left with a semi-circle. When the
cheese has melted, fold the outer thirds of the pancake
in and then over each other so you're left with a triangle,
and serve. Repeat until all the batter is used up.

Nothing beats a really good **ham, egg and chips**. Use whatever type of ham you have, whether it's home-cooked **gammon** or a dry-cured variety, like **prosciutto**. Clean **potatoes** rather than peeling them and then cut them into quarters lengthways for chunky wedges. Bring a large pan of salted water to the boil and simmer the potatoes until just cooked. Drain gently, blotting as much moisture as possible from the potatoes. Add to a roasting tray of hot **oil** and shuffle so that they are well coated. Season with **salt** and a good pinch of **smoked paprika**, then roast until golden and crisp. Just before the potatoes are ready, fry the **eggs** – for extra flavour, throw a few **sage leaves** into the hot oil before cracking in the eggs.

Toad in the hole is a classic one-tin supper: peel and cut some **apples** into large wedges. Heat oil in a large roasting tin and, when hot, add the apples and some **sausages**, shuffling carefully to coat in the **oil**. Roast in the oven at 200°C/Fan 180°C until starting to brown and then pour over a Yorkshire pudding batter (**plain flour**, **eggs**, **milk**, **salt and pepper**, all whisked together) and return to the oven until golden and puffed up. For an extra twist, add some **wholegrain mustard** to the batter mixture. **Onion gravy** is optional but recommended.

There are few things more satisfying or simpler than a baked potato, and **baked stuffed sweet potatoes** are a meal in themselves. Scrub **sweet potatoes** clean and then rub with a little **olive oil** and season with **salt** before roasting in a very hot oven (220°C/Fan 200°C) for 1 hour. Cut down the middle of the potato, scoop all the flesh out into a bowl and mix together with **crème fraîche**, sliced **spring onion**, crisp fried **bacon** pieces or **lardons** and season with **salt and pepper**. Spoon the mixture back into the potato skins and roast for a further 15 minutes, or until crisp. Serve a spoonful of **sour cream** or **crème fraîche** on the side with some **chilli sauce**.

BRAISED PORK BELLY WITH CHINESE MUSHROOMS

25g whole dried shiitake
    mushrooms
1 small bunch spring onions
2 tbsp vegetable oil
5cm piece fresh root ginger,
    peeled and finely chopped
3 garlic cloves, peeled and
    finely chopped
1 star anise
1 piece cassia bark
800g pork belly (ideally
    a 5-layered cut – skin/
    fat/meat/fat/meat),
    cut into cubes
3 tbsp Shaoxing rice wine
3 tbsp dark soy sauce
1 tbsp light soy sauce
2 tbsp caster sugar

1 : Soak the mushrooms in boiling water for at least 15 minutes.

2 : Chop all the spring onions into 4cm lengths except one. Finely slice this last one to garnish.

3 : Heat the oil gently in a large pan over a medium-high heat. Fry the lengths of spring onion with the ginger, garlic, star anise and cassia bark for 3–4 minutes, or until it smells great.

4 : Add the pork and cook until it starts to brown. You can do this in batches if your pan is a bit small.

5 : Add the mushrooms and their soaking liquid, the rice wine, soy sauces and sugar, and enough water to cover the pork. Cover the pan and gently simmer for 1½–2 hours, or until the pork is really tender and falling apart.

6 : Remove the lid, turn up the heat and cook uncovered over a high heat for 10–15 minutes to reduce the sauce so it becomes thick and syrupy.

7 : Adjust the seasoning to taste, scatter with the sliced spring onion and serve with steamed rice.

> **TIP** Serve with Salt and Pepper Tofu with Smacked Cucumber Salad (see page 167).

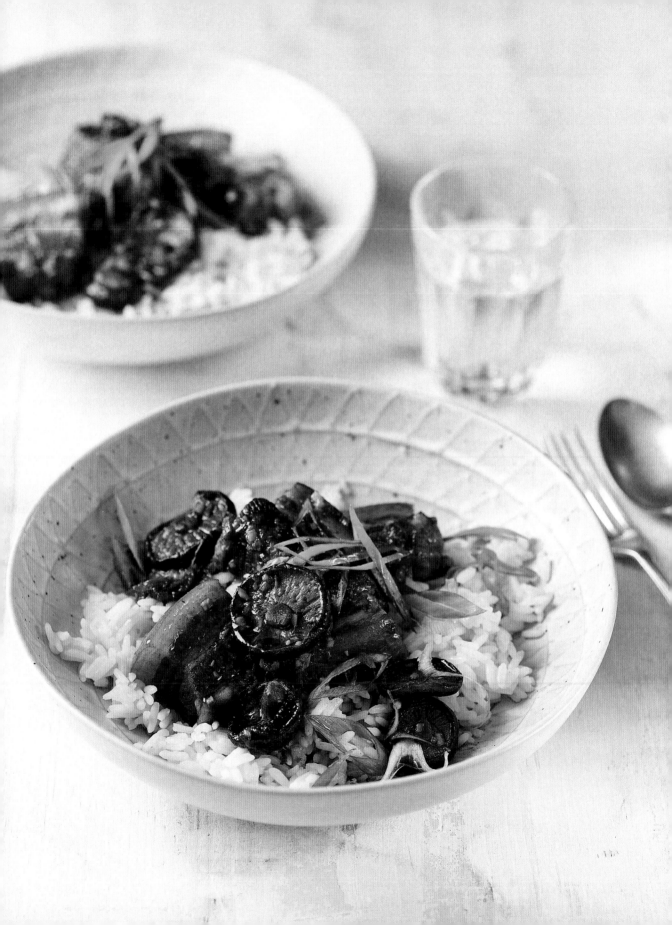

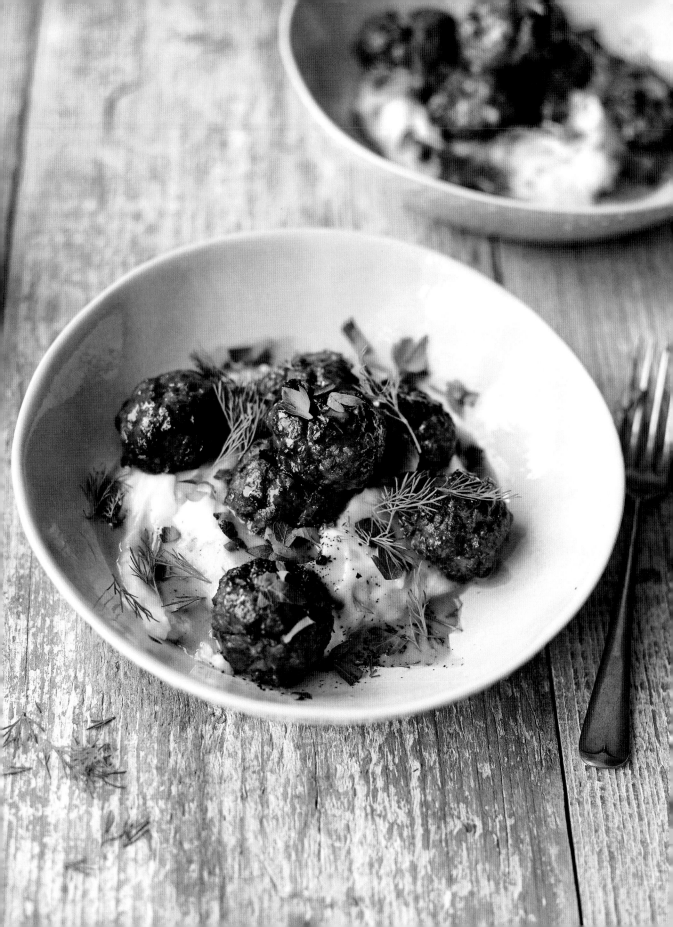

SWEDISH MEATBALLS
WITH DILL MASH

For the meatballs
200g Maris Piper
    potatoes, peeled
1 egg
3 tbsp butter
1 small red onion, peeled
    and finely chopped
250g minced beef
250g minced pork
½ tsp ground allspice
small bunch flat-leaf
    parsley, finely chopped
2 tbsp single cream
1 tsp salt
good pinch of pepper

For the allspice sauce
3 tbsp unsalted butter
1 small red onion, peeled
    and finely chopped
1 carrot, peeled and finely
    chopped
400ml beef stock
1 tbsp plain flour
pinch of ground allspice
150ml single cream
1 tbsp soy sauce
2 tsp redcurrant jelly

For the mashed potatoes
700g Maris Piper potatoes,
    peeled and cut into chunks
25g butter
50ml milk
2 tbsp freshly chopped dill ,
    plus a few sprigs to serve
salt and pepper

1. Preheat the oven to 220°C/Fan 200°C.

2. Make the meatballs Bring a large pan of salted
water to the boil and put the potatoes in to cook until
tender. Drain, mash with a potato masher and then
tip into a large bowl and mix with the egg.

3. Melt 1 tablespoon of the butter in a pan over a medium
heat. Add the onion and fry for about 5 minutes, until soft.
Remove from the pan and add to the potato mixture.

4. Set aside 1 tablespoon of the minced beef for the sauce.
Add the remaining beef and all the pork mince to the
potato mixture, along with the allspice, half the parsley,
the cream, salt and pepper. Mix together well, using
your hands.

5. Roll the meatballs into 3cm balls and set aside.

6. Make the allspice sauce Melt 2 tablespoons of the
butter in a pan over a medium heat. Add the onion and
carrot and sweat for 5 minutes. Add the reserved minced
beef and beef stock. Simmer for 15 minutes and then
strain into a jug.

7. Using the same pan, melt the remaining butter with
the flour and allspice. Slowly add the stock back into the
pan, whisking all the time, and allow to thicken. Finally,
add the cream, soy sauce and redcurrant jelly. Bring up
to a simmer and season to taste. Set aside and reheat
when ready to serve.

8. Cook the meatballs Use the remaining butter to
grease a large baking sheet and put in the preheated
oven for 3 minutes to heat. When hot, place all the

Recipe continues

MEAT

123

meatballs on the sheet and return to the oven. Roast for about 10 minutes, turning halfway, or until the meatballs are browned and cooked through. Remove and transfer to an ovenproof serving dish. Turn the oven off but place the meatballs inside to keep warm.

9 . Make the mash Bring a large pan of salted water to the boil and put the potatoes in to cook for 15 minutes, or until tender. Drain and pass through a potato ricer back into the pan. Add the butter and milk and mash well with a potato masher. Season to taste and stir in the chopped dill.

10 . Reheat the sauce and pour over the meatballs, sprinkle with the remaining parsley and dill and serve with the mash.

FAMILY TIP 'This is a really good, balanced meal, full of the flavours of Scandinavia. Use a combination of good-quality pork and beef mince and serve with cranberry sauce and steamed green vegetables.'

SPICY MEATBALLS WITH RAW COURGETTE SALAD

2 tbsp olive oil
1 red onion, peeled and
    finely chopped
2 garlic cloves, peeled
    and crushed
450g minced pork
100g streaky bacon,
    finely chopped
50g fresh white breadcrumbs
2 tbsp freshly chopped sage
a handful of freshly chopped
    flat-leaf parsley
½ egg, beaten, to bind
    (if required)
salt and pepper

For the tomato sauce
2 tbsp olive oil
1 large onion, peeled and
    finely chopped
3 garlic cloves, peeled and
    crushed
1 red chilli, sliced
2 x 400g tins chopped
    tomatoes
a few fresh thyme sprigs,
    leaves picked
2 tsp red wine vinegar
pinch of caster sugar
a handful of fresh basil leaves

For the courgette salad
3 large courgettes, ribboned
1 red chilli, finely chopped
juice of ½ lemon
pinch of caster sugar
4 tbsp extra-virgin olive oil

1 : Make the meatballs Heat half the oil in a pan over a medium heat and gently fry the onion for 5 minutes, or until soft. Add the garlic and fry for 1 minute more and then tip into a bowl to cool.

2 : Add the remainder of the ingredients to the bowl with plenty of seasoning and mush with your hands to mix. Add the egg if it needs help to come together. Shape into 16 meatballs and then chill.

3 : Make the tomato sauce Heat the oil in a flameproof casserole dish over a medium heat and fry the onion for 5 minutes. Add the garlic and chilli and cook for 1–2 minutes more.

4 : Stir in the tomatoes, thyme, vinegar, sugar and plenty of seasoning. Add a splash of water and the basil leaves, and gently simmer for 15–20 minutes.

5 : Heat the remaining oil for the meatballs in a frying pan and brown the meatballs all over in batches, dropping them into the sauce once they are browned. Cook in the sauce for 10 minutes until they are cooked through and the sauce has thickened.

6 : Make the courgette salad Combine the courgette with the chilli in a bowl. Mix the lemon juice with the sugar and some seasoning and then whisk in the olive oil. Pour over the courgettes.

7 : Serve the meatballs and sauce with the salad and some crusty bread or rice.

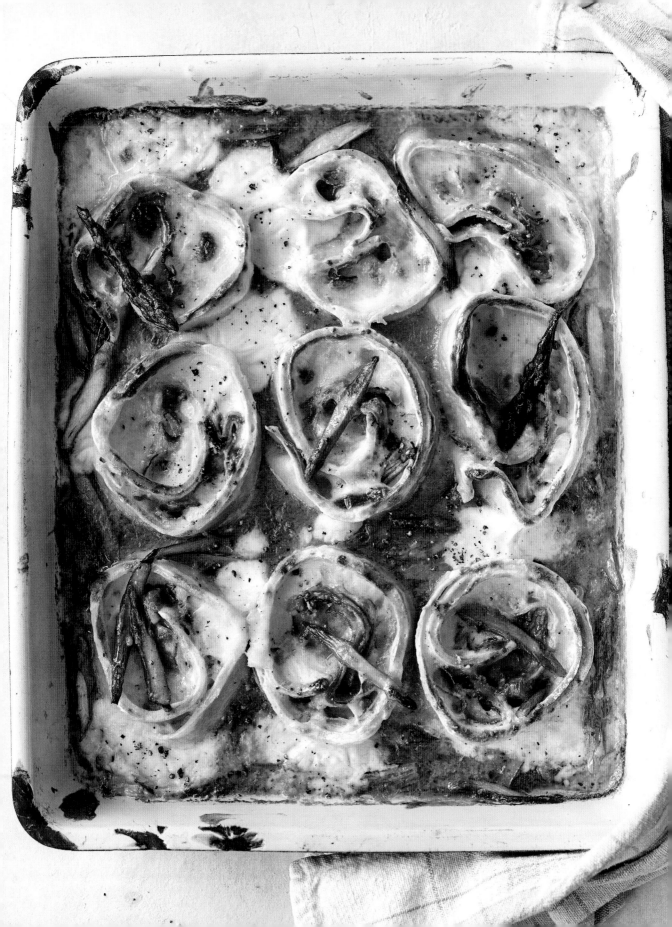

HAM & ASPARAGUS PASTA NESTS
ROTOLO

SERVES 4

250g asparagus, sliced
2 tbsp olive oil
1–2 garlic cloves, peeled
  and crushed
40g butter
20g plain flour
400ml chicken or vegetable
  stock, hot
250g mozzarella balls,
  broken into pieces
250g cooked ham (ideally an
  Italian rosemary variety),
  torn into pieces
6 tbsp freshly grated
  Parmesan
black pepper

For the pasta
200g Italian '00' flour
2 eggs

For the Béchamel sauce
40g butter
40g plain flour
500ml hot whole milk
freshly ground nutmeg
salt and freshly ground
  white pepper

1. **Make the pasta** Place the flour in a food-processor and pulse. Add the eggs and keep pulsing for 2–3 minutes, until the mixture resembles fine breadcrumbs. Tip the dough onto a lightly floured surface and knead briskly for 1 minute; it should be quite stiff and hard to knead. Wrap in clingfilm and leave to rest in the fridge for 20 minutes.

2. **Make the Béchamel sauce** Melt the butter in a pan over a medium heat. Add the flour and mix well. Cook for 2 minutes then add the hot milk, stirring continuously. Season with salt, white pepper and nutmeg. Leave to cool.

3. **Make the asparagus sauce** Sauté the asparagus in the olive oil and garlic over a medium heat for 2–3 minutes. Melt the butter in another pan over a medium heat. Add the flour and mix well before adding the hot stock, stirring continuously. Stir in the asparagus.

4. **Assemble the pasta nests** Take the pasta from the fridge and roll it out into a large round (about 40cm in diameter and as thin as you can make it). Bring a large pan of salted water to the boil and cook the pasta for 1–2 minutes and then drain on a tea towel.

5. Spread half of the cooled Béchamel onto the pasta, then top with the mozzarella, ham and 4 tablespoons of the Parmesan. Roll into a log and wrap in a tea towel. Leave in the fridge to firm up for 30 minutes, or as long as possible.

6. Preheat the oven to 200°C/Fan 180°C.

7. **Cook the pasta nests** Spoon half the asparagus sauce into a baking dish. Remove the pasta roll from the fridge and slice into 9 even pieces. Lay the slices on the asparagus sauce and spoon the remaining sauce and Béchamel over the top. Sprinkle with the remaining Parmesan and black pepper and bake for 20–30 minutes, or until browned on top.

MEAT

SMOKED CHILLI PORK TACOS WITH APPLE & AVOCADO SALSA

1 large bunch coriander
4 garlic cloves, peeled
1 green chilli
2 tbsp smoked paprika
1 tsp allspice berries
3 tbsp Chipotle Paste (see page 279 or use shop-bought)
2 tbsp cider vinegar
zest and juice of 1 large lemon
2 tbsp unsalted butter
1 large red onion, peeled and finely diced
1 large carrot, peeled and finely diced
½ red pepper, seeded and diced
2 fresh bay leaves
2 tsp cumin seeds
½ cinnamon stick
a sprinkle of light brown sugar
500g minced pork
500ml passata
vegetable oil, for frying
8 small flour tortillas
50g Manchego cheese, grated
salt and pepper

For the apple and avocado salsa
4 spring onions, chopped
1 green chilli, chopped
1 Granny Smith apple, peeled, cored and diced
2 avocados, diced
juice of 1 large lemon
1 small bunch coriander, chopped

1. **Make the chilli paste** Whizz half the bunch of fresh coriander with the garlic, green chilli, smoked paprika, allspice berries, chipotle paste, vinegar and lemon zest in a small food-processor. Add enough water to bring together into a paste.

2. **Make the chilli** Place the butter in a large pan over a low heat and add the onion, carrot, red pepper, bay, cumin seeds, cinnamon and a sprinkling of light brown sugar. After approximately 10 minutes, increase the heat and add the pork mince to colour.

3. Add the chilli paste to the pork and onion mixture, along with the passata, and bring to the boil. Reduce the heat to a simmer and continue to cook until the liquid has reduced by at least half.

4. Season and then add the remaining fresh coriander, and lemon juice to taste.

5. **Make the apple and avocado salsa** Combine all the ingredients in a large bowl and season to taste.

6. **Fry the tortillas** Heat a little oil in a pan and fry the tortillas for 30 seconds on each side until golden and crisp.

7. Serve the crispy tortillas with the smoked chilli pork and the apple and avocado salsa, sprinkled with the grated cheese.

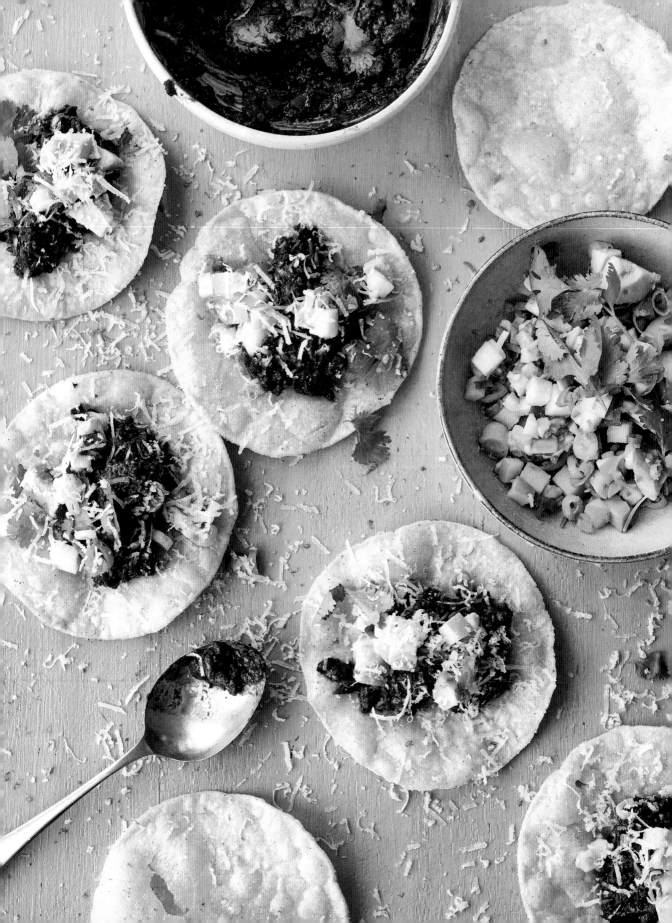

SOBRASSADA-STUFFED PORK TENDERLOIN WITH ROAST BROCCOLI & CIDER SAUCE

25g butter
1 small onion, peeled and
    finely diced
1 small eating apple, peeled
    and finely diced
1 small bunch oregano, chopped
1 small bunch basil, chopped
1 small bunch flat-leaf parsley,
    chopped
50g fresh white breadcrumbs
squeeze of fresh lemon juice
80g sobrassada sausage
1 x pork tenderloin (about 500g)
8 slices serrano ham
vegetable or olive oil, to rub
salt and pepper

For the roast broccoli
500g broccoli, broken into florets
125g full-fat cream cheese
2 tbsp Greek yoghurt
100g walnuts
squeeze of fresh lemon juice
a few fresh thyme, oregano
    and rosemary sprigs
1 tbsp paprika

For the cider sauce
2 banana shallots, peeled and
    finely diced
50g sobrassada sausage, diced
50g smoked non-spicy chorizo,
    diced
1 fresh bay leaf
200–250ml fresh chicken stock
200ml dry cider
50ml double cream
1 tbsp wholegrain mustard

1 . Make the sobrassada stuffing Melt the butter in a pan over a low heat. Add the onion and apple and fry for 2–3 minutes to soften. Tip into a bowl and mix with the herbs, breadcrumbs, lemon juice, the sobrassada and plenty of seasoning.

2 . Prepare the tenderloin Halve the tenderloin lengthways and bash it flat between sheets of clingfilm. Place the serrano ham on top of a sheet of clingfilm, overlapping the slices slightly to form a large square. Place one half of the fillet down the centre. Spread the sobrassada stuffing on top of the fillet and then cover with the remaining half fillet. Use the clingfilm to roll the ham around the fillets, ensuring that they are fully covered and held tightly together. Place in the fridge for 30 minutes to firm up.

3 . Preheat the oven to 200°C/Fan 180°C.

4 . Prepare the roast broccoli Put all the ingredients into a bowl, with salt and pepper to taste, mix well and tip onto a baking sheet.

5 . Cook the pork Remove the pork from the clingfilm, rub with oil and place on another baking sheet. Cook the pork for 30–40 minutes, or until cooked through. Cook the broccoli at the same time for 15–20 minutes, turning once or twice.

6 . Make the cider sauce Place a pan over a medium heat and fry the shallots with the cured meats and bay leaves until softened. Pour in the stock and cider and reduce. Add the cream and mustard, seasoning to taste.

7 . Leave the pork to rest before slicing and serving with the broccoli and cider jus.

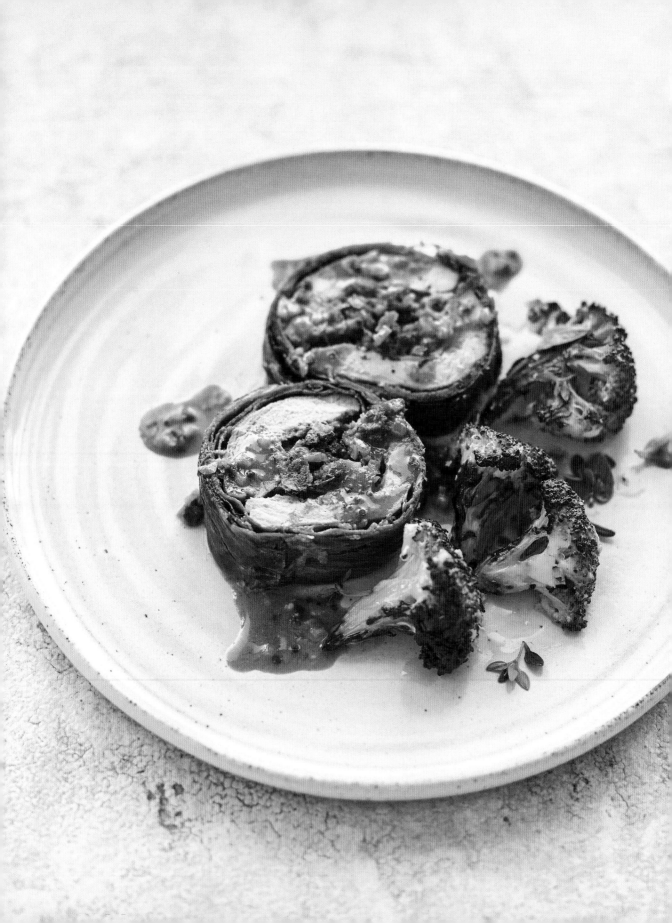

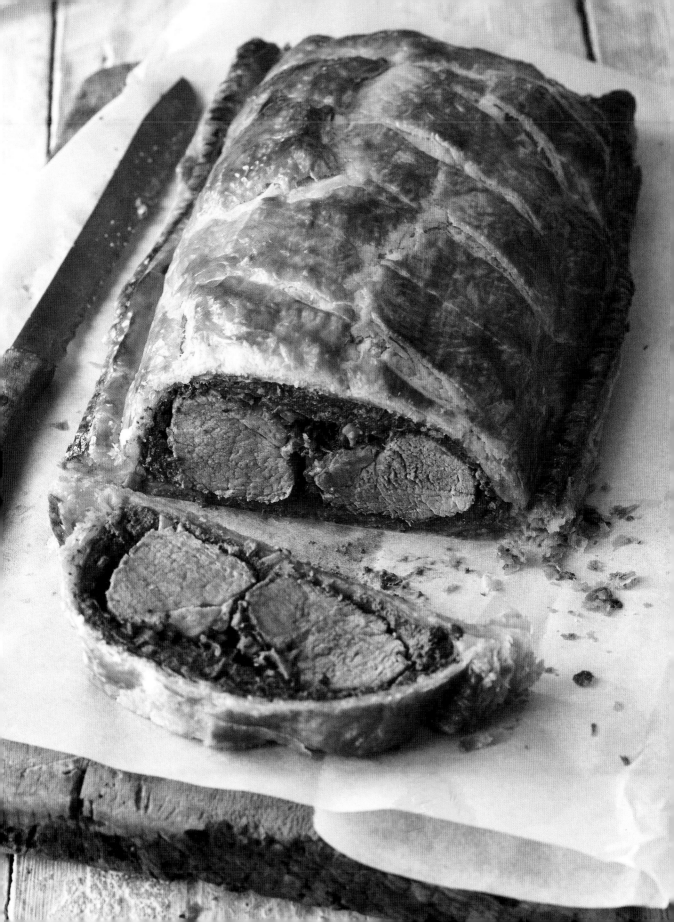

PORCHETTA WELLINGTON

2 pork tenderloins
(about 450g each)
1 tbsp olive oil
10 slices prosciutto
200g spinach leaves, wilted
and squeezed dry
2 x 375g packets all butter
puff pastry
plain flour, for dusting
2 eggs, beaten
salt and pepper

For the paté
100g unsalted butter
1 banana shallot, peeled
and chopped
250g chicken livers, trimmed
1 garlic clove, peeled and
chopped
1 tbsp brandy
½ tsp mustard powder

For the herb mix
2 tbsp olive oil
1 shallot, peeled and diced
4 garlic cloves, peeled
and chopped
150g chestnut mushrooms,
finely chopped
3 fresh thyme sprigs, leaves
picked
2 fresh rosemary sprigs, leaves
picked and finely chopped
1 tsp dried chilli flakes
finely grated zest of 1 lemon

1. **Make the paté** Melt 60g of the butter in a pan over a medium heat, then add the shallot and cook for 10–15 minutes, or until softened.

2. Add the chicken livers and garlic to the pan and cook for 2–3 minutes, turning, or until the livers are no longer pink.

3. Pour in the brandy, stir in the mustard powder and bubble for 1 minute, then season with salt and pepper.

4. Finally, place the remaining butter and the cooked liver mixture in a food-processor and whizz until smooth.

5. Spoon into a dish, cover with clingfilm so it touches the surface and then chill.

6. **Prepare the pork** Season and rub both pork loins in oil, sear in a hot pan until golden and set to aside to rest and cool.

7. **Make the herb mix** Heat the oil for the herb mix and gently fry the shallot over a low heat for 5 minutes. Add the garlic, mushrooms and herbs and fry over a high heat for a further 5 minutes. Add the chilli flakes and lemon zest, season and cool.

8. **Assemble the porchetta Wellington** Lay out two sheets of clingfilm overlapping and lay the prosciutto on top, so they overlap to make a large rectangle. Spread with the cool paté and then place the loins side by side on top. Carefully spread the herb mixture on top of the loins and tuck into all the gaps. Lay the wilted spinach on top of that.

Recipe continues

9 . Roll the clingfilm up on one side to form a tight sausage shape, so that the prosciutto encases the pork loins. Twist the ends to seal.

10 . Roll out one of the sheets of pastry on a lightly floured surface to a pound-coin thickness and then cut out a rectangle 4cm larger each side than the pork loin parcel. Unwrap the pork and place in the centre.

11 . Roll out the second piece of pastry to a pound-coin thickness. Brush the edges of the bottom piece with beaten egg. Gently lower the top pastry over the top and tuck in and press around the loins. Trim with a sharp knife to match the bottom pastry, seal the two together with a fork, then egg wash the entire Wellington and score the top with the back of a knife. Chill for 20 minutes.

12 . Preheat the oven to 200°C/Fan 180°C.

13 . **Cook the porchetta Wellington** Brush the pastry with a little more egg wash and cook for 35–40 minutes, or until golden.

14 . Allow to stand for 10 minutes before serving in thick slices.

> **TIP** Serve with Polenta & Balsamic-glazed Brussels Sprouts & Walnuts (see page 265) and Hasselback Potatoes (see page 270).

MOUSSAKA

80ml olive oil
1 large onion, peeled
  and finely sliced
4 garlic cloves, peeled
  and finely sliced
500g minced lamb
2 tsp ground cumin
1 tsp ground coriander
1 cinnamon stick
1 x 400g tin chopped tomatoes
2 tbsp tomato purée
3 fresh oregano springs,
  leaves picked
2–3 large aubergines, sliced
250ml Greek yoghurt
2 eggs, beaten
100g feta, crumbled
2 tbsp freshly grated
  Parmesan
salt and pepper

1 : **Prepare the mince** Heat 2 tablespoons of the oil in a large pan over a low heat and gently fry the onion for 10 minutes.

2 : Add the garlic and fry for 1 minute before adding the lamb mince. Increase the heat and fry for 2–3 minutes, stirring, until browned all over.

3 : Stir in all the spices and fry for 1 minute, then add the tomatoes, tomato purée and oregano. Season well.

4 : Lower the heat and bubble gently for 30–40 minutes, adding a splash of water if it starts to get a bit too dry.

5 : **Prepare the aubergine** Heat the rest of the oil in a large non-stick pan over a medium heat and fry the aubergine until golden on both sides and tender. Drain on kitchen paper and season.

6 : Preheat the oven to 200°C/Fan 180°C.

7 : Mix the yoghurt with the eggs and cheeses and season well.

8 : **Assemble the moussaka** Spread half the lamb mixture into the base of a 1.2-litre oven dish and then top with half the aubergine. Repeat. Pour the yoghurt mixture over the top of the second aubergine layer.

9 : **Cook the moussaka** Bake for 30–40 minutes, or until golden and bubbling. Serve with a green salad.

MEAT

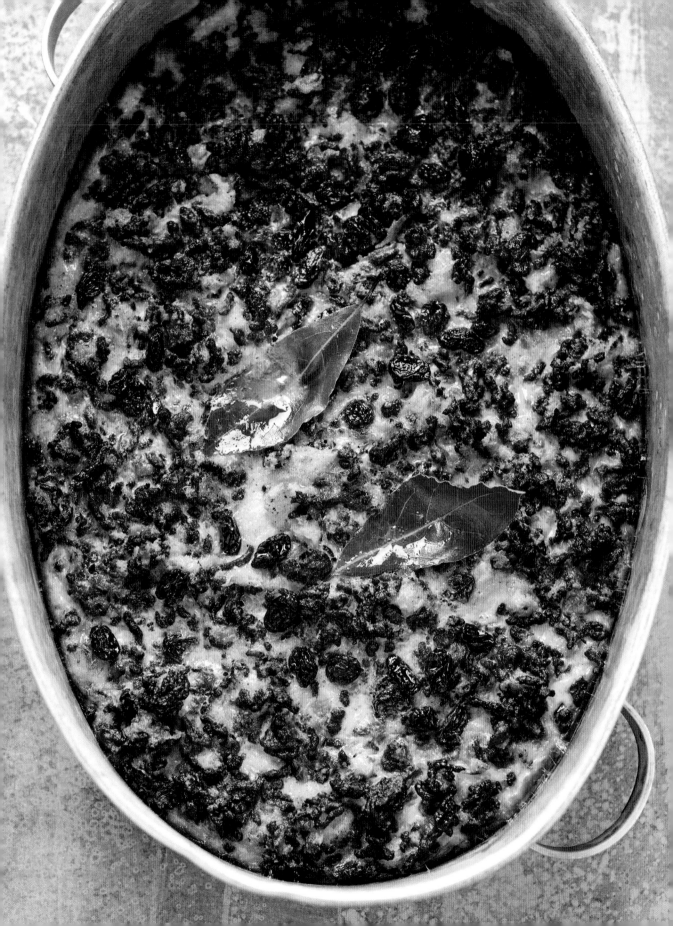

ROSEMARY'S BAKED SPICED LAMB WITH SAVOURY CUSTARD

2 tbsp rapeseed oil
500g minced lamb or beef
1 onion, peeled and chopped
1 ½ tsp medium curry powder
½ tsp turmeric
½ tsp salt
20g apricot jam
1 tbsp Worcestershire sauce
20ml apple cider vinegar
50g raisins
2 slices white bread,
   crusts removed
300ml whole milk
3 medium eggs
2 bay leaves

1. Heat 1 tablespoon of the oil in a large pan over a high heat and brown the mince off in batches. Remove from the pan and drain over a colander to remove excess fat.

2. Using the same pan, add the remaining oil and fry the onion until soft but not taking on colour. Stir in the curry powder, ¼ teaspoon of the turmeric, the salt, apricot jam, Worcestershire sauce and cider vinegar and cook for 2 minutes. Add the mince back to the pan and continue to cook for 5 minutes. Finally, add the raisins and stir well. Remove from the heat.

3. Place the slices of crustless bread in a bowl and pour over the milk. Allow to soak for about 1 minute and then remove the softened bread from the milk. Gently press any excess milk out (keeping it for the topping), break up the bread and stir through the mince. Ensure everything is well combined. Place this mixture in a large pie dish.

4. Preheat the oven to 180°C/Fan 160°C.

5. Beat the eggs into the reserved milk and add the remaining ¼ teaspoon of turmeric and a pinch of salt.

6. Pour evenly over the mince, tapping the pie dish to allow the custard to settle, and place the bay leaves on top. Bake for about 30–45 minutes, or until the custard is set with no liquid wobble in the centre.

7. Serve with a tomato and shallot salad.

> **TIP** A traditional South African dish – serve it with Coconut & Almond Pilaf Rice (see page 276).

MEAT

LAMB & VEGETABLE STEW WITH COUSCOUS

SERVES 4

1kg boned leg of lamb,
    cut into pieces
1 tsp ground ginger
1 tsp ground cumin
1 tbsp salt
6 tbsp olive oil
1 large onion, peeled and
    finely sliced
2 large carrots, peeled and
    finely chopped
3 fresh sage leaves
1 cinnamon stick
1 tsp black peppercorns
1 lamb stock cube
2 courgettes, trimmed
    and sliced
1 large aubergine, trimmed
    and cut into 2cm pieces
3 large potatoes, peeled and
    cut into 2cm pieces
1 x 400g tin chickpeas,
    drained and rinsed
400g couscous
1 tbsp butter
800ml chicken stock, boiling
a handful of chopped fresh
    coriander and parsley,
    to garnish

1. **Prepare the lamb** Rub the lamb pieces with the ginger, cumin and salt. Place a large pan over a high heat and add 2 tablespoons of the olive oil. Sear the meat all over then set aside.

2. Heat another tablespoon of the oil in the pan and fry the onion and carrots over a medium heat for 5 minutes, or until soft. Return the lamb to the pan and add the sage, cinnamon and black peppercorns. Pour in 500ml of water and add the stock cube. Bring to the boil, then cover and gently simmer for 45 minutes.

3. **Prepare the vegetables** Heat half the remaining oil in a pan and fry the courgette over a high heat until coloured and tender. Scoop out with a slotted spoon and put to one side. Add the remaining oil to the pan and fry the aubergine until tender, then add to the courgette.

4. When the lamb has been cooking for 45 minutes, add the potatoes and cook for a further 15 minutes.

5. Finally, stir in the courgette, aubergine and the chickpeas. Cook for another 15 minutes.

6. **Make the couscous** Place it in a large, heatproof bowl with the butter. Pour the boiling stock over the top, stir with a fork, and then leave for 5 minutes, or until the stock has been absorbed.

7. Serve the stew with the couscous on a platter alongside, garnished with fresh herbs.

> **FAMILY TIP** 'The depth of flavour in this recipe relies on two very important things: using a variety of vegetables and cooking with love. Cook in the company of your family and watch how the flavours transform!'

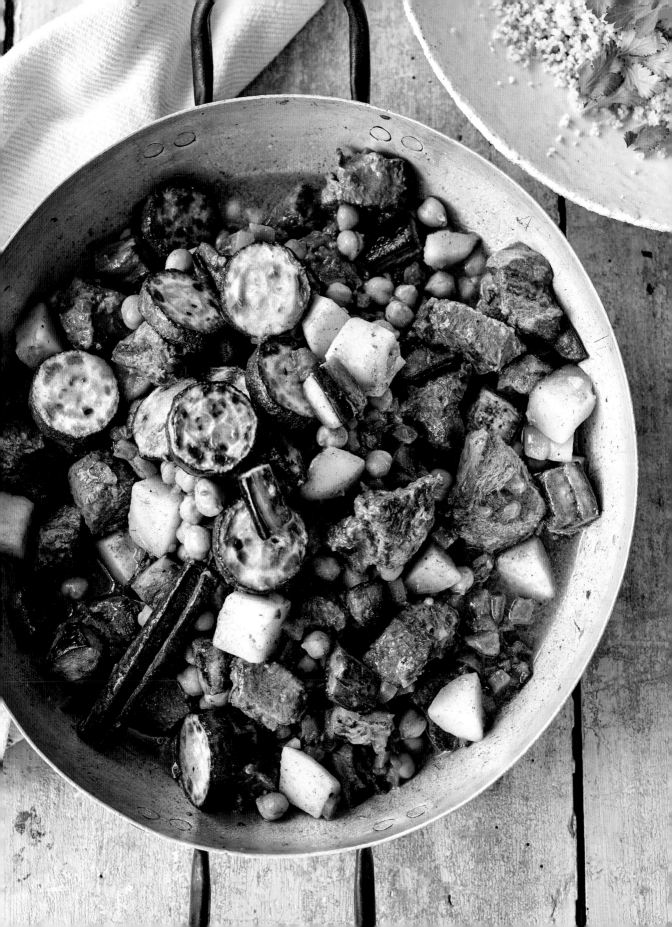

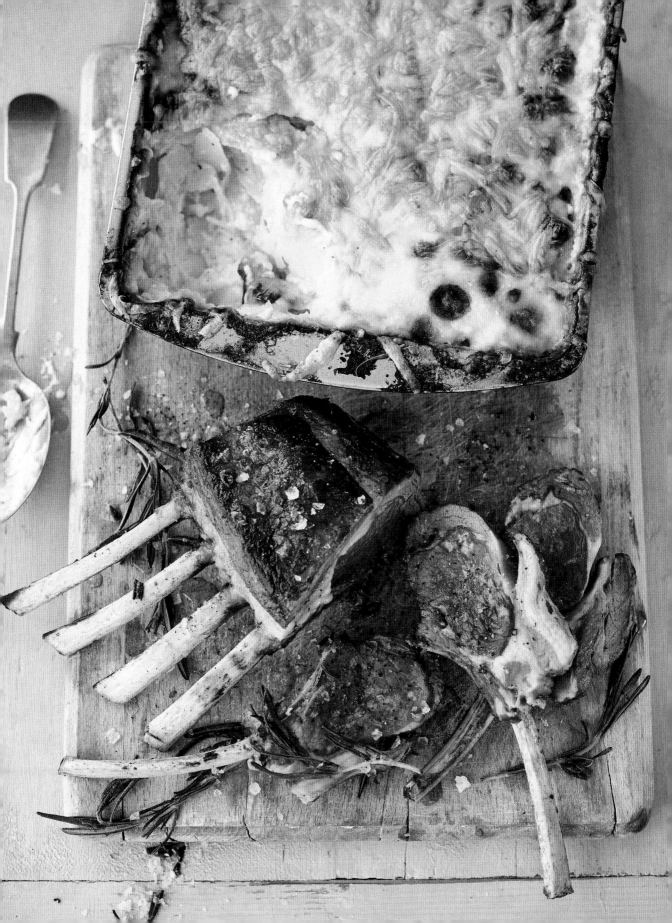

RACK OF LAMB WITH DAUPHINOISE POTATO

2 x 6-bone racks of lamb,
  French-trimmed
2–3 fresh rosemary sprigs

For the dauphinoise potato
butter, for greasing
750g Maris Piper potatoes,
  peeled
2 garlic cloves, finely sliced
good grating of nutmeg
200ml double cream
100ml milk
100g Emmenthal cheese,
  grated
salt and pepper

1 Preheat the oven to 170°C/Fan 150°C and butter a large ovenproof dish.

2 Make the dauphinoise potato Thinly slice the potatoes using a mandolin, and rinse to remove some of the starch. Drain and then layer the potato with the garlic, grated nutmeg and seasoning into the prepared ovenproof dish. Combine the cream with the milk and then pour over the potatoes.

3 Sprinkle with grated cheese and bake for 45–60 minutes, until the potatoes are soft and golden.

4 When the potatoes come out of the oven, turn the temperature up to 220°C/Fan 200°C.

5 Cook the lamb Pan-fry the racks of lamb over a high heat for about 2 minutes on each side to brown, and then transfer to a roasting dish. Cook in the hot oven for approximately 8 minutes, cover with foil and then leave to rest for 10 minutes before serving with the potatoes.

> **TIP** Serve with peas, carrots and parsnips.

ROSEMARY'S BUTTERFLIED LEG OF LAMB WITH WHOLE ROASTED GARLIC

SERVES 4

½ butterflied leg of lamb (about 800g–1kg), cut into 4 chunks
6 anchovy fillets in oil, finely chopped
4 garlic cloves, peeled and bashed, plus 2 whole heads
3 fresh rosemary sprigs, leaves stripped
2 tbsp olive oil
1 tbsp rapeseed oil
2 fresh lemon thyme sprigs
salt and pepper

1. **Prepare the lamb** Put the lamb in a dish and add the anchovies, bashed garlic cloves, rosemary and olive oil. Season with black pepper and mix to coat well. Marinate for at least 1 hour.

2. Preheat the oven to 200°C/Fan 180°C.

3. **Cook the lamb** Season the lamb with plenty of salt. Heat a large pan over a high heat and sear the lamb all over until a deep golden colour on all sides. Transfer to a roasting tin and then cook in oven for about 20–25 minutes. Allow to rest for 10 minutes before slicing.

4. **Make the roasted garlic** Slice the tops off the heads of garlic and rub with rapeseed oil. Place on a piece of tin foil along with the lemon thyme, wrap up the foil like a parcel and roast in the oven for 30 minutes alongside the lamb.

5. Serve slices of lamb with the roasted garlic.

> **TIP** Serve with Boulangère Potatoes (see page 271) and Braised Leeks (see page 256).

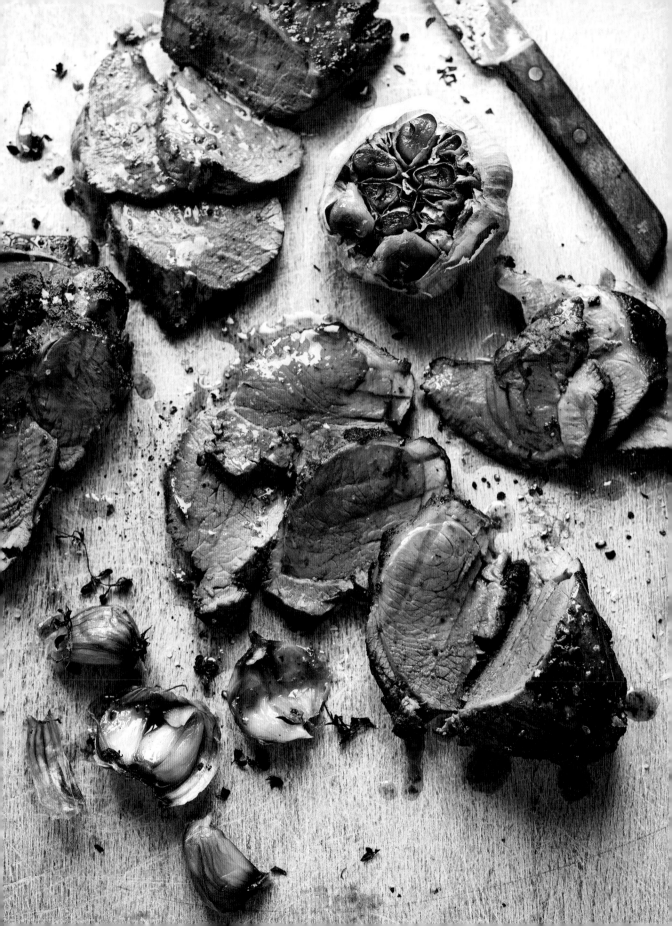

SAAG GOSHT WITH HOME-MADE CHAPATTIS

SERVES 6-8

For the saag gosht

75ml vegetable oil
2 medium onions, peeled
and finely chopped
1 garlic clove, peeled and
finely chopped
1 tsp grated fresh root ginger
1 small tomato, finely chopped
1 red chilli, finely chopped
1½ tsp turmeric
1 tsp ground cumin
2 tsp ground coriander
1kg boneless leg of lamb,
cut into chunks
250g spinach, tough stems
removed
100g fresh fenugreek (methi)
leaves, or a handful of dried
1 tsp garam masala
salt and pepper

For the chapattis

500g chapatti flour, ideally
gold chakki flour, or
250g plain flour and 250g
stoneground wholemeal
1 tsp salt

1. **Make the saag gosht** Heat the oil in a large flameproof casserole over a medium heat. Add the onions and garlic and cook for 5 minutes, or until golden brown. Stir in the ginger and tomato and fry for another minute. Season with salt and stir in the chilli, turmeric, cumin and coriander. Add a splash of water, reduce the heat, cover with a lid and leave to cook on low for 20 minutes.

2. Tuck the lamb into the dish and cook covered, over the low heat for about 70 minutes, or until tender.

3. **Make the chapattis** Place the flour in a large bowl. Mix with 200–250ml cold water to make a smooth dough. Separate the dough into 8 small round balls and then roll out each ball on a floured worktop.

4. Place a tawa or non-stick frying pan over a high heat and, when hot, cook the chapattis for 1–2 minutes on each side. Keep the cooked chapattis warm, wrapped in a clean tea towel, until ready to serve.

5. Just before serving, add the spinach, fenugreek and garam masala to the lamb, stir and cover. Allow to steam and wilt, stirring occasionally, for 5–10 minutes.

6. Serve the saag gosht with the chapattis.

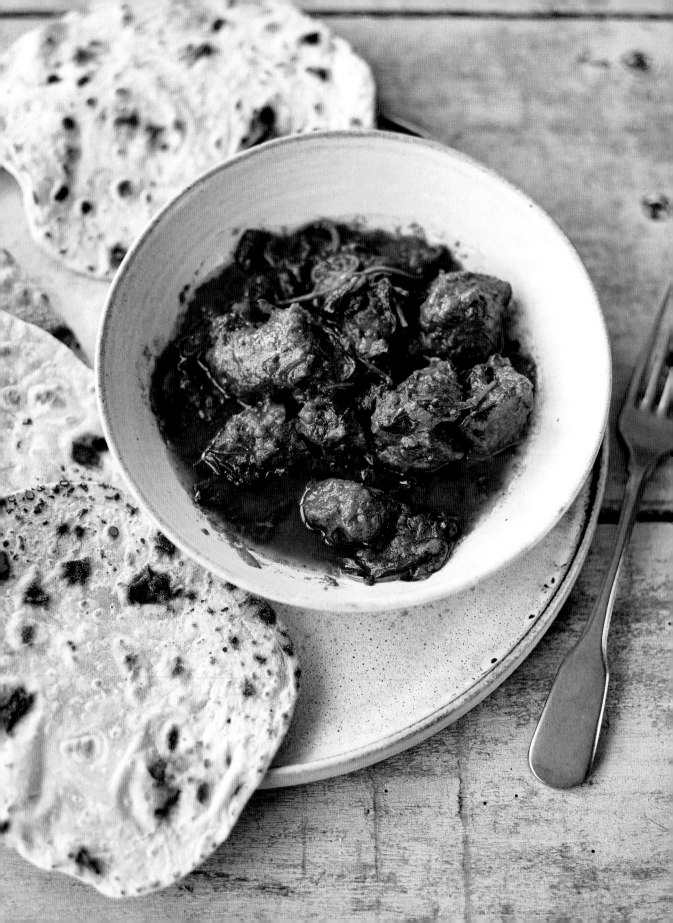

SEEKH KEBABS WITH SPICY CHILLI CORN

SERVES 4-6

For the seekh kebabs

1 medium onion, peeled
    and roughly chopped
15g fresh coriander
2 green chillies
1kg minced lamb
3 garlic cloves, peeled and
    crushed
2cm piece fresh root ginger,
    peeled and grated
1½ tsp Kashmiri chilli powder
1½ tsp garam masla
1 tsp salt
vegetable oil

For the spicy chilli corn

4 sweetcorn cobs
1 tbsp olive oil
1 tbsp garlic and ginger paste
large pinch of dried fenugreek
    (methi) leaves
1 green chilli, thinly sliced
½ tsp chilli powder
½ tsp turmeric
½ tsp salt
½ x 400g tin chopped
    tomatoes
knob of butter (about 20g)
2 lemons, quartered

1. **Make the seekh kebabs** Whizz the onion, coriander and chillies in a mini food-processor to form a paste.

2. In a large mixing bowl, place the lamb, the paste from the food-processor, the garlic, ginger, chilli powder, garam masala and salt. Using your hands, knead all the ingredients until they are incorporated and a paste-like consistency.

3. Oil your hands and shape the mince into sausages around 8 skewers. Place the kebabs in the fridge for 30 minutes; meanwhile, preheat the oven to 200°C/Fan 180°C.

4. Place the skewers directly onto an oven grill shelf, brush with oil and cook for 15–20 minutes, until lightly golden brown and cooked through. (You might want to place an oven tray beneath the skewers to catch the fat.)

5. **Make the spicy chilli corn** Cut each sweetcorn into 3 pieces and boil in plenty of water for 8–9 minutes, or until tender.

6. While the corn is boiling, heat the olive oil in a pan over a medium heat and add the garlic and ginger paste, the fenugreek, green chilli, chilli powder, turmeric and salt. Fry for about 30 seconds – not too long as you don't want it to colour.

7. Immediately add the tomatoes and cook until the sauce warms through – no more than 3 minutes.

8. Finish the sauce by stirring in the butter.

9. Drain the sweetcorn and place back into their pan. Pour over the sauce and mix well to get an even coating.

10. Serve the kebabs with the spicy sweetcorn and some lemon wedges.

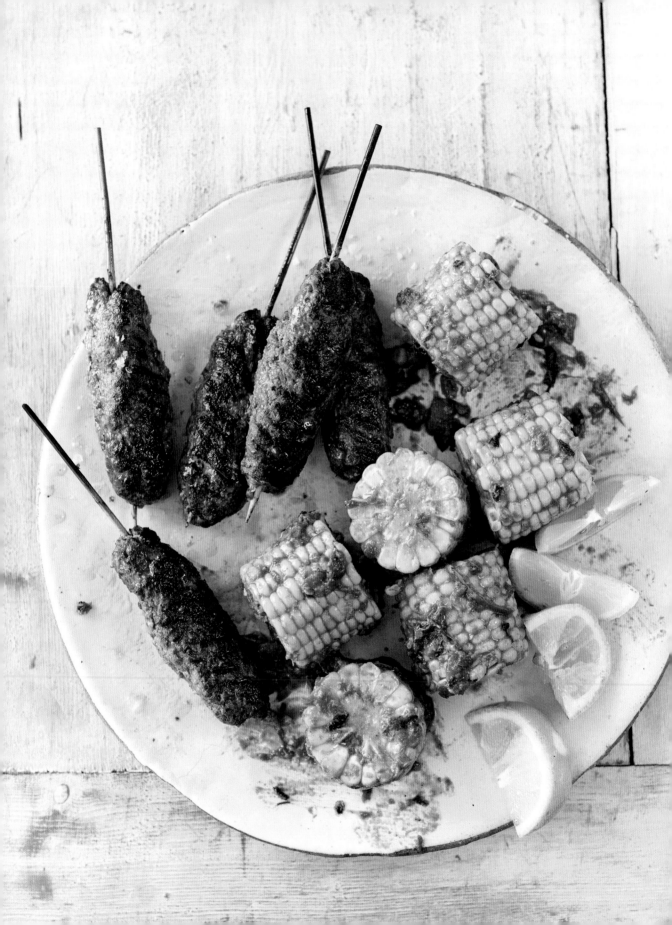

HANGER STEAK WITH CAULIFLOWER & ROASTED GRAPES

SERVES 4

150g red grapes
700g hanger steaks
    (or bavette or onglet)
salt and pepper

For the cauliflower mash
1 large cauliflower, broken
    into florets
400ml double cream
2 garlic cloves, peeled
75g butter
100g raclette cheese
1 tsp Marmite
15g Parmesan

1 : Preheat the oven to 180°C/Fan 160°C.

2 : Pick out about 200g of the small- and medium-sized cauliflower florets that have a good circular shape, and put to one side.

3 : **Make the cauliflower mash** Place the remaining florets and the stalk, roughly chopped, in a pan. Pour in the cream, add the garlic and 50g of the butter. Simmer over a medium heat for 10 minutes, then add the raclette cheese and plenty of seasoning. Cook for a further 5 minutes, or until the cauliflower is soft.

4 : Add the contents of the pan to a blender and whizz to a purée. Push through a sieve into a clean pan, ready to reheat to serve.

5 : **Make the roasted cauliflower** Bring a large pan of water to the boil, add the reserved florets and cook for 2–3 minutes, or until tender, then drain. Return to the pan with the remaining butter and the Marmite, and melt. Tip into a small roasting tin and cook in the oven for 20 minutes. Grate the Parmesan all over before serving.

6 : **Make the roasted grapes** While the florets are roasting, place the grapes in small bunches in another roasting tin and cook in the oven for 15 minutes, or until sticky and soft.

7 : **Cook the steaks** Heat a griddle pan over a very high heat and season the steak with salt and pepper. Cook for 1–2 minutes each side – this type of steak is best served very rare or it will become tough. Rest for 10 minutes before slicing and serving with the cauliflower mash, florets and grapes.

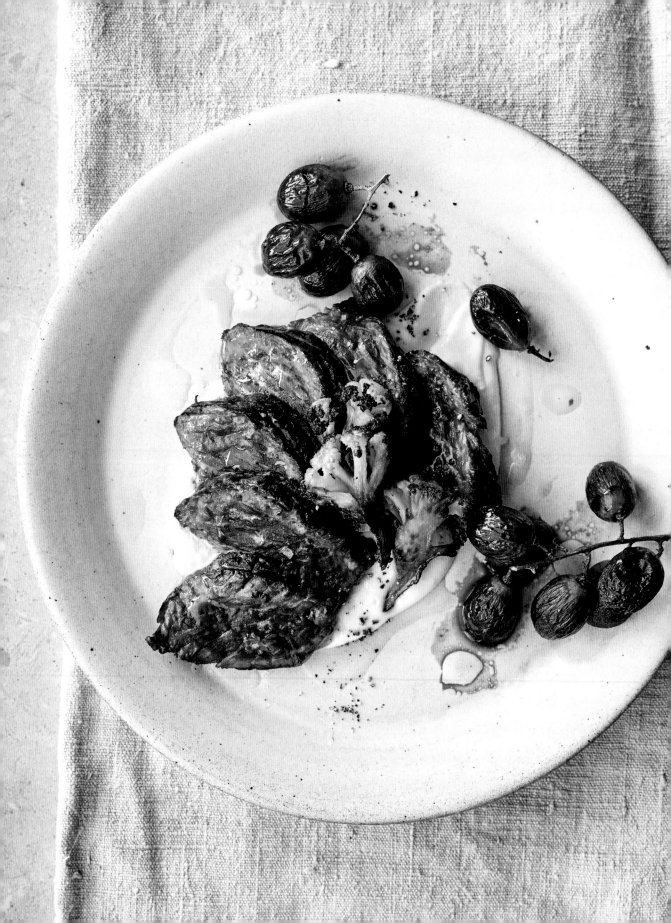

BEST-EVER LASAGNE

2 tbsp olive oil
1 large onion, peeled and
   finely chopped
1 small carrot, peeled and
   finely chopped
1 celery stick, finely chopped
2 garlic cloves, peeled and
   finely sliced
500g minced beef
50g chicken livers,
   finely chopped
3 fresh thyme sprigs,
   leaves picked
175ml red wine
1 x 400g tin chopped tomatoes
1 tbsp tomato purée
6–9 fresh lasagne sheets
   (depending on the size
   of the sheets)
salt and pepper

For the Béchamel sauce
50g unsalted butter
50g plain flour
600ml whole milk
good grating of fresh nutmeg
100g Parmesan, grated

1 : Preapare the mince Heat the oil in a pan over
a low heat and gently fry the onion, carrot and celery
for 15 minutes, or until really soft.

2 : Add the garlic and fry for 30 seconds then turn up
the heat and add the beef mince and chicken livers and
fry until browned all over.

3 : Add the thyme and red wine and bubble until reduced
by half. Stir in the tomatoes and the purée. Season, reduce
the heat and simmer gently for 1 hour, or until thickened
and really tender. Add a splash of water if it dries out
too much.

4 : Make the Béchamel Melt the butter in a pan over
a medium heat and add the flour. Cook for 1 minute then
gradually add the milk, stirring, until you have a thick
white sauce.

5 : Add the nutmeg and some seasoning and bubble
for 1–2 minutes before adding all but a handful of the
Parmesan; allow to melt.

6 : Preheat the oven to 200°C/Fan 180°C.

7 : Assemble the lasagne Spoon a third of the meat into
the bottom of an ovenproof dish (about 1.2 litre) and then
cover with 2 (or 3) of the lasagne sheets, before topping
with a third of the white sauce. Repeat twice more, ending
with a layer of white sauce. Scatter with the remaining
Parmesan and bake for 35–40 minutes, or until
golden and bubbling.

8 : Rest for 10 minutes before serving.

MEAT

ROAST RIB OF BEEF
WITH ROAST POTATOES, CARROTS
& HORSERADISH SAUCE

SERVES 6

2.5kg well hung (28 days
   minimum) rib of beef on
   the bone (1 large rib or
   2 smaller ones), spine off
rapeseed oil, to drizzle
1.5kg Maris Piper potatoes,
   peeled and halved
2 tbsp goose fat
3 garlic cloves, smashed
3 fresh thyme sprigs,
   leaves picked
salt and pepper

For the buttery carrots
60g salted butter
2 tsp soft light brown sugar
1 tsp salt
10 long skinny carrots,
   including green stems,
   peeled and trimmed

For the horseradish sauce
20g fresh horseradish,
   peeled and grated
1 tsp Dijon mustard
1 tsp white wine vinegar
squeeze of fresh lemon juice
½ tsp salt
150ml crème fraîche

1 : Preheat the oven to 110°C/Fan 90°C.

2 : Prepare the beef Rub the beef in rapeseed oil and
season all over. Heat a large pan over a high heat and
brown the meat on all sides. Don't leave it for too long
on one side or it will dry inside.

3 : Insert an ovenproof meat probe and place the beef in
a roasting tin. Roast in the oven for 4–5 hours. When the
internal temperature reaches 55°C the beef is ready.

4 : Make the roast potatoes Bring a pan of salted water
to the boil and par-boil the potatoes for 5–6 minutes. Drain,
bash them around in the pan and season with salt.

5 : Take the beef out of the oven and turn the temperature
up to 200°C/Fan 180°C. Cover the beef with foil and then a
tea towel and leave to rest for 1 hour while the potatoes cook.

6 : Place the goose fat in a roasting tray and put in the
oven to heat. Add the potatoes and roast for 50 minutes.
Add the garlic and thyme 20 minutes before the end.

7 : Make the buttery carrots Melt the butter in a pan
with 150ml water. Add the sugar, salt and the carrots and
cook for 10–12 minutes, or until tender and the liquid has
reduced and coats the carrots all over.

8 : Make the horseradish sauce Combine all the
ingredients except the crème fraîche and leave to rest
for 15 minutes. Finally, stir in the crème fraîche.

9 : Cut the beef off the bone, carve and serve with the
roast potatoes, carrots and horseradish sauce.

TIP Serve with Oxtail and Bone Marrow
Gravy (see page 281).

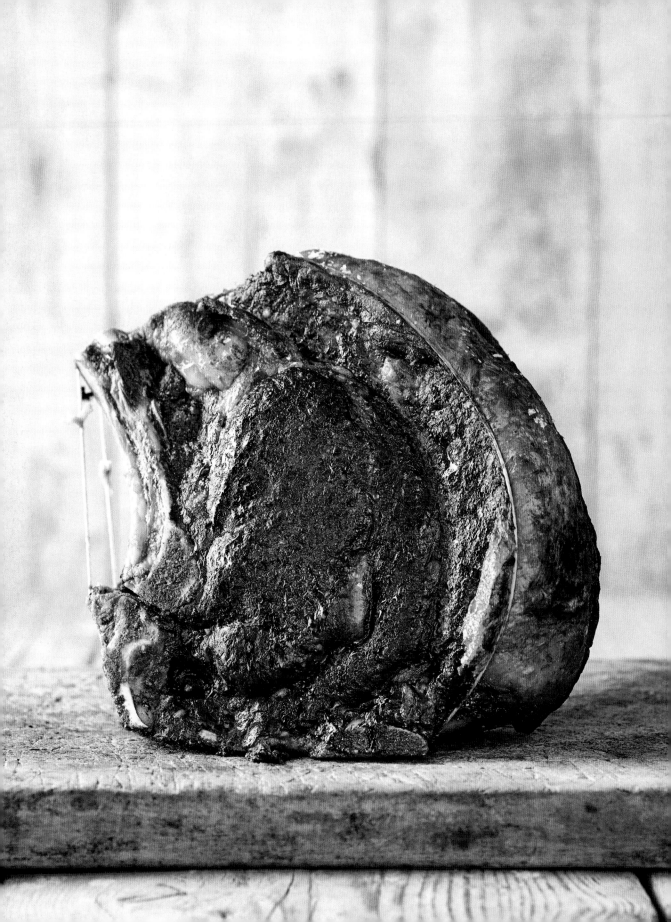

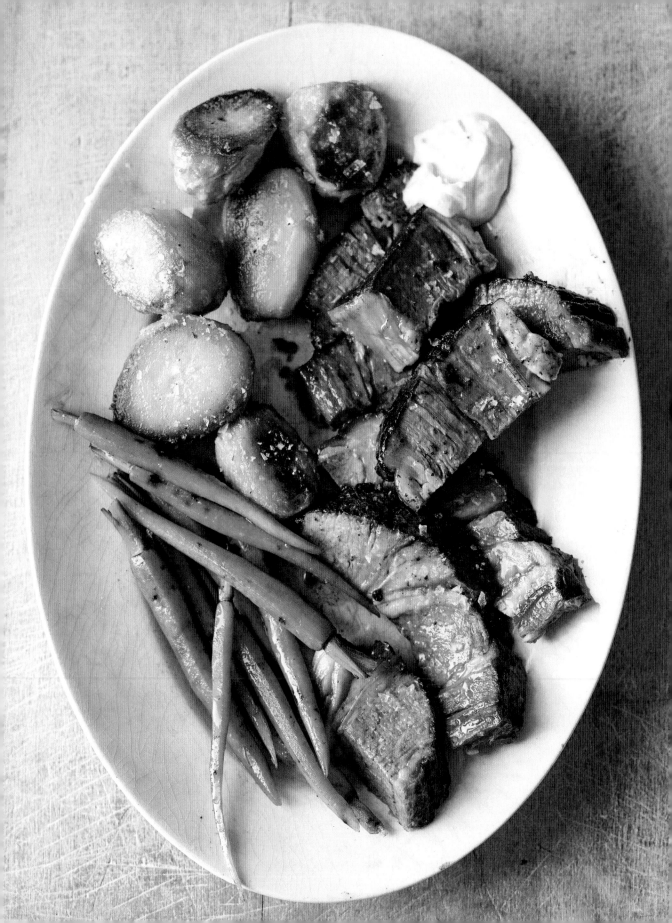

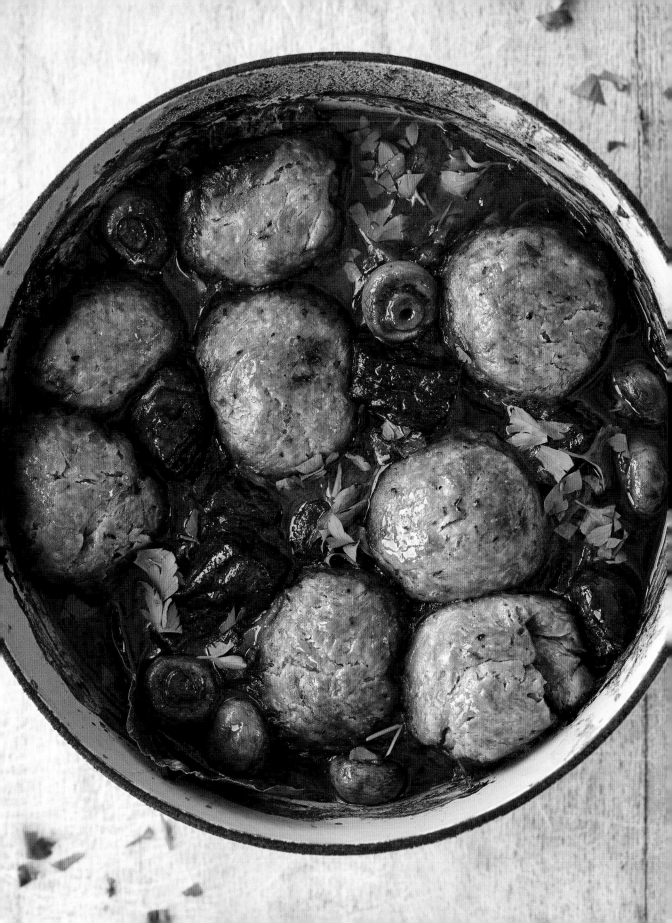

ROSEMARY'S STEAK & KIDNEY PIE WITH HERBY DUMPLINGS

SERVES 4

800g braising steak, diced
200g ox kidney, cut into pieces
2 tsp plain flour
3 tbsp oil
1 onion, peeled and diced
200ml red wine
400ml fresh beef stock
200g tomatoes, chopped
2 tsp soft light brown sugar
a small handful of fresh herbs
    (rosemary, thyme, bay leaf)
2 tbsp unsalted butter
200g button mushrooms
2 tbsp freshly chopped
    flat-leaf parsley, to serve
salt and pepper

For the herby dumplings
150g self-raising flour
pinch of salt
75g vegetable suet
1 tsp dried mixed herbs
1 tsp freshly chopped
    flat-leaf parsley

1. Preheat the oven to 150°C/Fan 130°C.

2. Season the beef and kidney and dust in plain flour.

3. **Make the pie** Heat half the oil in a flameproof casserole over a medium heat and fry the meat in batches until browned all over. Set aside.

4. Add the remainder of the oil to the casserole and cook the onion over a medium heat for 10 minutes, or until soft and starting to caramelise.

5. Pour in the red wine and bubble until reduced by two thirds.

6. Add the stock, tomatoes, sugar and the handful of herbs and season well. Return the meat to the pan and bring to a simmer. Cover and cook in the oven for 2–2½ hours, or until the meat is very tender.

7. **Make the herby dumplings** Mix all the dry ingredients for the dumplings together and add about 60ml water, or enough to make a soft, not sticky dough. Shape into 8 balls.

8. Melt the butter in a pan over a medium heat and fry the button mushrooms until brown.

9. Remove the casserole from the oven, stir in the mushrooms and pop the dumplings on top. Cover the casserole with a lid and continue to cook for about 20 minutes, or until the dumplings are golden and puffed.

10. Serve sprinkled with parsley.

> **TIP** Serve with mashed potato, horseradish sauce and Braised Red Cabbage in Cider (see page 262).

MEAT

DRY-SPICED VENISON WITH WILD MUSHROOMS & SPINACH

SERVES 4

4 x 200g venison steaks
½ shallot, peeled and
    finely chopped
25g unsalted butter
200g wild mushrooms, cleaned
a handful of fresh coriander,
    chopped to garnish
350g fresh spinach
a squeeze of lemon

For the dry rub

3 cardamom pods, bashed
    and seeds extracted
1 tsp cumin seeds
1 tsp coriander seeds
½ dried chilli
4 curry leaves
2.5cm cinnamon stick
1 clove
pinch of ground ginger

For the sauce

2 tbsp olive oil
1 white onion, peeled
    and chopped
1 carrot, peeled and diced
2.5cm fresh root ginger,
    finely chopped
2 garlic cloves, peeled and
    finely chopped
1 red chilli, finely chopped
1 tsp ground cumin
1 tsp ground coriander
1 tbsp tomato purée
500ml fresh beef stock
250ml fresh chicken stock
2 tsp grated chocolate
    (100 per cent cocoa solids,
    if you can find it)
salt and pepper

1. **Marinate the venison** Grind all the ingredients for the dry rub in a pestle and mortar and then rub all over the venison fillet steaks.

2. **Make the sauce** Place the oil in a pan over a medium heat and gently fry the onion and carrot, before adding the ginger, garlic, chilli, dried spices and tomato purée.

3. Add the stocks and simmer until the liquid has reduced by about half and then strain with a fine sieve.

4. Return to the pan and place over a high heat and reduce down again to sauce consistency. Add the chocolate and season to taste, if necessary.

5. **Cook the venison** Place a large pan over a high heat and brown the venison on all sides for 1–2 minutes. Turn the heat down and cook for 1–2 minutes more, turning once. Leave to rest for 5–10 minutes.

6. **Cook the wild mushrooms** Fry the shallots in half the butter over a medium heat for 1 minute before adding the mushrooms and frying for a further 3 minutes. Tip into a serving dish and garnish with the fresh coriander.

7. **Cook the spinach** Using the same pan, melt the remaining butter and then fry the spinach until lightly wilted. Season to taste with salt pepper and lemon juice.

8. Slice the venison and serve with the wild mushrooms, spinach and sauce alongside.

FAMILY TIP 'Don't move the venison around too much in the pan, you want to get some char; that's where the flavour is.'

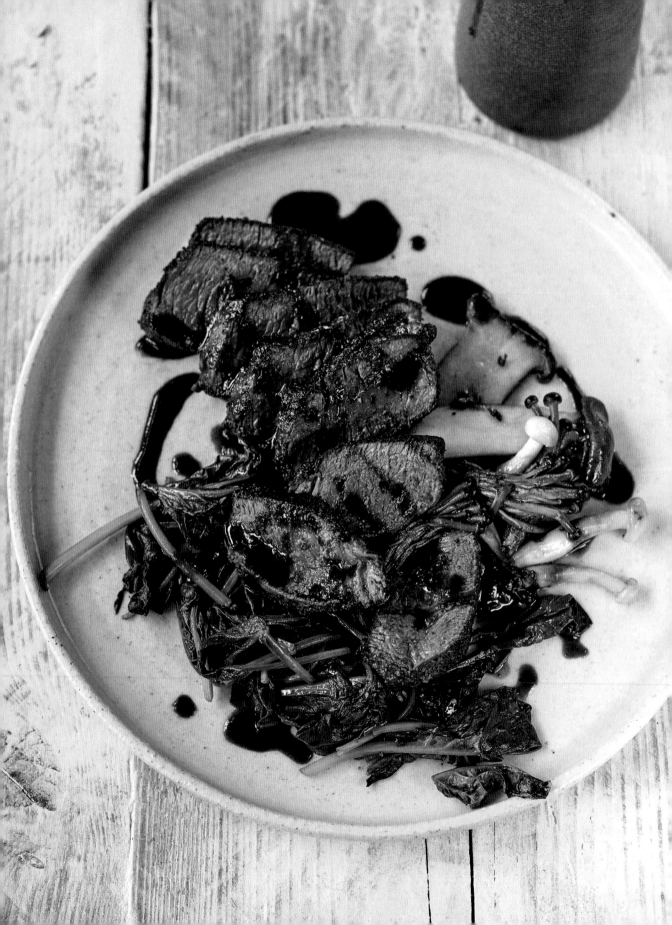

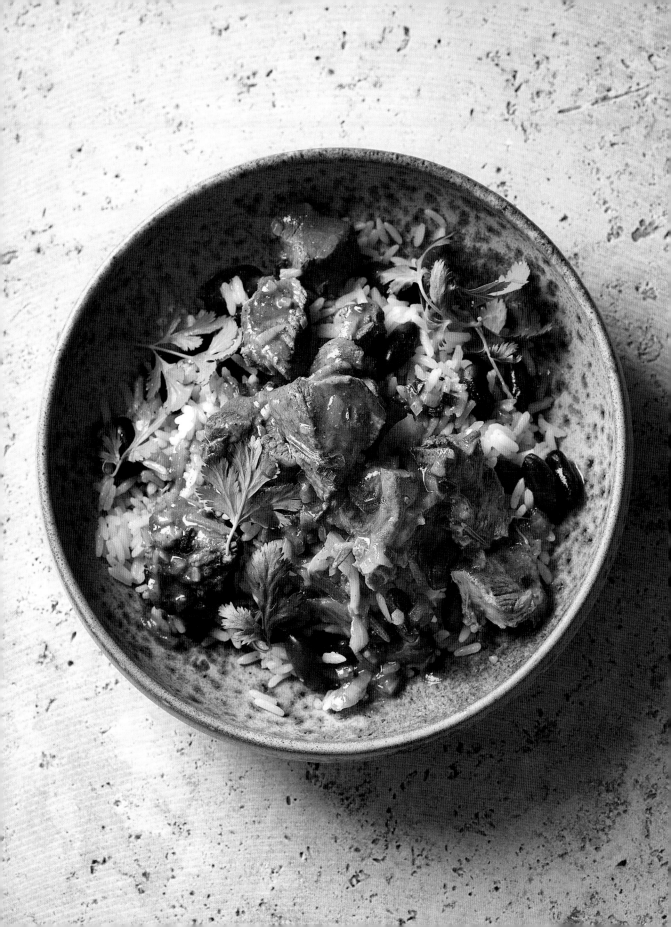

CURRIED GOAT & RICE

SERVES 6

3 large onions, peeled, 1 finely chopped, 2 finely sliced
5 garlic cloves, peeled and bashed
1 small bunch chives, snipped
60ml white wine vinegar
¼ tsp ground cloves
1kg goat thigh, cut into chunks
3 tbsp sunflower oil
3 tbsp mild curry powder
1 lamb stock cube
2 fresh rosemary sprigs
2 fresh oregano sprigs
a handful of fresh parsley
1 small bunch coriander, chopped
salt and pepper

For the rice
300g easy-cook long grain rice, rinsed
200ml coconut milk
40ml sunflower oil
2 chicken stock cubes
1 x 400g tin kidney beans, drained and rinsed
pinch of salt

1 **Marinate the goat** In a bowl large enough to hold all the meat, mix the chopped onion, garlic and chives with the vinegar and cloves. Add the goat and marinate for about 20 minutes.

2 **Make the curry** Heat the oil in a large flameproof casserole dish over a medium heat. Add the sliced onions and fry for 10 minutes. Stir in the curry powder and cook for 1 minute.

3 Tip in the goat and crumble in the lamb stock cube. Stir in the rosemary, oregano and parsley, add 700ml water and season well. Mix everything together and bring to the boil. Reduce the heat, cover with a lid and leave to simmer for 1 hour.

4 Remove the lid and continue to simmer for a further 1–1½ hours, or until the meat is very tender and the sauce reduced.

5 **Make the rice** Place all the ingredients in a pan with 450ml water. Stir well and bring to a boil. Reduce the heat, cover and gently simmer for 6 minutes.

6 Take off the heat and leave to stand, covered, for a further 5–6 minutes, or until tender and the liquid has been absorbed.

7 Fluff up the rice, stir coriander through the curry and serve alongside plantain chips and coleslaw.

> **FAMILY TIP** 'Music has always been central to our cooking – the music is always loud, our hands are always busy and so are our hips. Cooking is a celebration.'

SIMPLE RECIPE IDEAS

At its most simple a **frittata** needs nothing more than a large handful of grated **cheese**, some freshly **ground black pepper** and **eggs**. Use 6 large eggs to make a frittata for 4 people: beat the eggs in a bowl until combined then season with **salt**, pepper and add cheese. Melt **butter** in a large frying pan over a low-medium heat and pour in the egg mixture. Cook for 10–15 minutes and then finish the top under a hot grill. You can add almost anything to this basic recipe: **roasted red peppers** and fried **chorizo**; leftover **roasted vegetables** and crumbled **goats' cheese**; **frozen peas** and finely chopped **herbs**; **caramelised onion** and crispy **lardons**.

Store-bought puff pastry is a supper saviour, and it's handy to have some stashed in the fridge or freezer. **Savoury puff pastry tarts** couldn't be easier to put together and are perfect for a picnic, packed lunch, or easy dinner. Roll out ready-made **puff pastry** until around 0.75cm thin. Roll or slide onto a baking sheet then prick with a fork, leaving an unpricked border of around 1cm. Top with grated **Gruyère**, very thinly sliced **potatoes** and a sprinkling of chopped **rosemary**; or cover with slices of **spicy sausage** and then top with sliced **baby plum** or **cherry tomatoes**, **mozzarella** and a few blobs of **pesto**. Brush the pastry edges with a little beaten **egg** or **milk**, and cook until golden and crisp.

> **FAMILY TIP** 'Turmeric is always useful in the kitchen and to have to hand, especially if you cut yourself as it helps stop the bleeding and prevents infection; as well as having health benefits, it tastes pretty good too!'

Egg fried rice is typically made with leftovers but it is still very simple to assemble even if you don't have rice at the ready. Cook **rice** according to packet instructions and leave to cool. Meanwhile, chop **tenderstem, purple sprouting** or regular **broccoli** into small chunks and fry in a little **oil**. When just cooked, add sliced **spring onions** and **frozen peas**. Cook for 2–3 minutes then add the cooked rice and mix together. When the rice is hot, make a well in the pan and crack in **eggs**. Leave for a second then stir the eggs with a wooden spoon to scramble and mix them into the rice and vegetables. Add a splash of **soy sauce**, **sesame oil** and a little **chilli oil**, if liked, mixing together and adjusting to taste. You could also add some strips of **chicken breast** or **thigh** for a non-vegetarian version: just fry the raw meat in the pan for a few minutes before adding the broccoli.

Home-made pizza is a firm favourite: using ready-made bases means more time to prepare the toppings, but if you want to make dough from scratch, use **320ml water, 500g strong bread flour** and **1 x 7g sachet of instant yeast** (to make two large or four small pizzas). Add the water to the yeast, mix together and leave to froth. Whisk the flour with a pinch of **salt** and **sugar**. Pour the frothy yeast mixture into the flour and mix together until a dough forms, then knead until smooth. Cover and leave in a greased bowl until it's risen to double its size. Divide the dough into two or four then roll out until 0.5cm thick. Decorate with your choice of toppings and cook for around 10 minutes in a hot (240°C/Fan 220°C) oven until crisp and melted. A few topping ideas: **potato**, **mozzarella** and **rosemary**; **broccoli**, **sausage** and **fennel seeds**; fresh **spinach**, **Parmesan** and **egg**; **roasted vegetables** and **pesto**.

FAMILY TIP 'Prepping is a very important part of home cooking. We marinate all of our meat, so that there is always lots of flavour.'

SIMPLE RECIPE IDEAS

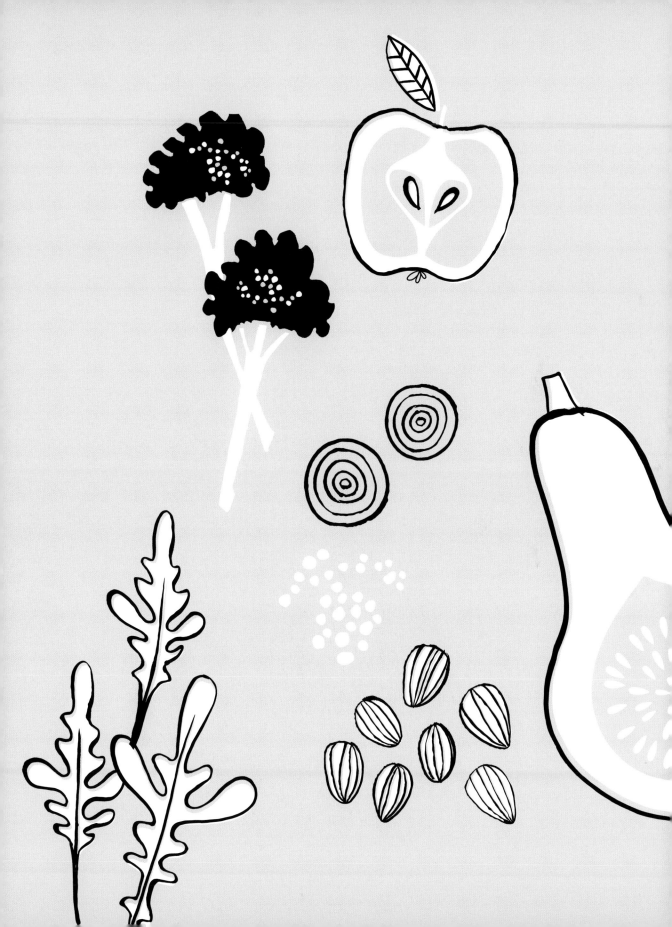

VEGETARIAN

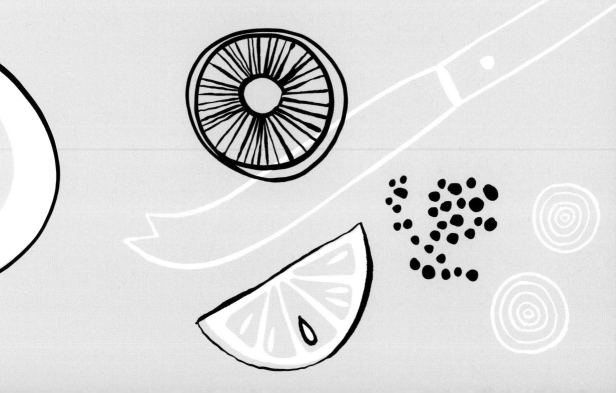

SIMPLE RECIPE IDEAS

To make a **no-soak dal**, add **red lentils** to a large pan with **chilli powder**, **ground coriander**, **ground ginger**, **ground turmeric**, a **cinnamon stick**, **coconut milk**, **chopped tomatoes**, chopped **fresh coriander**, **salt** and enough **water** to cover everything by 5cm. Cook over a medium-high heat for 15 minutes, or until the lentils are cooked. Check the seasoning before serving topped with a **tarka**: add **oil** to a pan and fry sliced **garlic** with **cumin** and **mustard seeds** until they pop.

It's fun to make your own wraps at the table and **Falafel wraps** make a lovely, fresh meal. Fry **falafels** until crisp and make a crunchy salad by mixing together thinly sliced **white cabbage**, peeled **carrot**, chopped **tomato**, **cucumber** and **jarred pickled chillies**, a squeeze of **lemon juice** and a pinch of **salt**. Meanwhile, mix together **tahini**, **plain yoghurt**, a little crushed **garlic** and enough **water** to make a pouring consistency. Lay out some warmed **tortillas** and let everyone build their own wrap.

Black bean quesadillas are a real favourite: drain **tinned black beans** and mix together with finely chopped **red onion**, chopped **roasted red peppers**, **ground cumin** and **coriander**. Mash slightly and season to taste. Spread the mixture onto one **tortilla**, sprinkle over some grated **Cheddar** and then top with another tortilla, sandwiching them together. Heat a little **oil** in a frying pan large enough to fit the tortilla, and then carefully lower it in. Fry for a few minutes on each side, pressing down and turning with a spatula, until the tortilla is golden and the inside melted. Slide out of the pan, cut into triangular slices and serve with **guacamole** and **chilli sauce** or **salsa**.

> **FAMILY TIP** 'Saffron will never fail to add that touch of luxury to a dish'

Sweetcorn fritters: add **sweetcorn kernels** (tinned or fresh) to a large bowl with crumbled **feta**, chopped **fresh parsley**, **flour**, **salt**, **pepper**, **dried chilli flakes** and a beaten **egg** and mix together until incorporated. Be generous with the seasoning! Heat **oil** in a frying pan over a medium heat and drop in spoonfuls of the mixture, spacing apart. Press down lightly with a spatula to flatten and then leave for 3–4 minutes, or until crisp and golden. Turn and cook the other side. Grated **courgette**, **beetroot** or **carrot** make wonderful fritters, too.

To make **roasted cauliflower couscous**, add **couscous** to a heatproof bowl and pour over boiling **stock**. Cover the bowl with a clean tea towel and leave to sit for a few minutes. Once the liquid has been absorbed, fluff up the grains with a fork. Separate a large **cauliflower** into florets (halve or quarter any large ones) and chop the stalk into chunks. Place in a roasting tray, drizzle with **olive oil** and season with **salt** and a sprinkle of **turmeric**. Roast in a hot oven for 20 minutes. Remove from the oven and add a tin of drained **chickpeas**, mixing everything together. Roast for another 20 minutes. Remove from the oven and tip the cauliflower and chickpea mixture into the couscous, adding chopped **parsley** and **lemon juice** to taste. Swap in other veg such as **broccoli**, **courgettes**, **butternut squash** or **carrots** in place of the cauliflower, or try **cumin** or dried **chilli flakes** instead of **turmeric**.

FAMILY TIP 'We usually try to use whatever is in the fridge or freezer to create a new dish and to avoid waste, and this makes us more imaginative in our cooking as it challenges us to try new things.'

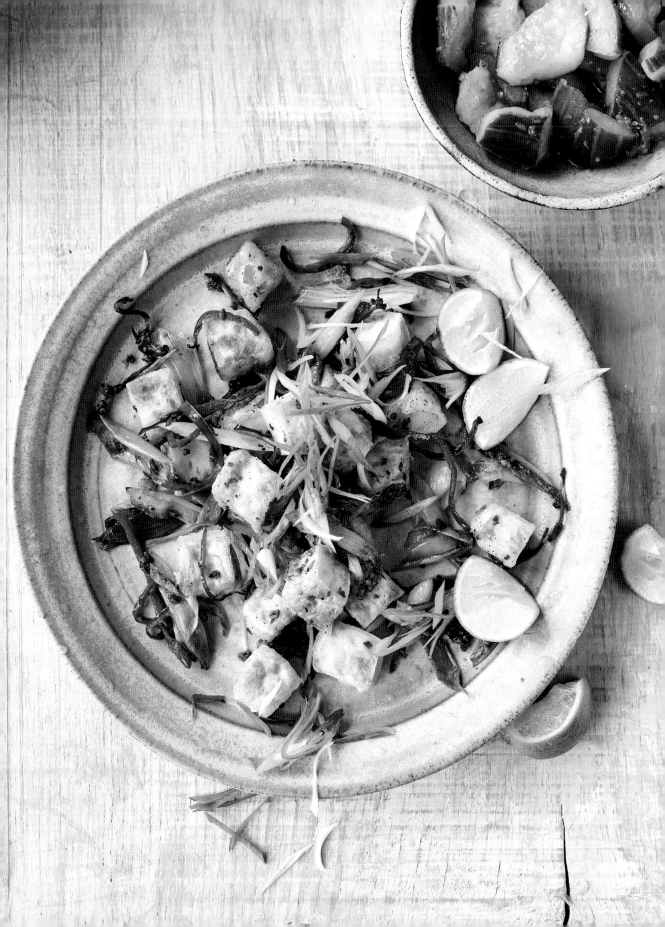

SALT & PEPPER TOFU WITH SMACKED CUCUMBER SALAD

SERVES 4

For the salt and pepper tofu
1 x block firm tofu
   (about 340g), cut into
   1cm cubes
cornflour, to coat
vegetable oil, for frying
3 garlic cloves, peeled and
   finely chopped
2 large chillies, red and
   green, thinly sliced
2 large spring onions, cut into
   3cm pieces, plus 1 extra
   finely sliced, to garnish
½ tsp Sichuan peppercorns,
   coarsely ground
1 tsp white pepper
1 tsp caster sugar
1 tsp sea salt
1 lime, cut into wedges

**For the smacked
  cucumber salad**
1 large cucumber
2 tsp salt
1 garlic clove, peeled and
   very finely chopped
2½ tbsp rice vinegar
2 tsp sugar
2 tsp chilli oil
2 tsp sesame oil
1 tsp light soy sauce

1. **Prepare the cucumber** Lay the cucumber on a chopping board and smack lightly with a rolling pin. Roughly chop, put in a colander and sprinkle with the salt. Leave for 30 minutes, then rinse and pat dry with kitchen paper.

2. Meanwhile, dust the tofu in cornflour and heat 4cm of oil in a wok to 180°C, or until a cube of bread browns in 20 seconds.

3. **Cook the tofu** So the wok is not overcrowded, drop the tofu into the oil in batches and move it around with chopsticks to stop the pieces sticking together. When they are crisp and golden (about 2 minutes), take them out with a slotted spoon and drain on kitchen paper. Bring the oil back up to temperature before repeating with another batch. Carry on until all the tofu is cooked.

4. Pour away most of the oil, leaving about 2 tablespoons, and fry the garlic, chillies and spring onions until fragrant.

5. Mix the peppercorns with the white pepper, sugar and salt and add to the wok, along with the cooked tofu. Stir-fry for 2 minutes.

6. **Make the salad** Mix the garlic with the vinegar, sugar, oils and soy sauce in a bowl. Toss the cucumber in the dressing and leave it to marinate for 10 minutes before serving.

7. Serve the tofu garnished with the sliced spring onion and lime wedges, alongside the cucumber salad.

FAMILY TIP 'If you think you don't like tofu, you're doing it wrong.'

VEGETARIAN

ROSEMARY'S VEGETABLE LASAGNE

1 large butternut squash
200g mozzarella, sliced
40g freshly grated Parmesan
75g breadcrumbs
salt and pepper

For the tomato sauce
1 tbsp rapeseed oil
1 red pepper, seeded and
   thinly sliced
2 garlic cloves, peeled
   and crushed
1 red chilli, finely diced
   (optional)
800g ripe tomatoes, chopped
   (or 2 x 400g tins chopped
   tomatoes)
a handful of fresh basil
   leaves, chopped

For the spinach filling
400g ricotta cheese
30g freshly grated Parmesan
50ml sour cream
3 shallots, peeled and sliced
1 tbsp rapeseed oil
500g spinach leaves, wilted,
   squeezed dry and chopped
grating of nutmeg

For the mushroom filling
1 tbsp rapeseed oil
500g chestnut mushrooms,
   sliced
2 garlic cloves, peeled and
   finely chopped
1 tbsp finely snipped thyme

1 **Make the tomato sauce** Heat the oil in a large pan over a medium heat and fry the pepper for 5 minutes, or until starting to soften. Add the garlic and chilli, if using, and continue to cook for 1 minute. Add the tomatoes and simmer for 20–30 minutes, or until the sauce thickens and any excess moisture has evaporated.

2 **Make the spinach filling** Mix the ricotta, Parmesan and sour cream together in a large bowl and season well. Meanwhile, heat the oil in a small pan over a medium heat and fry the shallots for 5 minutes, or until soft. Stir in the wilted spinach and season with some grated nutmeg. Add to the ricotta mixture, mix well and taste for seasoning.

3 **Make the mushroom filling** Heat the oil in a pan over a high heat and fry the mushrooms for 5–6 minutes, or until there is not much moisture left in the pan. Stir in the garlic and thyme, season and remove from the heat.

4 Preheat the oven to 180°C/Fan 160°C.

5 Cut the butternut squash in half and peel. Discard the seeds and cut the flesh into wide slices 0.5cm thick.

6 **Assemble the lasagne** In a medium-sized oven dish, spread some tomato sauce on the base and then lay slices of squash to cover. Top with half the mushroom filling and then half the spinach and ricotta filling and repeat. Finish with a layer of squash and spread with a thin layer of tomato sauce. Cover with a layer of mozzarella and then sprinkle with Parmesan and breadcrumbs.

7 Bake for 30–40 minutes, or until the top is golden and a knife slides through the squash with no resistance.

8 Serve with a fresh rocket salad.

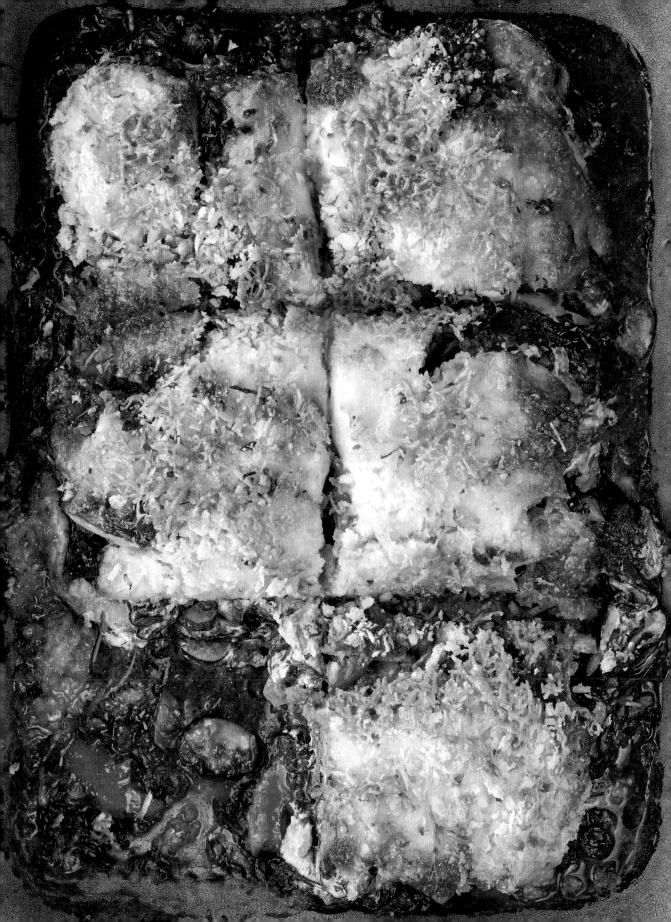

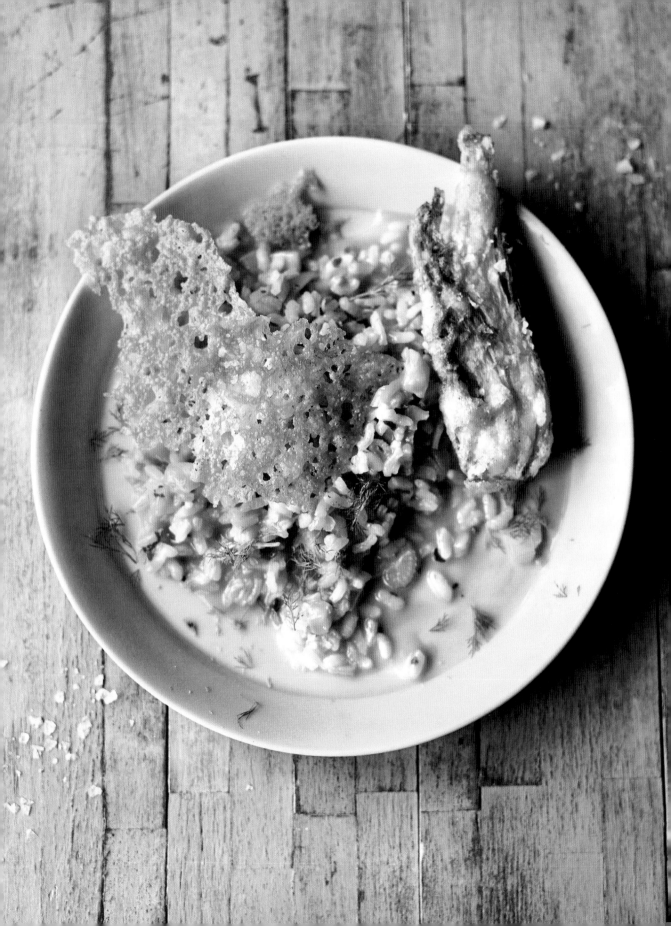

FENNEL & LEMON RISOTTO
WITH PARMESAN CRISPS & FENNEL FRITTERS

2 tbsp olive oil

1 garlic clove, peeled
and chopped

1 tsp fennel seeds, ground

½ tsp dried chilli flakes

2 large fennel bulbs, 1½ finely
chopped and ½ cut into
thin wedges, fronds kept
for garnish

140g Parmesan, finely grated

1 large onion, peeled and
finely sliced

280g Arborio rice

250ml white wine

700ml–1 litre chicken
stock, hot

zest and juice of 1 lemon

salt and pepper

For the fennel fritters

250ml soda water, ice cold

1 large egg

good pinch of cayenne pepper

1 tsp baking powder

2 tbsp cornflour

100g plain flour

1 litre vegetable oil, for
deep-frying

1. Heat 1 tablespoon of the olive oil in a large pan over a medium heat and sauté the garlic with the ground fennel seeds and chilli flakes for 1–2 minutes. Add the finely chopped fennel and cook for 15–20 minutes, or until soft.

2. Make the Parmesan crisps Preheat the grill to medium high. Using half the Parmesan, spread piles of cheese onto a silicon sheet and place under the grill until melted and golden – if the cheese is spread too thin it will burn. Remove and leave to cool before breaking into pieces.

3. Make the risotto Heat the remaining olive oil in a large frying pan over a medium heat and cook the onion until soft. Stir in the rice and cook for 1–2 minutes. Pour in the white wine and let it bubble until all the liquid has gone. Stir in the stock, ladleful by ladleful, waiting until each ladleful has been absorbed before adding more. Continue adding the stock until the rice is tender but still creamy (about 25–30 minutes). Stir in the cooked chopped fennel, along with the lemon zest and juice and plenty of seasoning. Finally, stir in remaining grated Parmesan. Cover and take off the heat while you make the fritters.

4. Make the fennel fritters Combine the soda water with the egg in a bowl. Place this bowl in a separate bowl full of ice, to keep it as cold as possible, and then slowly stir in the cayenne pepper, baking powder, cornflour and plain flour to make a batter.

5. Heat the oil in a high-sided pan or wok until it reaches 180°C, or a cube of bread browns in 20 seconds. Dip the fennel wedges in the batter, then deep-fry in batches until golden – this will take 1–2 minutes. Drain on kitchen paper.

6. Garnish the risotto with fennel fronds and the Parmesan crisps and serve with the deep-fried fennel wedges alongside.

VEGETARIAN

FALAFEL WRAPS WITH HOME-MADE HUMMUS

SERVES 4

300g dried chickpeas, soaked
    overnight with 1 tsp
    bicarbonate of soda
½ tbsp sunflower oil
50g minced lamb
a good handful of fresh
    parsley, leaves picked
1 litre vegetable oil, for
    deep-frying
2 large Middle Eastern
    flatbreads
1 beef tomato, sliced
2 pickles, sliced
a squeeze of fresh lemon juice
sumac, to garnish
salt and pepper

For the falafel
a handful of fresh coriander,
    leaves picked
a handful of fresh parsley,
    leaves picked
1 garlic clove, peeled
1 tsp ground cumin
1 tsp coriander seeds
25g sesame seeds

For the hummus
1 tbsp tahini
1 garlic clove, peeled
a drizzle of olive oil
2 tbsp natural yoghurt
juice of 1 lemon
1–2 ice cubes

For the sauce
3 tbsp tahini
3 tbsp natural yoghurt
a good squeeze of fresh lemon
    juice

1. **Prepare the chickpeas** Drain the chickpeas and tip half of them into a pan, keeping the other half to one side for the falafels. Cover with water and bring to the boil. Reduce the heat and simmer for 45–50 minutes, or until tender. Alternatively, use a pressure cooker and cook for 20 minutes. Drain, reserving the cooking liquid.

2. **Make the falafel** Put the reserved uncooked chickpeas in a food-processor with the remaining ingredients and whizz. Add a little warm water if the mixture is too thick. Season to taste. Shape into 20 falafels and set aside until ready to fry.

3. **Make the hummus** Whizz the cooked chickpeas in the food-processor with the tahini, garlic, olive oil, yoghurt, lemon juice and some seasoning. Add 1 or 2 ice cubes and whizz again until smooth.

4. **Make the sauce** Mix the tahini with the yoghurt and lemon juice and season to taste.

5. Heat the sunflower oil in a small pan over a medium heat. Fry the mince until golden brown, breaking the meat up as it cooks.

6. Spoon half of the hummus into a dish and top with the cooked lamb and garnish with the sumac and half the parsley. Keep the remainder of the hummus to serve alongside the falafel.

7. Heat the vegetable oil in a high-sided pan until it reaches 170°C, or a cube of bread browns in 30 seconds.

Recipe continues

VEGETARIAN

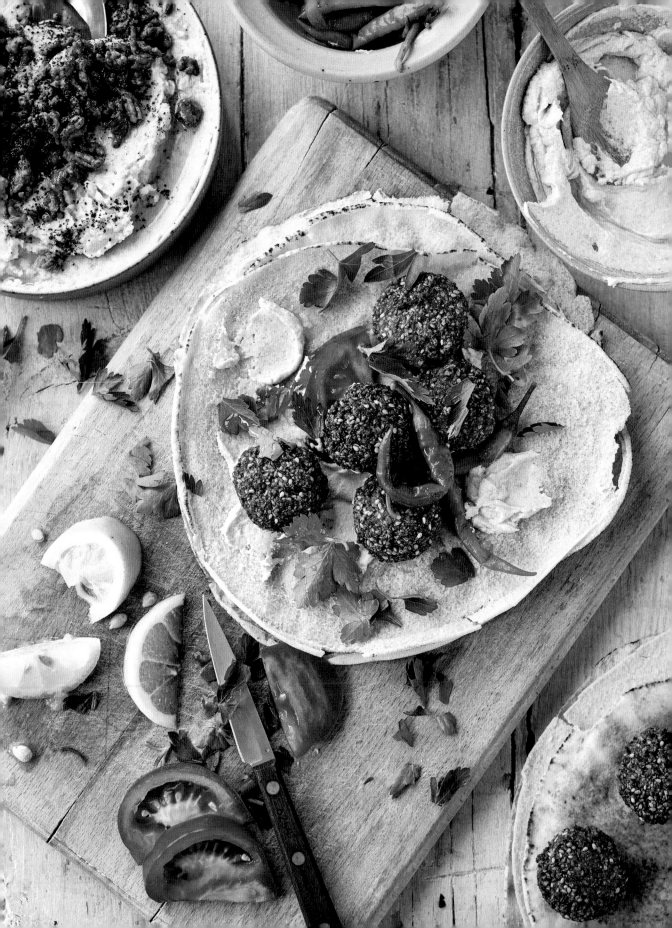

8 . **Fry the falafels** Carefully place a few balls of falafel into the hot oil and fry them for 2–3 minutes, or until the outside is brown and crisp. Remove with a slotted spoon and drain on kitchen paper. Continue to cook the falafel in batches until they are all done.

9 . **Make the wraps** Split the large flatbreads in half around the circumference so you end up with 2 circles. Lay one half on top of the other so they are slightly overlapping. Spoon falafel sauce along the middle, top with 5 falafel, half the tomato and pickle, some parsley and a good squeeze of lemon. Wrap up carefully and repeat with the second flatbread.

10 . Place a griddle over a high heat and, when hot, cook the wraps until hot and charred.

11 . Cut each flatbread in half and serve with the hummus and the remaining falafels alongside.

FAMILY TIP 'You don't need a deep-fat fryer if you've got a decent wok. A wok can deal with the high temperature of the oil, but don't try this in a cheap frying pan.'

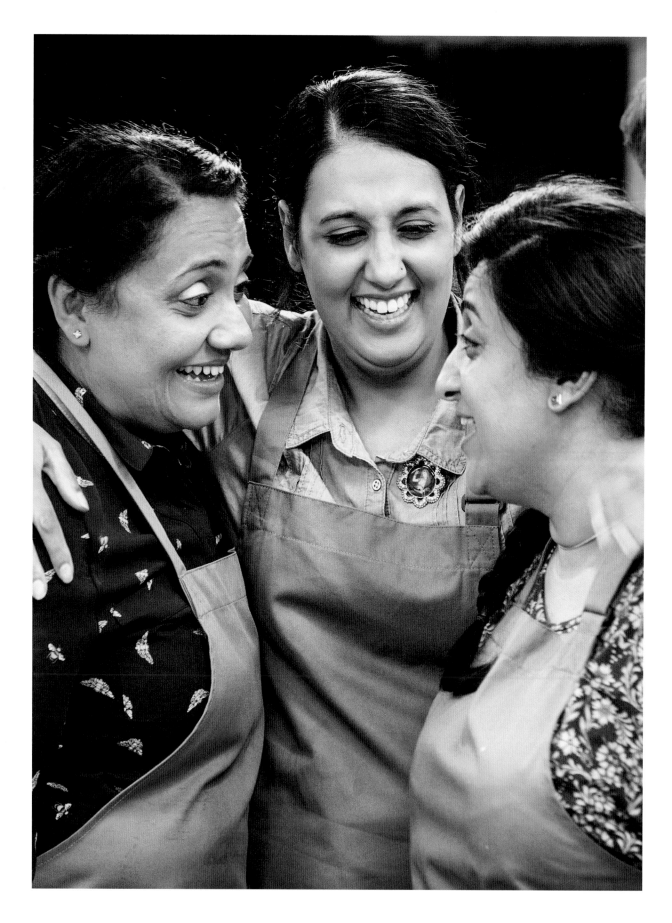

ROASTED VEGETABLE & LENTIL SALAD WITH GOATS' CHEESE

2 beetroot, peeled and
    quartered
½ butternut squash,
    peeled, seeded and sliced
1 whole head of garlic,
    cloves separated
a few fresh thyme sprigs,
    leaves picked
1 tsp cumin seeds
1 tsp coriander seeds
olive oil, to drizzle
200g tenderstem broccoli
½ tsp smoked paprika
pinch of cayenne pepper
200g Puy lentils
350ml chicken stock
100g goats' cheese, crumbled
juice of ½ lemon
3 tbsp crème fraîche
a handful of freshly chopped
    flat-leaf parsley
a few fresh mint sprigs,
    leaves picked and torn
2 tsp balsamic vinegar
2 tbsp extra-virgin olive oil
salt and pepper

1 : Preheat the oven to 200°C/Fan 180°C.

2 : **Roast the vegetables** Place the beetroot, squash, garlic, thyme, cumin and coriander seeds in a large roasting tin, drizzle with lots of oil and season well. Roast for 40–50 minutes until tender, turning every now and then.

3 : Put the broccoli in another roasting tin with the paprika and cayenne pepper, a good drizzle of oil and some seasoning, and roast for 20 minutes.

4 : **Cook the lentils** Put the lentils in a large pan with the chicken stock. Bring to the boil then gently simmer for 20 minutes until tender. Drain off any liquid.

5 : Scatter the goats' cheese over the broccoli and roast for a further 10 minutes, or until lightly golden.

6 : Stir the lemon juice, crème fraîche and herbs into the lentils and season well.

7 : Toss the roasted beetroots and squash with the balsamic vinegar.

8 : **Assemble the salad** Tip the lentils onto a large platter and top with the roasted veg and extra-virgin olive oil, and serve.

FAMILY TIP 'Cooking shouldn't be a chore, it's always fun in our kitchen. I think when you're having a laugh with the people you love it shows in the food you produce.'

VEGETARIAN

STUFFED VEGETABLES
MAHSHI

8 small courgettes
8 baby aubergines
6 mini peppers
1 tbsp vegetable oil
1 whole head of garlic,
    cloves separated
2 tbsp tomato purée
800ml warm water
2 fresh mint sprigs,
    leaves picked
toasted pitta bread, to serve

For the stuffing
200g pudding rice
250g minced lamb (shoulder
    with minimal fat)
good pinch of saffron
1 tsp each salt, pepper and
    ground cumin
½ tsp ground cardamom
1 tbsp vegetable oil

For the garnish
2 spring onions, finely sliced
1 small bunch coriander,
    chopped
1 small bunch parsley, chopped
1–2 fresh mint sprigs, leaves
    picked and chopped
1 x small bag rocket

1 : Prepare the vegetables Carefully hollow out the courgettes, auberbines and peppers, discarding the flesh on the inside.

2 : Make the stuffing Mix the ingredients together in a large bowl.

3 : Fill the cored vegetables with the stuffing mixture.

4 : Measure the oil into a large pan then lay the stuffed vegetables in the bottom, in a single layer if you can, then tuck in the cloves of garlic.

5 : Mix the tomato purée with the water, then pour into the pan.

6 : Cook the vegetables Cover the pan with a lid, bring to the boil, then reduce the heat and leave to simmer over a low heat for 40 minutes.

7 : Serve the stuffed vegetables and the cooking juices garnished with the spring onions, herbs and rocket scattered over the top, and with toasted pitta breads to soak up the juices.

> **TIP** Cook the vegetables on a bed of lamb chops for a meaty alternative.

VEGETARIAN

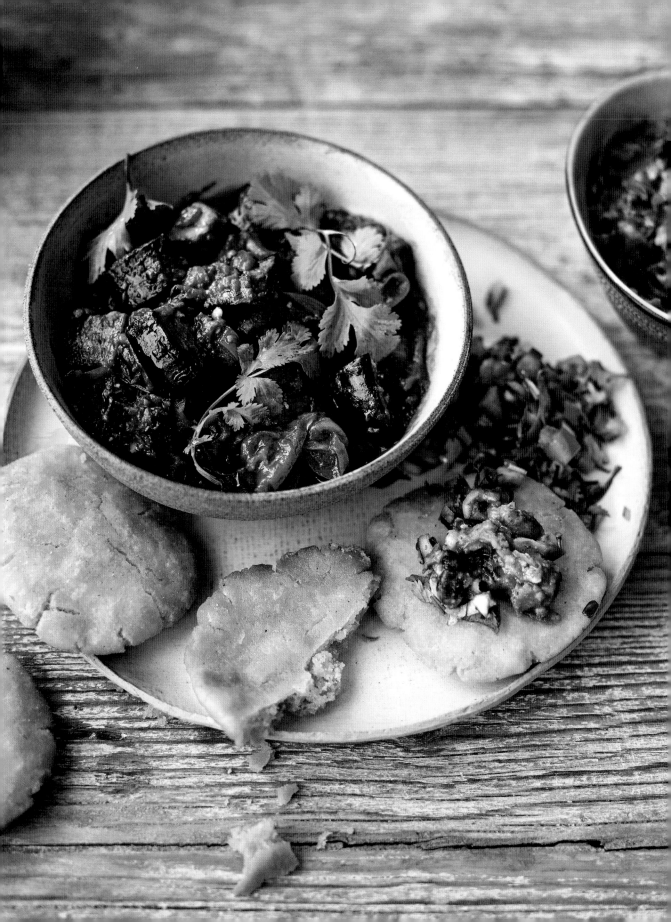

Buy ready-made refried beans and salsa and skip steps 3 and 5

VEGETARIAN GORDITAS
MEXICAN PASTRIES WITH ROASTED AUBERGINE, REFRIED BEANS & SALSA

SERVES 4

For the roasted aubergine

1 large aubergine, cut into small chunks
5 garlic cloves
3 fresh thyme sprigs
50ml olive oil, plus extra for frying
1 large onion, peeled and finely sliced
1 x 400g tin chopped tomatoes
½ red pepper, seeded and finely sliced
2 tbsp demerara sugar
2 tbsp tomato purée
½ tbsp soy sauce
5 tbsp Chipotle Paste (see page 279 or use shop-bought)
juice of ½ lime
½ bunch fresh coriander, leaves picked and stalks finely chopped
salt and pepper

For the refried beans

1 tbsp olive oil
1 onion, peeled and finely chopped
2 large garlic cloves, peeled and crushed
1 red chilli, finely chopped
1 x 400g tin mixed pulses, drained and rinsed
½ small bunch coriander, leaves picked and stalks finely chopped
1 tbsp Chipotle Paste (see page 279 or use shop-bought)
½ small bunch flat-leaf parsley, chopped

1. Preheat the oven to 200°C/Fan 180°C.

2. Make the roasted aubergine Place the aubergine in a roasting tin with 2 of the garlic cloves – left whole and unpeeled – and the thyme. Season with salt and pepper and coat everything in the oil. Roast in the oven for 30–40 minutes, turning every so often, until lovely and soft and golden.

3. Make the refried beans While the aubergine is roasting, heat the oil in a pan over a medium heat. When hot, fry the onion for about 5–10 minutes, until starting to turn golden. Add the garlic and the chilli and cook for a further minute. Add the drained pulses, coriander stalks and chipotle paste. Cook for another 10–12 minutes. Season with salt and pepper.

4. To finish the roasted aubergines, heat a splash of oil in a pan over a medium heat and fry the onion for about 5 minutes, or until translucent. Peel and crush the remaining garlic cloves and add to the pan. Fry for a further 2 minutes before adding the chopped tomatoes, red pepper, sugar, tomato purée and soy sauce. Bring to the boil, season and simmer to reduce by about a third. Add the chipotle paste, lime juice and coriander stalks and bring back to the boil. Finally, add the roasted aubergine cubes and the coriander leaves, and check the seasoning.

5. Make the salsa Mix all the salsa ingredients together and leave to one side.

Recipe continues

For the salsa
½ small bunch coriander,
    chopped
1 large red onion, peeled
    and diced
½ chilli, diced
juice of ½ lime
1 tomato, diced

For the gorditas
250g masa harina flour
good pinch of salt
1 tsp baking powder
200–250ml hot water
250ml olive oil, for
    shallow frying

6 . Make the gorditas Combine the masa harina, salt and baking powder in a large bowl. Make a well in the centre and slowly add the water until you have a workable dough. Shape into 8 pieces and roll each one into a 10cm circle.

7 . Heat the oil in a non-stick frying pan and fry the gorditas in batches for 2–3 minutes, turning, until golden brown. Drain on kitchen paper.

8 . Stir the coriander leaves and parsley through the refried beans, then serve with the gorditas, the warm aubergine sauce and the salsa.

FAMILY TIP 'We would always recommend adding a few spices, trying it and then adding more. Don't worry too much, just keep whacking stuff in until it tastes good!'

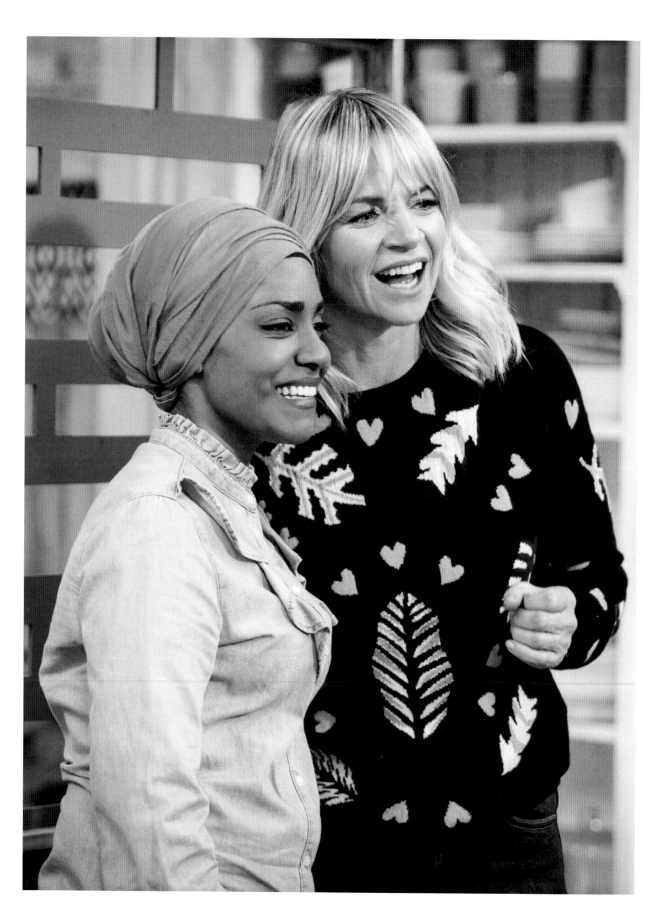

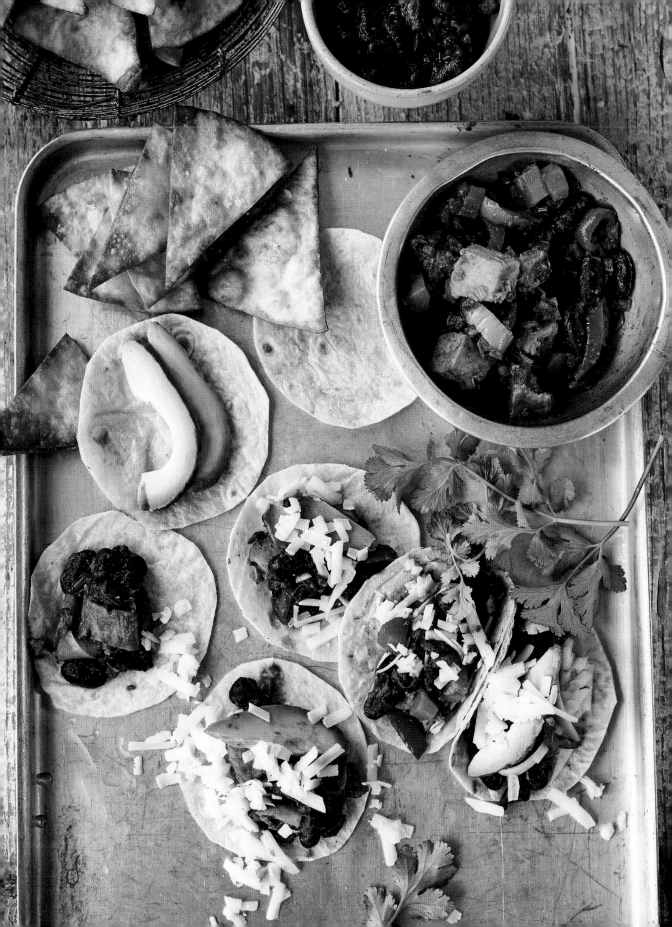

Buy ready-made tortilla chips, wraps and refried beans and skip steps 7–9

VEGETABLE MEXICAN CHILLI
WITH MINI TACOS & TORTILLA CHIPS

SERVES 4

2 small sweet potatoes, peeled and cut into cubes
2 tsp chilli powder
pinch of ground cinnamon
2 tsp paprika
4 tbsp olive oil
1½ red onions, peeled and finely diced
2 celery sticks, finely diced
2 carrots, peeled and finely diced
2 garlic cloves, peeled and crushed
1 red chilli, finely chopped
1 red pepper, seeded and sliced
1 yellow pepper, seeded and sliced
150g chestnut mushrooms, quartered
1 aubergine, cut into bite-sized pieces
1 tsp ground coriander
1 tsp ground cumin
2 x 400g tins kidney beans in chilli sauce
1 x 400g tin plum tomatoes
few dashes of Worcestershire sauce
few dashes of Tabasco sauce
dash of red wine vinegar
200ml vegetable stock
1 small bunch coriander, leaves picked and stalks chopped
salt and pepper

1. Preheat the oven to 200°C/Fan 180°C.

2. Make the chilli Put the sweet potato in a roasting tin and sprinkle with half the chilli powder, the cinnamon and half the paprika. Season and drizzle with half the oil. Roast in the oven for 20 minutes until tender.

3. Meanwhile, heat the remaining oil in a large pan over a medium heat and fry the onions, celery and carrots gently for 10 minutes until softened. Add the garlic and chilli and fry for a minute more before adding all the remaining vegetables. Cook for a further 10 minutes, until everything is starting to soften, particularly the aubergine.

4. Add the remaining chilli powder and paprika, the ground coriander and cumin, and plenty of seasoning, and cook for 1–2 minutes more.

5. Add 1½ tins of the kidney beans to the pan, keeping the remainder to one side for the mini tacos.

6. Add the tomatoes, Worcestershire sauce, Tabasco, red wine vinegar and the stock. Bring to the boil, reduce the heat and leave to simmer for 20–30 minutes.

7. Finally, add the coriander stalks to the chilli with the roasted sweet potato and cook for a further 5 minutes.

8. Make the home-made tortilla chips and mini tacos While the chilli is cooking, heat the vegetable oil in a high-sided pan or wok until it reaches 180°C, or a cube of bread browns in 20 seconds.

Recipe continues

vegetable oil, for deep-frying
3 large flour tortillas
1 tbsp olive oil
½ red onion, peeled and
finely diced
good pinch of chilli powder

To finish
1 ripe avocado, finely sliced
50g Cheddar, grated
sour cream, to serve
rice, to serve

9 . Cut 4 x 10cm discs out of one of the flour tortillas and set aside. Cut the other 2 tortillas into small triangles and, together with any trimmings left from the first tortilla, deep-fry in batches for 1–2 minutes, or until crisp. Drain on kitchen paper.

10 . Heat the olive oil in a small pan over a medium heat and fry the onion for 10 minutes, or until softened. Stir in the chilli powder, reserved kidney beans, season and leave to bubble for 1-2 minutes.

11 . Preheat the grill to medium high.

12 . Put the tortilla rounds on a baking sheet and top each one with some of the bean mixture. Cover with the avocado slices and sprinkle with the cheese. Place under the preheated grill until the cheese has melted. Top each taco with a small amount of sour cream and garnish with the reserved coriander leaves.

13 . Serve the tacos and tortilla chips with the vegetable chilli and rice.

FAMILY TIP 'Know your audience – go easy on the chilli elements if members of your family don't like spicy food.'

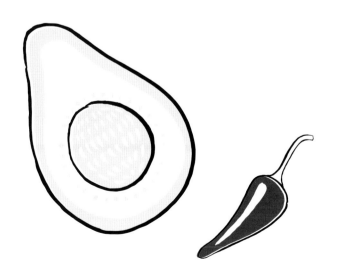

ROASTED AUBERGINES
BAINGAN KA BHARTA

4 aubergines, lightly oiled and pierced with a knife in a few places
2 tbsp sunflower oil
2 tbsp unsalted butter
3cm piece fresh root ginger, peeled and grated
3 garlic cloves, peeled and very finely chopped
1 onion, peeled and finely chopped
2 tsp cumin seeds
1 tsp turmeric
1 tsp salt
5 large vine-ripened tomatoes, sliced
2 tsp garam masala

1 : Cook the aubergines over a charcoal fire or bbq until the skin is blackened and the flesh tender. Otherwise, preheat the oven to 200°C/Fan 180°C and cook the aubergines for 40 minutes.

2 : Remove the skin from the aubergines and keep the pulp.

3 : Heat the oil and butter in a pan over a medium heat and add the ginger, garlic and onion. Cook for 15 minutes until really soft and tender and the oil starts to separate. Add the cumin seeds and turmeric and cook for 1 minute more.

4 : Add the salt and tomatoes and cook for 5 minutes.

5 : Finally add the aubergine pulp and garam masala. Mix together and serve.

FAMILY TIP 'Whether it's a meal for one, a family get-together or entertaining friends, cooking is never a chore but always a delight.'

VEGETARIAN

POMEGRANATE & CHICKPEA CURRY ANARDANA CHANA

200g dried chickpeas
100g chana dal
2 tbsp sunflower oil
2 onions, peeled and diced
3cm piece fresh root ginger,
    peeled and grated
1½ tsp cumin seeds
1 cinnamon stick
2 black cardamom pods
2–3 cloves
1 tsp freshly chopped green
    chilli (to taste)
1 tsp salt
1½ tbsp anardana powder
    (crushed pomegranate),
    or 1 tbsp pomegranate
    molasses
1 tsp garam masala
50g pomegranate seeds,
    to garnish
a handful of freshly chopped
    coriander, to garnish

1. Soak the chickpeas and chana dal separately in cold water overnight.

2. Drain the chickpeas and place in a pan. Cover with water and bring to the boil. Reduce the heat and leave to simmer for 45 minutes, or until tender. Drain and keep to one side.

3. Meanwhile, heat the oil in a pan over a medium heat. When hot, add the onions and cook for a few minutes until starting to soften. Add the ginger, spices, chilli and salt. Drain the dal and add them to the pan with 250ml water. Bring to the boil, then leave to simmer for 20–25 minutes, or until the dal are tender. Add a little more water if needed.

4. Stir in the anardana, garam masala and the chickpeas, bring back to the boil and adjust the seasoning.

5. Serve garnished with the pomegranate seeds and coriander.

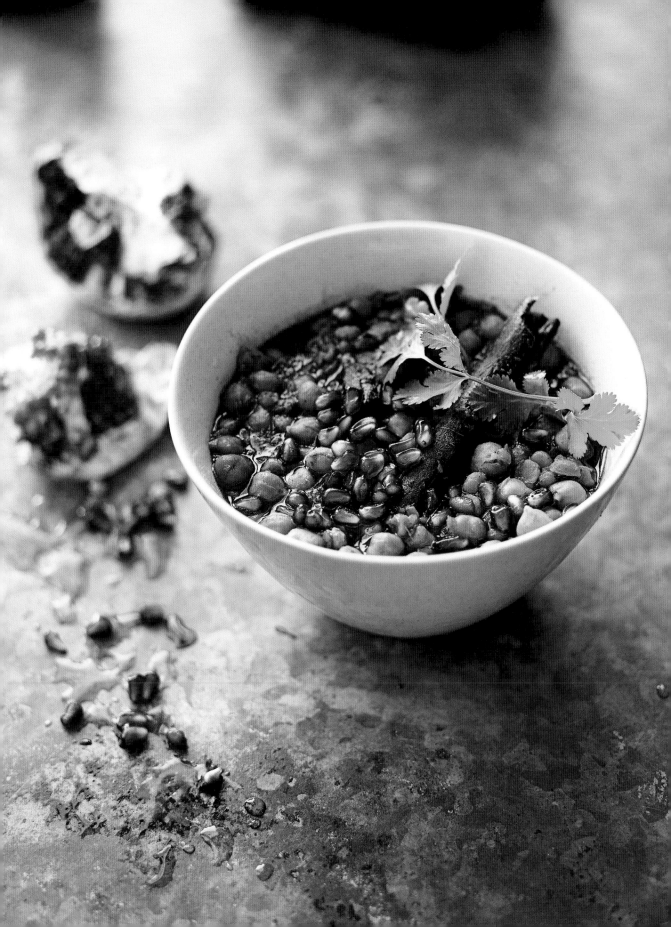

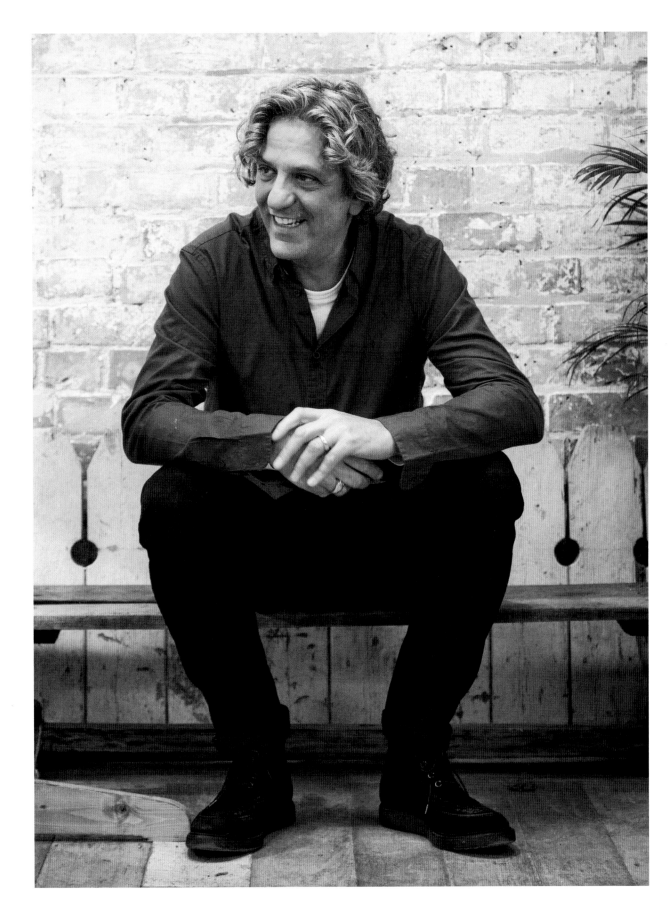

YOGHURT CURRY & FRITTERS
PUNJABI KADHI & PAKORAS

50g gram/chickpea flour
150g live yoghurt
1 tsp salt
2 tbsp vegetable oil
1 tsp black mustard seeds
2 tsp cumin seeds
1 tsp black peppercorns
1 cinnamon stick
3 cloves
2 onions, peeled and finely
    sliced lengthways
3 tbsp grated fresh root ginger
3 tbsp grated garlic
1 tsp turmeric
1 red chilli, finely chopped
a handful of fresh fenugreek
    (methi) leaves
2 tsp garam masala

For the pakoras
200g gram/chickpea flour
2 onions, peeled and
    finely sliced
3 potatoes, coarsely grated
2 tbsp grated fresh root ginger
1 tbsp garam masala
a handful of chopped
    fresh coriander
1 tsp salt
vegetable oil, for deep-frying

For the tarka
4 tbsp vegetable oil
3–4 whole dried red chillies
10–12 curry leaves
1 tsp yellow mustard seeds

1 Make the yoghurt curry Whisk the gram flour, yoghurt and salt together in a bowl until smooth. Add 750ml water and mix again.

2 Heat the oil in a large pan over a low heat, add the whole spices and cook for 1 minute. Add the onions and cook for 3–4 minutes, or until softened but not coloured. Add the ginger, garlic, turmeric, chilli and fenugreek and cook for 10 minutes more. Add the yoghurt mixture and bring to the boil. Reduce the heat and leave to simmer, stirring every so often to stop it catching, for about 20–25 minutes. It should thicken up nicely – if it is too thick you can add a little more water.

3 Make the pakoras Mix all the ingredients except the oil with enough water to bring it together to form a thick batter.

4 Heat a deep pan of vegetable oil to 170°C, or until a cube of bread browns in 30 seconds.

5 Fry dollops of the pakora mixture for 4–5 minutes, turning, until golden brown. Drain on kitchen paper. Add to the kadhi with the garam masala and cook for 5 minutes more.

6 Make the tarka Just before serving, heat the oil for the tarka in a small pan and add the whole red chillies, curry leaves and mustard seeds and cook for 30 seconds.

7 Serve the curry and pakora with the tarka spooned over the top.

TIP Serve with Salmon Curry (see page 83), Roasted Aubergines (see page 185) and Missi Roti (see page 274).

VEGETARIAN

TARKA DAL

For the dal
175g mung dal
175g masoor dal
2 tsp freshly chopped green
    bird's-eye chillies (to taste)
1 tsp turmeric
2 tsp salt (to taste)
2 tsp garam masala
fresh coriander, to garnish

For the tarka
2 tbsp sunflower oil
30g butter
2½ tsp cumin seeds
5 garlic cloves, peeled and
    finely diced
3cm piece fresh root ginger,
    peeled and grated
1 onion, peeled and diced
2 tomatoes, diced

1. **Make the dal** Wash and rinse the dal. Place in a large pan and pour over 1.7 litres of water. Add the chilli, turmeric and salt and bring to the boil. Reduce the heat and leave to simmer for 10–15 minutes, or until the dal is cooked through.

2. **Make the tarka** Heat the oil and butter in a small pan over a medium heat. Add the cumin seeds, garlic, ginger, onion and tomatoes, and cook for 12–15 minutes.

3. Stir the tarka and the garam masala into the dal, bring it back to the boil and then remove the pan from the heat. Garnish with coriander before serving.

> **FAMILY TIP** 'Cumin is such a simple, staple spice and is used in most curry and rice dishes in our home.'

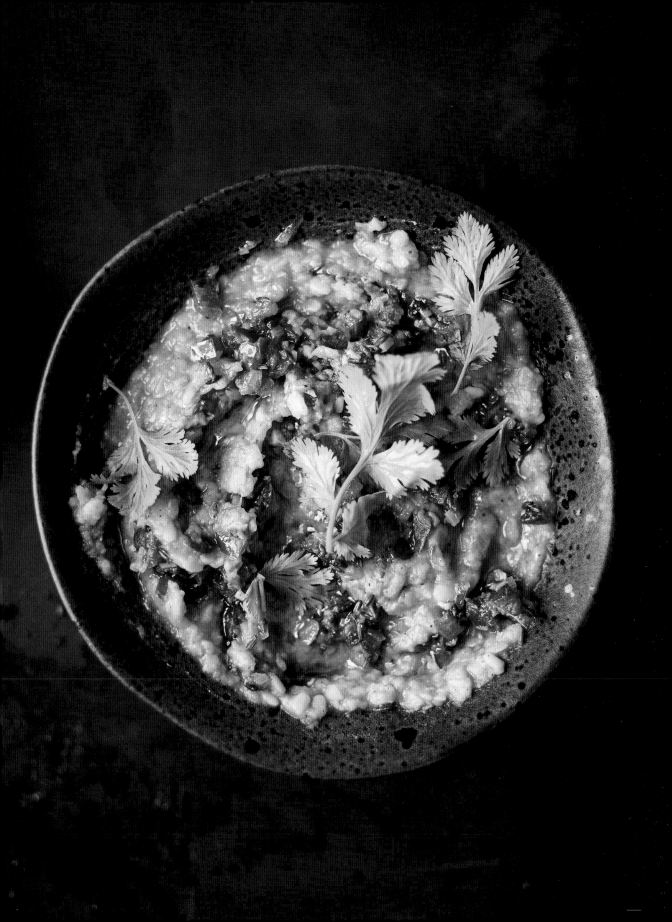

AUBERGINES WITH CHILLI
CA TIM NUONG

SERVES 4

2 medium aubergines
6 tbsp vegetable oil
3 banana shallots, peeled
   and finely sliced
2cm piece fresh root ginger,
   peeled and julienned
2 garlic cloves, peeled
   and finely chopped
4 fresh Thai chillies,
   finely sliced, to garnish
a large handful of fresh
   coriander leaves

For the sauce
6 tbsp dark soy sauce
2 tbsp rice vinegar
2 tbsp soft brown sugar
1 tsp dried chilli flakes
1 tsp cornflour

1: **Make the sauce** Mix all the ingredients together with 4 tablespoons of water and set aside.

2: **Prepare the aubergines** Cut the aubergines in half lengthways then into 2cm slices. Place in a bowl with 1 tablespoon of the oil and toss to coat.

3: **Cook the aubergines** Heat 4 tablespoons of the oil in a pan over a medium-high heat. Add the aubergines and fry till lightly browned on each side and lovely and soft. Remove and set aside.

4: Add the remaining oil to the pan and fry the shallots until slightly browned. Add the ginger and cook for 1 minute before adding the garlic and frying for 1 further minute.

5: Return the aubergine to the pan, add the sauce and bring it up to a boil. Reduce the heat slightly and leave to simmer for 1–2 minutes, or until the sauce has thickened.

6: Serve sprinkled with the red chilli and coriander leaves.

TIP Serve with Red Prawn Curry (see page 70) and Chicken in Pandan Leaves (see page 102).

VEGETARIAN

192

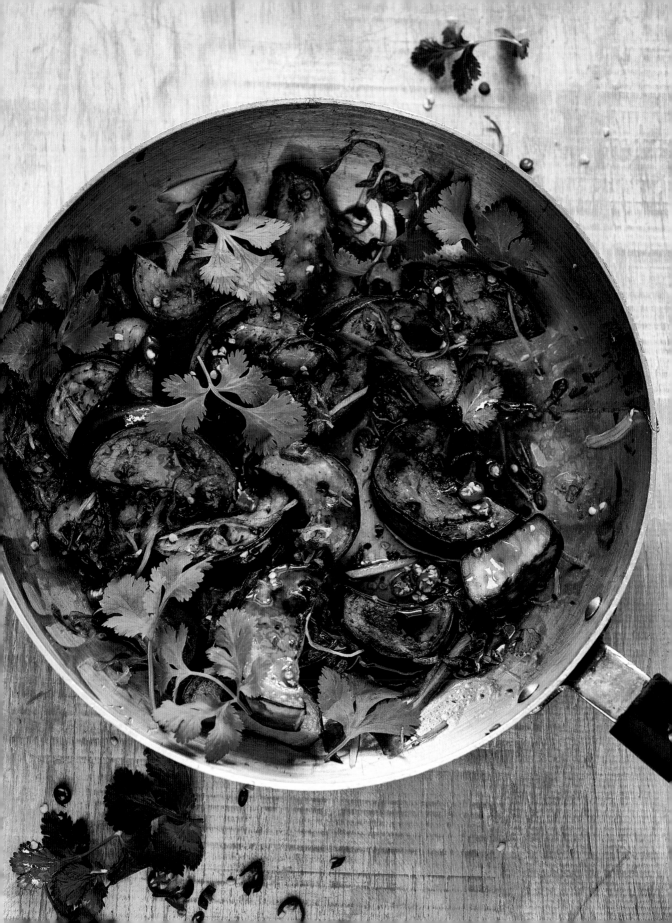

DESSERTS

SIMPLE RECIPE IDEAS

If you have a well-stocked baking cupboard, a **fruit crumble** is an easy option. Use fruit in season, like **rhubarb**, or **mixed berries** from the freezer and put in an ovenproof dish. Place cold diced **butter**, **flour**, **sugar**, **oats** and a pinch of **salt** in a bowl and rub with your fingertips until the mixture resembles breadcrumbs – don't overwork or the butter will get greasy. For an optional twist, add **flaked or chopped nuts** (**almonds**, **pistachios** or **hazelnuts** work well), or ground spices like **cinnamon** or **cardamom** to the crumble mixture. Sprinkle the crumble over the fruit and bake in the oven at 180°C/ Fan 160°C until golden and bubbling. Serve with **ice cream**, **cream** or **custard**.

Chocolate fridge cake is perfect for using up odds and ends and is as good for pudding as it is for a 4pm treat – plus there's no baking involved! Line a baking tin with clingfilm, leaving enough hanging over the edges for you to be able to fully cover the top. Melt **chocolate** (milk, dark, white – whatever you have) with **butter** and **golden syrup** in a bain marie. Once melted, mix in **dried fruit**, chopped **nuts** and broken up **biscuits** (chopped up pieces of chocolate bars, cereal and marshmallows all work well, too). Pour into the tin, smoothing the surface with a spatula or palette knife. Cover with the clingfilm, then put in the fridge to cool and set. How long this takes will depend on how deep the baking tin is and how much else there is in the fridge! Cut into squares to serve.

For crisp, **caramelised fruit tarts**, roll out shop-bought **puff pastry** until very thin (around 0.5cm). Roll or slide onto a baking sheet then prick with a fork, leaving an unpricked border of 1–2cm. Top with fruit (cored, thinly sliced **apples**, **pears**, **peaches**, or **frozen soft fruit**) then fold the pastry border over it. Brush the border with beaten **egg** or **milk**, sprinkle with **caster sugar**, then bake in the oven at 190°C/Fan 170°C until the pastry is golden and the fruit juicy.

Ice cream sundaes with salted caramel sauce are an indulgent but simple treat. Melt **butter**, **light brown sugar**, **caster sugar** and **golden syrup** in a heavy-based pan over a low heat, stirring occasionally. When bubbling, remove from the heat and add **double cream** and crunchy **sea salt**, to taste, stirring to combine. Serve warm poured over some **vanilla ice cream**, sliced **bananas** or other fruit. Add crumbled up **biscuits** for extra crunch.

> **FAMILY TIP** 'Love your ingredients – be excited about them, taste them and don't be scared of using them.'

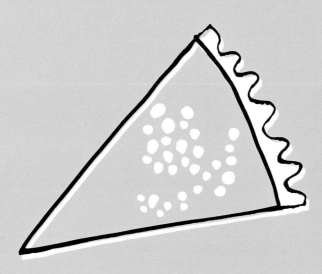

DOTTY GRANDMA'S APPLE CRUMBLE WITH CARDAMOM CUSTARD

SERVES 4

150g butter, at room
    temperature
60g caster sugar
1 tbsp plain flour
70g flaked almonds
½ tsp ground cinnamon
60g panko breadcrumbs
5 large Royal Gala apples,
    peeled, cored and
    coarsely grated
juice of 1 lemon

For the cardamom custard
5 cardamom pods, ground
    to a powder in a pestle
    and mortar
300ml whipping cream
1 tsp vanilla extract
2 egg yolks
1½ tbsp caster sugar
½ tsp cornflour

1. Preheat the oven to 180°C/Fan 160°C.

2. Make the crumble Beat the butter and sugar together in a large bowl. Mix the flour, almonds, cinnamon and breadcrumbs together and then rub into the butter and sugar mixture using your fingertips to form a thick, crumbly dough.

3. Make the apple base Place the grated apple and lemon juice in the base of a 20cm ovenproof dish, top with the crumble mixture and spread it out as evenly as possible.

4. Bake for 30 minutes, or until brown on top.

5. Make the cardamom custard Place a pan over a medium heat and add the cream, cardamom and vanilla. Bring to the boil, reduce the heat and simmer for 3 minutes. Set aside to cool slightly and then strain into a bowl through a fine sieve.

6. Whisk the egg yolks, sugar and cornflour together in a large bowl. Add the warm cream, whisking constantly. Pour this mixture back into the pan and cook over a low heat for 6–8 minutes, or until the custard thickens.

7. Serve the apple crumble with the cardamom custard.

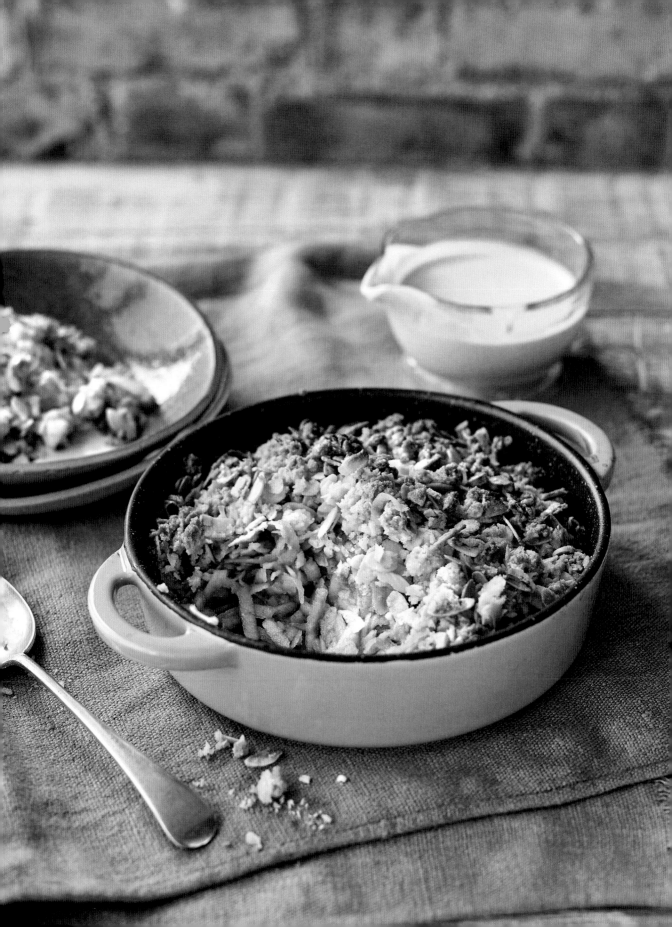

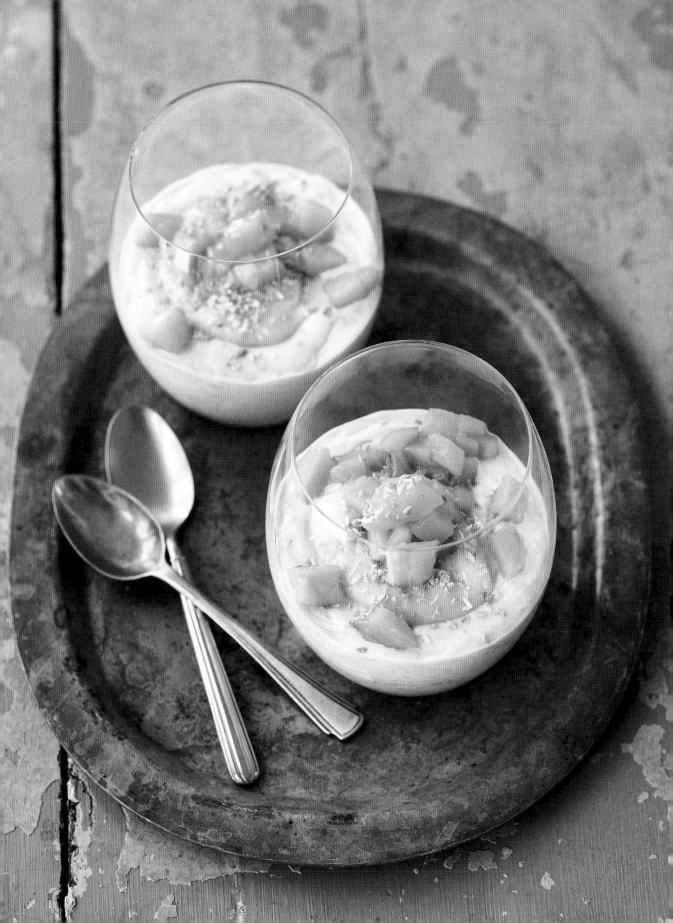

Buy ready-made lime curd and skip step 3

MANGO & CARDAMOM POSSET
WITH TOASTED COCONUT & LIME CURD

SERVES 4

250ml double cream
75g golden caster sugar
zest and juice of 1 lemon
4 cardamom pods, bashed
1 large ripe mango, peeled
    and stoned
25g desiccated coconut,
    toasted in a pan
    until golden

For the lime curd
150g caster sugar
150g butter
3 large eggs, beaten
zest of 2 limes and juice
    of 5 limes

1. **Make the posset** Bring the cream, sugar, lemon zest and cardamom to the boil in a pan over a high heat and cook for 3 minutes.

2. Cut a few slices off the mango, cut into dice and keep for garnish, then blitz the remainder in a blender with the lemon juice. Add to the cream mixture and then pour through a sieve into a jug. Pour into individual glasses and chill for at least 30 minutes to set.

3. **Make the lime curd** Weigh the sugar and butter into a pan. Add the eggs and the lime zest and juice and gently cook over a low heat, whisking all the time until stiff. Once you can see a trace of the whisk in the pan, set aside to cool.

4. When the posset has set, layer some of the lime curd on top and then add some diced mango and sprinkle with the toasted coconut to garnish.

TIP This recipe will make more curd than you need so keep any extra in a jar in the fridge.

ROSEMARY'S LEMON MERINGUE PIE

SERVES 8

For the pastry
250g plain flour
pinch of salt
125g butter, cut into cubes
1 tbsp caster sugar
2 large egg yolks
3 tbsp cold water

For the filling
80g cornflour
325g caster sugar
150ml fresh lemon juice
zest of 1 lemon
80g butter, cut into cubes
4 large egg yolks

For the meringue
225g caster sugar
3 large egg whites

1. **Make the pastry** Sift the flour and salt into a medium bowl. Rub the cubed butter into the flour with your fingertips until you get a fine crumb. Stir in the sugar. Mix the yolks and cold water together, then measure 3 tablespoons of liquid and pour over the dry ingredients. Using a cutlery knife or a palette knife, start bringing the pastry together. If you have dry crumb add more liquid, but only enough to bring it together; you do not want to over work or make the pastry too sticky or it will become tough. Roll into a thick disc, wrap in clingfilm and place in the fridge to rest for 10 minutes.

2. Roll out the pastry on a floured surface to 2–3mm thick and use it to line a 23cm loose-bottomed tart tin, making sure you line the tin evenly; there will be an overhang. Place on a baking sheet. Chill in the fridge for 10 minutes.

3. Preheat the oven to 190°C/Fan 170°C.

4. Line the pastry case with greaseproof paper and baking beans and bake the pastry case blind for 15–20 minutes. Remove the beans and paper and continue to bake the case for a further 5–8 minutes, until a pale golden colour. Leave to cool. One cooled, trim off excess pastry.

5. **Make the filling** Combine the cornflour and sugar in a medium pan and stir in the lemon juice and 300ml water until smooth. Cook over a high heat, stirring frequently for a few minutes until the mixture thickens.

Recipe continues

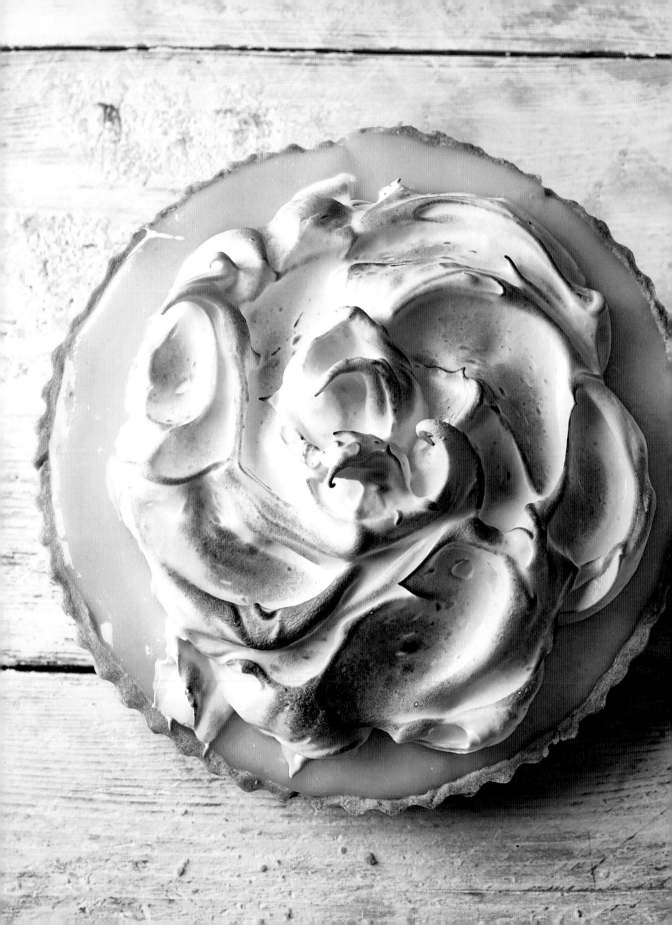

6 . Reduce the heat, gently simmer for 1–2 minutes then remove from the heat. Stir in the lemon zest, butter and egg yolks and mix to combine. Set aside to cool. The mixture should be smooth, thickened and set.

7 . **Make the Italian meringue** Place the sugar in a pan with 75ml water and gently bring to the boil – use a thermometer to ensure the sugar syrup reaches 120°C.

8 . Place the egg whites in a mixer with a balloon whisk and, when the syrup reaches 110°C, start whisking the whites until they reach stiff peaks. Once the sugar reaches 120°C pour it over the egg whites while continuing to whisk, being careful not to pour the syrup over the mixing attachment or against the bowl, and ensuring the sugar does not caramelise or become grainy. Whisk until the meringue is shiny, stiff, stable and cool.

9 . **Assemble the pie** Spoon the lemon filling into the cooked and cooled pastry case, spreading it out evenly. Remove from the tin. Spoon the Italian meringue over the top – you can make it smooth or rustic looking. Using a blowtorch, torch the meringue to add a golden colour.

BANANA & PASSION FRUIT SOUFFLÉ

SERVES 4

150ml whole milk
150ml cream
3 large eggs, separated
25g cornflour
100g caster sugar
1 large or 2 medium bananas
4 passion fruit, halved and
    seeds scooped out
juice of ½ lemon
icing sugar, for dusting

For the ramekins
butter, for greasing
caster sugar, for dusting

1 : Preheat the oven to 190°C/Fan 170°C and butter
4 x 150ml ramekins and dust with caster sugar.

2 : Combine the milk and cream in a pan over a medium
heat and bring to the boil.

3 : In a bowl, whisk the egg yolks into the cornflour
and 50g of the caster sugar. Add a little of the hot
milk and cream to the egg mixture and whisk. Pour
this solution back into the pan with rest of the milk
and cream and return to the heat until it forms a
thick crème pâtissière.

4 : Whizz the bananas, passion fruit and half the
lemon juice together in a blender and stir this into
to the crème pâtissière.

5 : In a separate clean bowl, whisk the egg whites until
holding their shape and then gradually whisk in the
remaining 50g of sugar until you have a glossy meringue.

6 : Add a third of this meringue mix to the crème
pâtissière and mix well. Carefully fold the remainder
of the meringue into the crème pâtissière and then
spoon into the prepared ramekins.

7 : Bake for approximately 15 minutes until risen
and golden.

8 : Dust with icing sugar before serving.

> **TIP** Serve with Salted Caramel Ice Cream
> (see page 242).

SUMMER BERRY
SHORTBREAD CAKE

SERVES 10

For the shortbread base
100g unsalted butter, chilled,
    plus extra for greasing
175g plain flour, plus extra
    for dusting
¼ tsp fine sea salt
50g desiccated coconut
2 tbsp golden caster sugar
1 egg yolk (reserve white
    for cake)
½ tsp vanilla extract
100g raspberry jam

For the cake
175g unsalted butter, melted
150g natural yoghurt
3 eggs, plus reserved white
150g plain flour
¼ tsp fine sea salt
2 tsp baking powder
175g golden caster sugar
100g desiccated coconut
150g mixed raspberries
    and blueberries
50g flaked almonds

1. Lightly butter a 23cm square cake tin and line with baking parchment.

2. Make the shortbread base Measure the flour, butter and salt into a food-processor and pulse to make fine crumbs. Add the coconut and sugar and pulse again.

3. Beat the egg yolk with the vanilla and add to the machine with 1 tablespoon of water. Keep the motor running to make a soft dough.

4. Roughly press into the prepared tin with your hands, dust with a little flour and press with the back of a spoon to push into the corners and flatten. Prick with a fork and chill for 10 minutes.

5. Preheat the oven to 200°C/Fan 180°C.

6. Bake the shortbread base for 15 minutes or until pale golden. Remove from the oven and lower the temperature 180°C/Fan 160°C.

7. Cool the base for a couple of minutes and then spread with the jam.

8. Make the cake Beat the melted butter and yoghurt in a bowl with a fork and then add the eggs and reserved egg white.

9. Sift the flour, salt and baking powder into a large bowl then stir in the sugar and coconut.

10. Pour the wet cake ingredients into the dry and mix well with a spatula. When well combined, spread over the jammy biscuit base, level the top and then scatter with the berries and flaked almonds.

11. Bake for 35–45 minutes.

12. Cool in the tin then cut into bars.

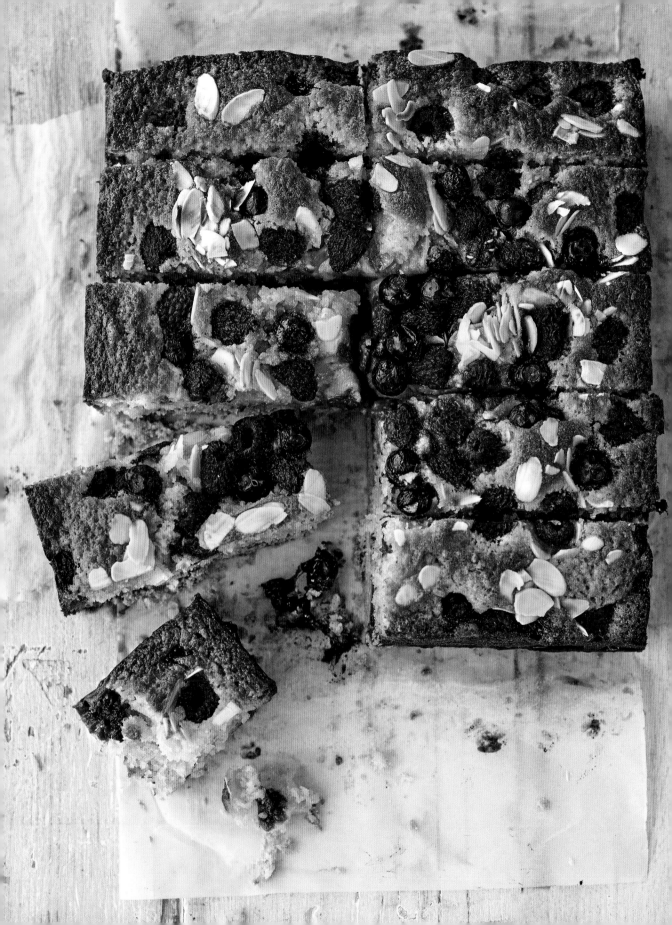

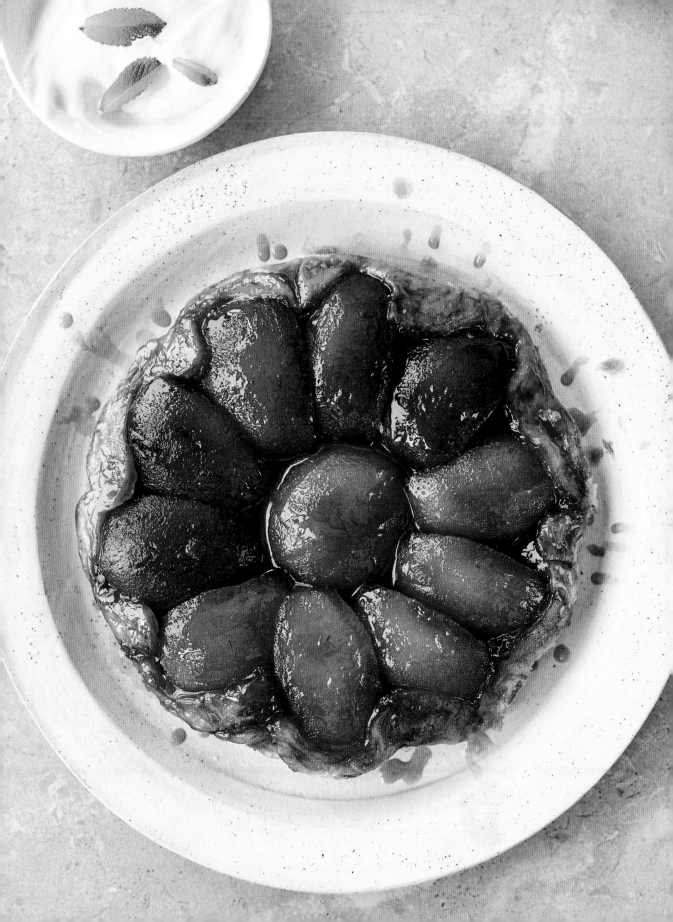

TARTE TATIN
WITH CALVADOS CREAM

SERVES 4

1 x 375g block all butter
   puff pastry
100g caster sugar
60g unsalted butter, cubed
   plus extra melted butter
   for brushing
600g Braeburn apples, peeled,
   cored and cut into quarters

For the Calvados cream
175ml double cream
½ tbsp icing sugar
1 tbsp Calvados
1 fresh mint sprig, to decorate

1. Preheat the oven to 200°C/Fan 180°C.

2. **Prepare the pastry** Roll out the pastry to the thickness of a pound coin and then cut a disc slightly larger than the size of a 20cm ovenproof frying pan or skillet and set aside.

3. Place the frying pan over a medium heat, pour in the caster sugar and melt until it turns light brown and starts to smoke a little; do not stir during the process, simply move the pan around a little if required – it will take 5 minutes or so.

4. Remove from the heat and add the 60g of butter. Stir to melt and combine and set aside. Arrange the apples in the pan, round side down, starting from the outer edge of the pan and working towards the centre.

5. Put the pan back on the heat and cook the apples in the caramel for 10 minutes.

6. Brush the melted butter over the apples and cover with the puff pastry, tucking it in at the sides. Pierce the pastry several times and then cook in the oven for 20–25 minutes, or until risen and golden brown.

7. Remove from the oven, leave to cool for 10 minutes before turning out onto a deep plate.

8. **Make the Calvados cream** Place the cream and icing sugar in a bowl and whip until it starts to form soft peaks. Add the Calvados and stir gently.

9. Serve the tarte tatin with the Calvados cream in a small bowl, topped with the sprig of mint.

CARDAMOM CHEESECAKE WITH ROSE WATER SYRUP

SERVES 4

250g digestive biscuits
100g unsalted butter, melted
105g icing sugar
280g cream cheese
½ tsp ground green cardamom
1 tsp ground ginger
210ml double cream
50g pistachios, crushed
50g caster sugar
¼ tsp rose water
1 tbsp fresh lemon juice
sugared rose petals,
   to decorate
summer fruits, to decorate

1 . **Make the biscuit base** Place the biscuits in a food-processor and whizz to make crumbs. Add the melted butter and mix together. Press the biscuit mixture into the base of a 23cm fluted loose-bottomed tart tin and put in the freezer for 15 minutes to firm up.

2 . **Make the cheesecake** Beat the icing sugar and cream cheese together in a large bowl. Add the ground cardamom and ginger.

3 . In a separate bowl, beat the double cream until stiff and then beat in the cream cheese mixture.

4 . Spread on top of the biscuit base and place back in the freezer for about 15 minutes.

5 . **Make the rose water syrup** Bring 50ml water to the boil in a small pan with the sugar over a medium heat, stir until dissolved. Add the rose water and allow to cool.

6 . Scatter the pistachios on top of the cheesecake and then decorate with the rose water syrup, petals and summer fruits.

FAMILY TIP 'Combining Middle Eastern and Indian flavours, this recipes requires little skill but delivers maximum results.'

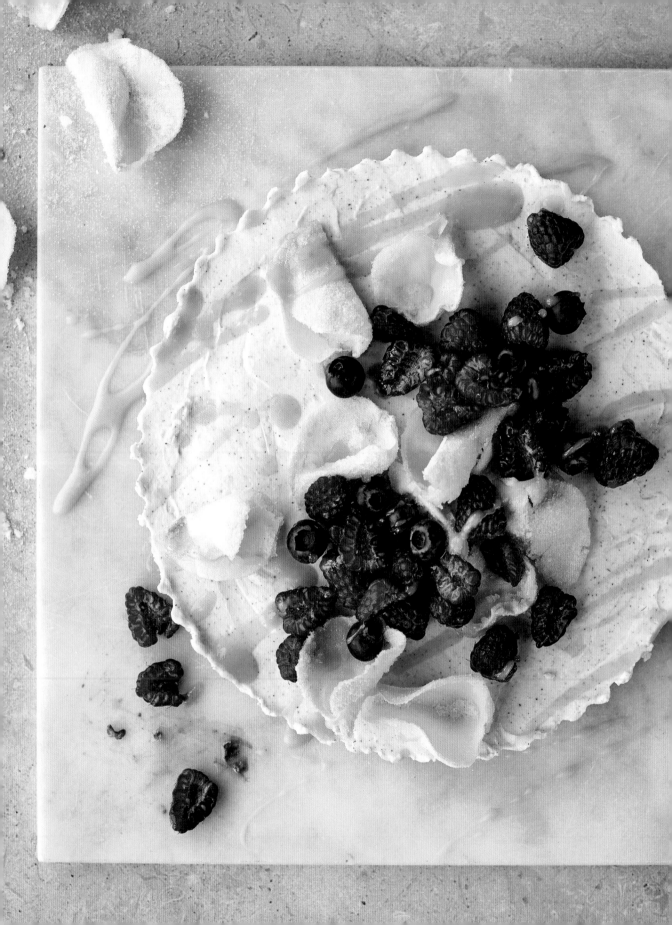

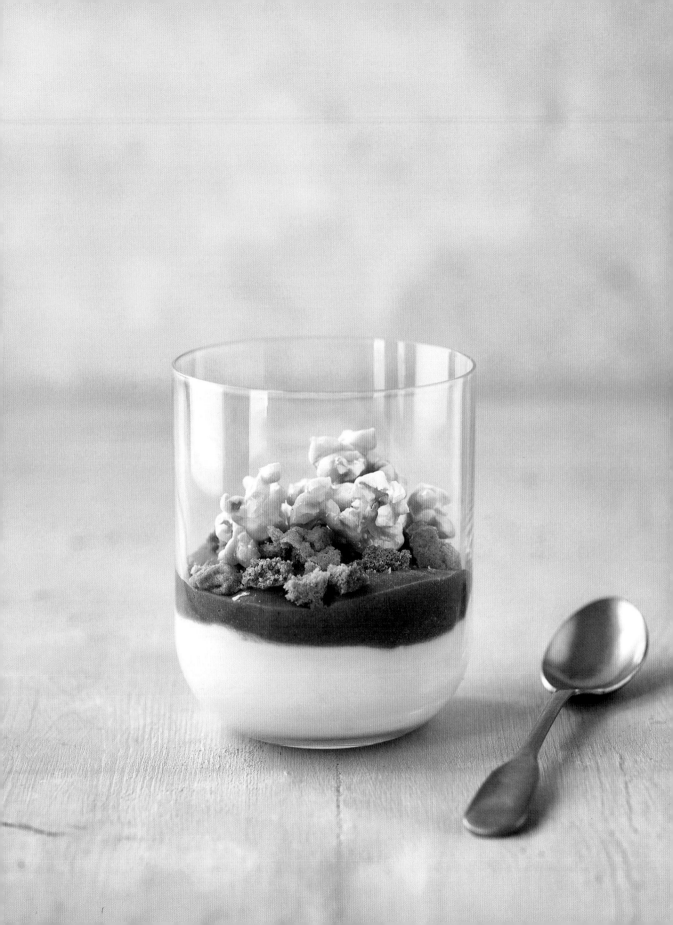

Buy ginger biscuits and caramel popcorn and skip steps 3–5

CHEESECAKE WITH SALTED CARAMEL POPCORN, BLACKBERRY CURD & GINGERNUT CRUMBLE

SERVES 4

250g mascarpone cheese
125ml double cream
125ml natural yoghurt
zest and juice of 1 lemon

For the blackberry curd
100g blackberries
1 large egg
zest and juice of 1 lemon
1 tbsp caster sugar
50g butter

For the ginger nut crumble
35g unsalted butter
1 tbsp soft brown sugar
35g plain flour
½ tsp baking powder
1 tsp ground ginger
¾ tbsp golden syrup
1 ball of stem ginger in syrup,
  finely chopped

For the salted caramel
50g caster sugar
10g unsalted butter
½ tsp sea salt
½ tsp vanilla extract

For the popcorn
a knob of butter
drop of rapeseed oil
1 tbsp popcorn kernels

1. Make the cheesecake Whisk together the mascarpone, cream and yoghurt to thicken, add half the lemon juice and all the zest. Spread into a serving dish and leave to chill in the fridge.

2. Make the blackberry curd Push the blackberries hrough a sieve and then add to a large pan with the egg, lemon zest, juice and sugar. Add the butter and place over a medium heat. Stir until thick and then remove from the heat. Leave to chill in the fridge.

3. Make the ginger nut crumble Preheat the oven to 200°C/Fan 180°C and line a baking sheet with greaseproof paper. Cream the butter and sugar in a large bowl. Add the remaining ingredients and mix well. Place 12 heaped teaspoons of the mixture on the lined sheet, leaving room to spread. Cook for 10 minutes and then leave to cool. Break into crumble.

4. Make the salted caramel Place the sugar and 100ml water in a pan over a high heat. Bring up to a temperature of 185°C without stirring. You can do this by eye – when the caramel has reached a lovely golden brown colour, it is ready. Remove from the heat and carefully add the butter (the hot sugar will spatter and could burn you). Keep stirring until the caramel stops bubbling and spitting.

5. Make the popcorn Heat the knob of butter and drop of oil in a large pan over a medium heat, add the popcorn kernels, cover with a lid and leave to pop. When the popcorn has finished popping, stir in the salted caramel.

6. Layer the cheesecake mix in serving glasses with the blackberry curd on top. Decorate with the crumbled ginger nut and popcorn then serve.

DESSERTS

Use shop-bought candied peel and nut brittle and skip steps 4 and 5

ALMOND CAKE WITH PEARS POACHED IN RED WINE

SERVES 4

For the almond cake
110g butter, plus extra
    for greasing
130g caster sugar
3 eggs
2–3 drops almond extract
110g ground almonds
40g plain flour

For the pears
300ml red wine
130g caster sugar
pared zest of 1 lemon
1 cinnamon stick
4 ripe pears

**For the candied peel
    and nut brittle**
2 oranges
150g caster sugar
50g mixed nuts, roughly
    chopped

1. Preheat the oven to 160°C/Fan 140°C and butter and line a 20cm loose-bottomed sandwich tin.

2. Make the almond cake Beat the butter with a wooden spoon or in a food-processor to soften. Add the caster sugar gradually, beating all the time, until soft and light. Add the eggs and almond extract, beating well, and fold in the ground almonds and flour. Tip the cake mixture into the prepared tin and bake for 35 minutes, or until an inserted skewer comes out clean. Cool the cake in the tin for 10 minutes, then turn out onto a wire rack.

3. Make the pears poached in red wine Place a pan over a medium heat and pour in the wine and 300ml water. Stir in the caster sugar, lemon zest and cinnamon stick. Bring to the boil and leave to bubble for 1 minute. Keeping the stalks on the pears, peel and remove the 'eye' from the base. Place the pears in the syrup over the heat and leave to poach over a gentle heat for about 30 minutes, or until tender to the point of a sharp knife.

4. Make the candied peel Pare the zest of the oranges and cut into strips. Place the zest in a pan of water over a high heat and bring to the boil. Change the water and bring to the boil again. Meanwhile, make a sugar syrup in a small pan with 50g of the sugar and 100ml water. Place the zest in the sugar syrup and boil for 20 minutes. Drain.

5. Make the nut brittle Put the remaining sugar in a pan over a low heat and slowly melt, swirling the pan occasionally, until it caramelises. Meanwhile, spread the nuts out onto baking parchment, then pour the caramel over the top. Allow to cool then chop into brittle.

6. Decorate the cake with the peel and brittle then serve with the poached pears.

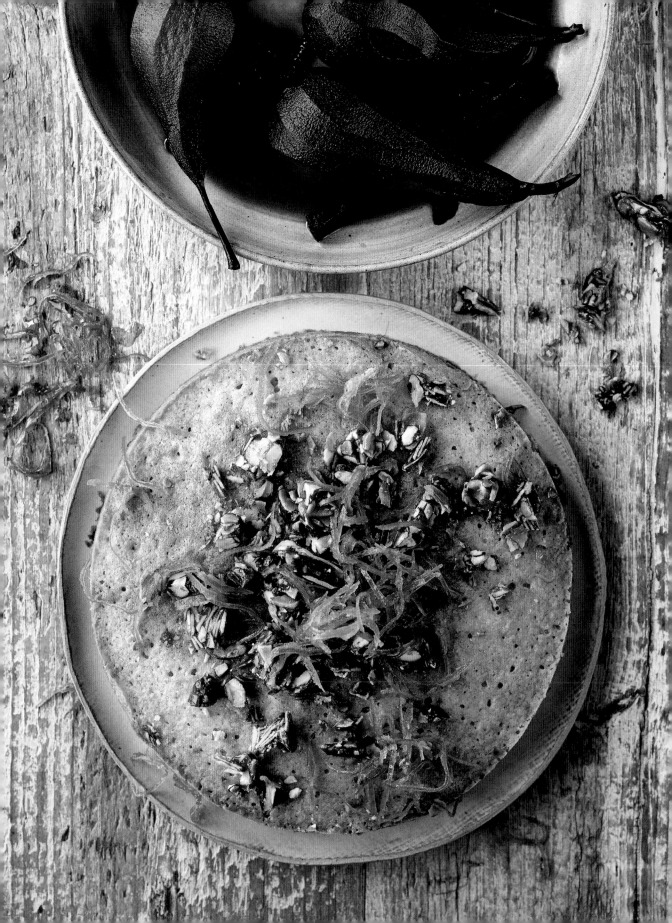

APPLE CAKE

175g butter, softened,
    plus extra for greasing
150g soft brown sugar
3 large eggs, beaten
225g self-raising flour,
    plus extra for dusting
1 tsp ground cinnamon
1 tsp mixed spice
zest and juice of 1 large lemon
milk, to loosen
150g Bramley apples, peeled
    and diced

For the caramelised apples
50g unsalted butter
500g Bramley apples,
    peeled and diced
½ tsp ground cinnamon
pinch of salt
75g caster sugar

1 : Preheat the oven to 180°C/Fan 160°C and butter and line a 20cm square cake tin.

2 : Make the apple cake Cream the butter and sugar together with an electric whisk until light and fluffy.

3 : Beat the eggs in one at a time and then sift in the flour and spices and fold into the mixture.

4 : Stir in the lemon zest and a little milk if it is too thick.

5 : Toss the apple pieces lightly in flour and then add to the mix. Scrape into the prepared tin and bake for 35–40 minutes, or until golden and a skewer inserted into the centre comes out clean.

6 : Make the caramelised apples Melt the butter in a pan over a gentle heat. Once melted, add the apples, cinnamon and salt. Cook until the apples are soft but not broken down.

7 : Add the sugar and 100ml of water and bubble to form a caramel.

8 : Once the cake is cooked, use a skewer to make some holes in the surface and then strain over the caramel from the apple pan.

9 : Leave the cake to cool a little and then slice into squares and serve with the caramelised apples.

> **TIP** Serve alongside Baked Apples with Blackberry Jam (see opposite) and Burnt Honey Custard (see page 245).

BAKED APPLES WITH BLACKBERRY JAM

SERVES 4

For the blackberry jam
300g blackberries
20g icing sugar, plus extra
    for sprinkling
1 vanilla pod, slit lengthways

For the baked apples
4 eating apples, cored and the
    skin scored round the middle
2 tsp ground cinnamon
50ml apple juice
fresh lemon juice (to taste)
200g blackberries
approximately 400ml
    blackberry liqueur

1 : Preheat the oven to 200°C/Fan 180°C.

2 : Make the blackberry jam Add the blackberries
to a pan with the icing sugar and the vanilla pod and
a small amount of water. Cook until the blackberries
are soft but not totally broken down.

3 : Make the baked apples Place the apples on a
baking sheet and spoon some of the blackberry mixture
into the cavity of each, leaving the remainder in the pan.
Sprinkle the apples with more sugar, the cinnamon and
pour over some of the apple juice. Bake for 20–25 minutes,
or until tender.

4 : Make the macerated blackberries Mix the
200g blackberries with the liqueur and leave to infuse.

5 : Continue cooking the blackberries remaining in
the pan until they break down and become a bit jammy,
but not too reduced. Pass through a sieve and add the
lemon juice or more icing sugar, to taste.

6 : Serve the baked apples with the macerated blackberries
and blackberry jam.

TIP Serve with Apple Cake (see opposite)
and Burnt Honey Custard (see page 245).

Buy a ready-made sweet pastry case and skip steps 1–4

TORTA NERA
CHOCOLATE, WALNUT & ALMOND TART

SERVES 8

For the sweet pastry
100g butter, plus extra
for greasing
200g plain flour
pinch of salt
50g caster sugar
2 egg yolks

For the filling
230g walnuts
200g caster sugar
3 eggs
50g butter, melted
65g amaretti biscuits,
roughly crushed
75g dark chocolate, grated
1 tbsp plain flour
1 tbsp instant coffee powder
dissolved in a little hot water
50ml Amaretto liqueur

whole walnuts, to decorate
icing sugar, for dusting
mascarpone cheese, to serve

1. Butter a 23cm deep, fluted, loose-bottomed tart tin.

2. Make the pastry Place the butter in a bowl with the flour and salt and rub in with your fingertips until the mixture resembles coarse breadcrumbs. Add the sugar and mix in the egg yolks. Bring together without kneading and wrap the pastry in clingfilm. Rest in the fridge for 30 minutes.

3. Preheat the oven to 200°C/Fan 180°C.

4. Roll out the pastry on a lightly floured surface and use it to line the prepared tart tin. Cover the pastry with greaseproof paper and fill with baking beans. Bake blind for 10–12 minutes. Remove the beans and greaseproof paper and return to the oven to bake for a further 5–6 minutes, or until lightly golden.

5. Reduce the oven temperature to 180°C/Fan 160°C.

6. Make the filling Whizz the walnuts and 100g of the sugar in a food-processor until finely ground.

7. Whisk the eggs with the remaining sugar. Carefully stir in the melted butter, the ground walnuts, amaretti biscuits, chocolate, flour, coffee and Amaretto. Mix together well.

8. Cook the tart Spoon the filling into the tart case, decorate with the whole walnuts and place in the middle of the oven to cook for 25 minutes.

9. Serve warm with a dusting of icing sugar and a small scoop of mascarpone.

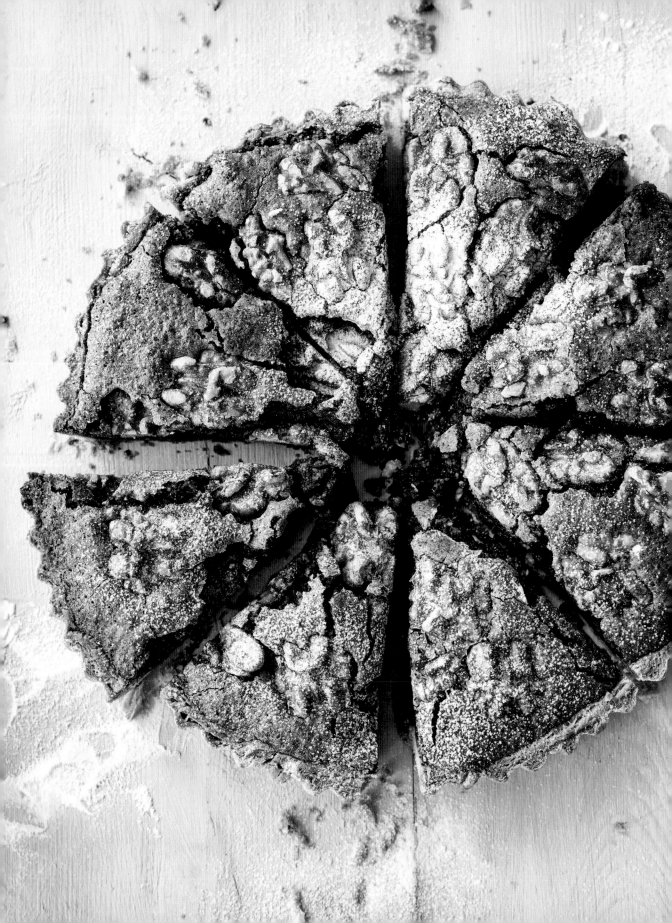

ROSEMARY'S FIG FRANGIPANE WITH TOASTED ALMONDS

SERVES 6

4–6 figs (not quite ripe)
2 tbsp redcurrant jelly
30g slivered almonds, toasted
icing sugar, for dusting

For the pastry
80g unsalted butter,
    cold and cubed
50g icing sugar, sifted
190g plain flour, plus extra
    for dusting
1 egg yolk

For the frangipane
100g unsalted butter, softened
100g icing sugar
100g ground almonds
2 eggs
1 tbsp double cream

1. **Make the pastry** Put the butter, icing sugar and flour in a food-processor and whizz until the mixture resembles breadcrumbs. Add 1 tablespoon of cold water and the egg yolk and process to a dough.

2. Tip onto a floured surface – if it is too soft, wrap in clingfilm and place in the fridge for 30 minutes. Roll out the dough to 3mm thickness and use it to line a 20cm loose-bottomed fluted tart tin, making sure you press well into the corners. Chill for 1 hour.

3. Heat the oven to 190°C/Fan 170°C.

4. Line the pastry with greaseproof paper and fill with baking beans or rice. Bake for 15 minutes. Remove the greaseproof paper and beans and put back in the oven for a further 3–5 minutes, or until lightly golden and sandy to the touch.

5. Turn the oven temperature down to 180°C/Fan 160°C.

6. **Make the frangipane** Combine all the ingredients in a bowl and beat well.

7. **Cook the tart** Spread the frangipane filling into the pastry case and press the fig halves into it, cut side up. Bake for about 30 minutes.

8. Leave to cool for 10 minutes before removing from the tin and cooling completely on a wire rack.

9. To finish, heat the redcurrant jelly until smooth and brush over the figs. Sprinkle with toasted slivered almonds and dust with icing sugar to serve.

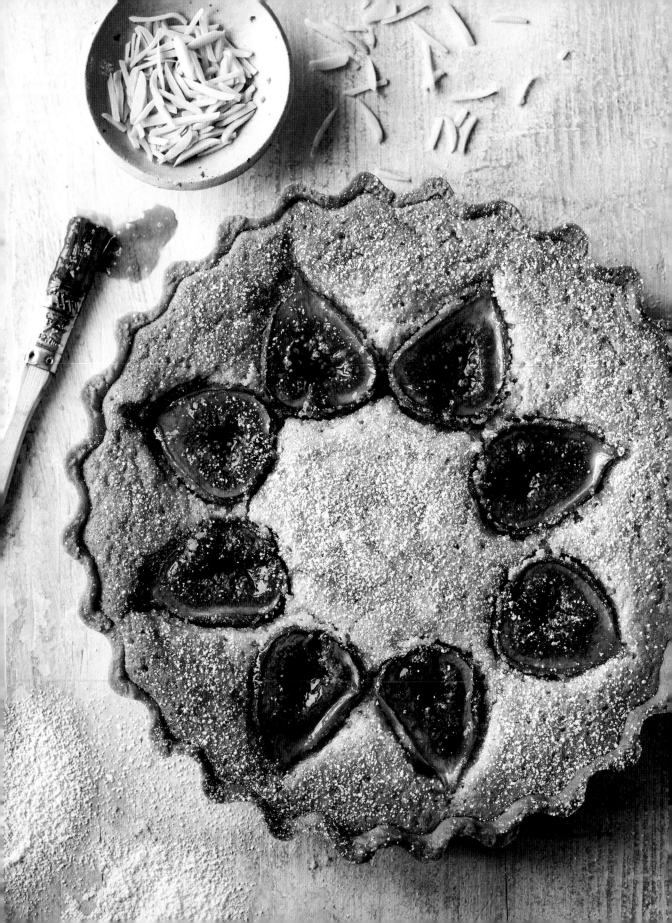

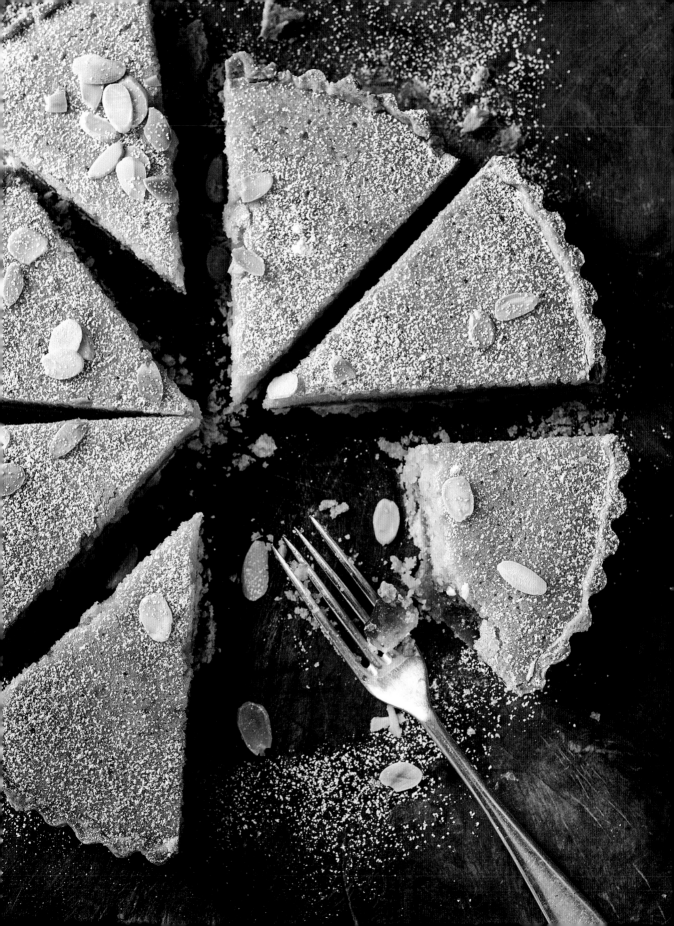

Buy good-quality jam and a ready-made sweet pastry case and skip steps 1–5

BAKEWELL TART

SERVES 8

For the sweet pastry
150g plain flour, plus
    extra for dusting
pinch of salt
75g butter, cubed
½ tbsp caster sugar

For the raspberry jam
250g raspberries
200g jam sugar
juice of ½ lemon

For the frangipane
4 medium eggs, plus
    2 medium egg yolks
115g caster sugar
150g butter, melted and cooled
150 ground almonds
1 tsp almond extract

3 tbsp flaked almonds and
    icing sugar, to decorate

1. Make the pastry Sift the flour and salt into a bowl. Rub the cubed butter into the flour with your fingertips until you get a fine crumb. Stir in the sugar. Add 2½ tablespoons of cold water and, using a cutlery knife or a palette knife, start bringing the pastry together; if you have a dry crumb add more liquid, but only enough to bring it together; you do not want to over work or make the pastry too sticky or it will become tough. Roll into a disc, wrap in clingfilm and place in the fridge to rest for 10 minutes.

2. Make the raspberry jam Place the raspberries in a medium pan and gently heat until they start to soften. Add the sugar and lemon juice and continue to heat until the sugar has dissolved. Bring to the boil and cook for 8–10 minutes, stirring occasionally, until starting to thicken. Whilst still hot, carefully strain the jam through a sieve into a bowl and set aside. Place the bowl on top of a bowl of iced water until completely cooled, stirring occasionally.

3. Roll out the pastry on a floured surface to 3mm thick and use to line a 23cm loose-bottomed tart tin, making sure it's evenly lined and has an overhang of pastry. Chill for 10 minutes. Prick the base with a fork to stop the pastry puffing up during the blind bake.

4. Preheat the oven to 190°C/Fan 170°C.

5. Place the lined pastry dish on a baking sheet, then line the pastry case with greaseproof paper and baking beans. Bake the pastry case blind for 20 minutes. Remove the beans and paper and continue to bake the case for a further 5–8 minutes, until a pale golden colour. Leave to cool. Once cool, trim off the excess pastry.

Recipe continues

6 : Reduce the oven temperature to 180°C/Fan 160°C.

7 : **Make the frangipane** Beat the eggs, egg yolks and sugar well together, then mix in the melted butter, ground almonds and almond extract.

8 : **Assemble the tart** Spread 8 tablespoons of the cooled raspberry jam on the base of the cooled pastry case and top with the frangipane to create an even layer that covers the jam. Ensure that the frangipane mix doesn't come over the top of the pastry.

9 : Bake for about 35 minutes until the filling is golden brown and a skewer inserted in the centre comes out clean.

10 : While the tart is cooking, gently heat a dry frying pan with an even layer of flaked almonds, gently toast them until they start to colour, then remove them from the pan onto kitchen paper.

11 : Once the tart is cooked through, remove from the oven and allow it to cool before removing from the tin (including the base) on to a plate or board.

12 : Decorate the tart with a light dusting of icing sugar and the toasted flaked almonds.

ROSEMARY'S SPICED PEARS WITH APPLE & RASPBERRY COMPOTE, SAFFRON CARDAMOM MASCARPONE & OAT CRUMBLE

SERVES 4

4 pears
750ml red wine
100g caster sugar
1 cinnamon stick
2 star anise
4 cloves
pared zest of 1 orange

For the apple & raspberry compote
2 Braeburn apples, peeled, cored and cut into 1cm dice
juice of 1 lemon
50g butter
1 vanilla pod, slit lengthways and seeds scraped out
125g raspberries

For the oat crumble
50g plain flour
50g unsalted butter
50g demerara sugar
25g caster sugar
25g rolled oats

For the saffron cardamom mascarpone
1 tbsp honey
pinch of saffron
125g mascarpone cheese
½ tsp ground cardamom

1. **Make the spiced pears** Peel the pears and carefully remove the 'eye' from the base. Bring the red wine, caster sugar, aromatics and orange zest to a boil in a pan over a medium heat, stirring to dissolve the sugar. Add the pears, cover the pan with a circle of greaseproof paper and allow to simmer for 20–25 minutes, or until the pears have softened and taken on the red wine colour. Remove from the heat and leave to steep overnight in the liquid, if you have time; this will give a better flavour and colour.

2. **Make the apple & raspberry compote** Place the apples in a small bowl with the lemon juice; toss them through so the apples do not discolour.

3. Measure the butter into a small pan over a medium heat and, when sizzling, add the apples and cook until they start to soften. Add the seeds from the vanilla pod and stir. Once the apples have softened, remove from the heat and gently stir through the raspberries. Leave to cool.

4. Preheat the oven to 150°C/Fan 130°C.

5. **Make the oat crumble** Place all the ingredients in a food-processor and whizz. Tip onto a baking sheet and cook in the oven for about 45 minutes, turning every 10 minutes, until you have a lovely golden crunchy crumble.

6. **Make the saffron cardamom mascarpone** Place the honey and 1 tablespoon of water in a small pan and place over a gentle heat. Add the saffron and leave to infuse for at least 10 minutes. Leave to cool. Whisk the mascarpone so there are no lumps, then add the saffron honey and the cardamom. Mix well.

7. To serve, place each pear on a plate and add a sprinkle of crumble, some compote and a spoonful of mascarpone.

STICKY TOFFEE PUDDING

SERVES 8

100g unsalted butter,
  plus extra for greasing
200g dates, stoned
1 tsp bicarbonate of soda
200g soft dark brown sugar
3 eggs
½ tsp vanilla extract
200g plain flour
2 tsp baking powder

For the toffee sauce
120g unsalted butter
130g soft light brown sugar
100g soft dark brown sugar
500ml double cream

For the custard
200ml double cream
50ml whole milk
2 tsp vanilla extract
4 egg yolks
75g caster sugar

1 . Preheat the oven to 180°C/Fan 160°C.

2 . Butter a 20cm square tin and line the base with non-stick baking parchment.

3 . Make the pudding Place the dates and 150ml water in a medium pan and simmer for about 5 minutes, until softened and beginning to break down. Whizz in a food-processor to a moist and gooey paste. Add the bicarbonate of soda and leave to cool.

4 . Cream the butter and dark brown sugar together until pale and fluffy. Beat the eggs in one at a time, then add the vanilla and fold in the flour and baking powder. Finally, tip in the cooled date mixture, stirring well to combine. Pour into the prepared tin and bake for about 50 minutes, or until cooked through. A skewer inserted into the centre should come out clean.

5 . Make the toffee sauce Slowly melt the butter in a pan over a gentle heat. Add the sugars and caramelise slowly. Finally, stir in the cream and simmer for 3 minutes.

6 . Make the custard Heat the cream, milk and vanilla extract in a small, heavy pan until bubbles form at the edges. While this is heating, whisk together the egg yolks and sugar until smooth. Slowly pour ½ cup of hot milk mixture into the egg yolks, whisking constantly. Gradually add egg yolk mixture back into the remaining milk mixture, whisking constantly. Continue to cook over a low-medium heat, stirring constantly, until the mixture coats the back of a spoon.

7 . To serve, turn the whole pudding out and pour over half of the toffee sauce, reserving the remainder to be served in a jug alongside the custard.

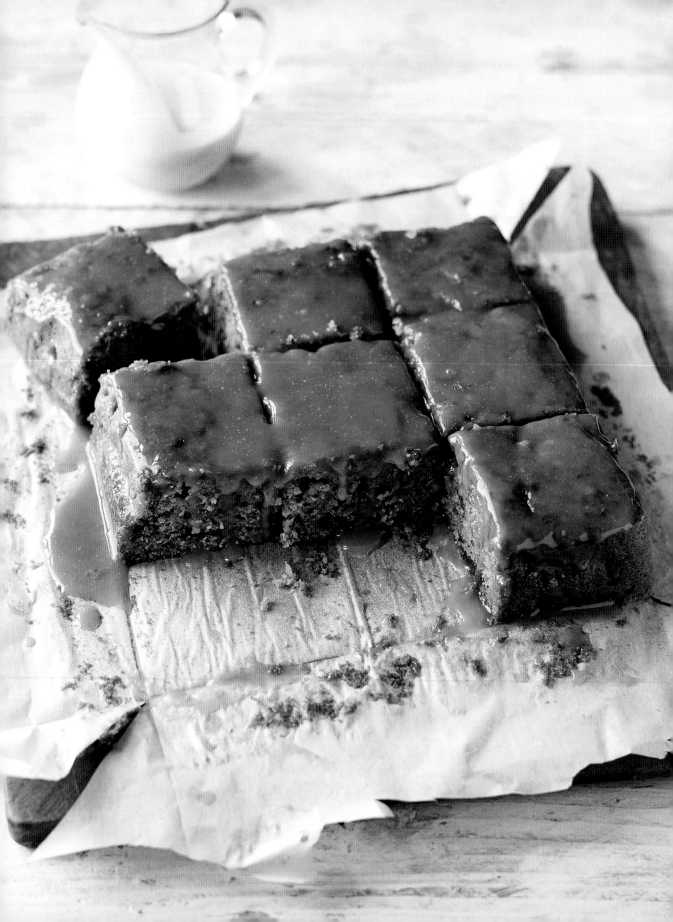

ROSEMARY'S CHOCOLATE BRIOCHE BREAD & BUTTER PUDDING

SERVES 4–6

2 medium eggs, plus
   2 medium egg yolks
1 tsp vanilla extract
1 tsp ground cinnamon
¼ tsp grated nutmeg
500ml double cream
1 brioche loaf (about 400g),
   cut into 1cm slices and
   then triangles
100g unsalted butter, melted
40g walnuts, chopped
80g sultanas
125g dark chocolate,
   coarsely grated
30g white chocolate,
   coarsely grated
soft light brown sugar or
   demerara, for sprinkling

1. Preheat the oven to 160°C/Fan 140°C.

2. **Make the custard** Whisk the eggs, egg yolks and vanilla extract with the cinnamon and nutmeg.

3. Meanwhile, bring the cream to the boil in a pan over a medium heat, whisking all the time.

4. Add the boiled cream to the egg mixture and leave to one side to cool.

5. **Assemble the pudding** Brush both sides of each triangle with melted butter and then place a layer in an oval dish at a slant. Sprinkle with half the walnuts and half the sultanas and half the grated chocolate. Repeat with a second layer and finish with the remainder of the nuts, sultanas and chocolate. Very carefully, pour the cooled egg mixture over the brioche and allow to soak in for 10 minutes, before sprinkling with brown sugar.

6. Bake for 30 minutes, or until the mixture is just set but still a little bit wobbly.

7. Leave to stand for 10–15 minutes and then serve warm.

> **TIP** Serve with Crème Anglaise
> (see page 245).

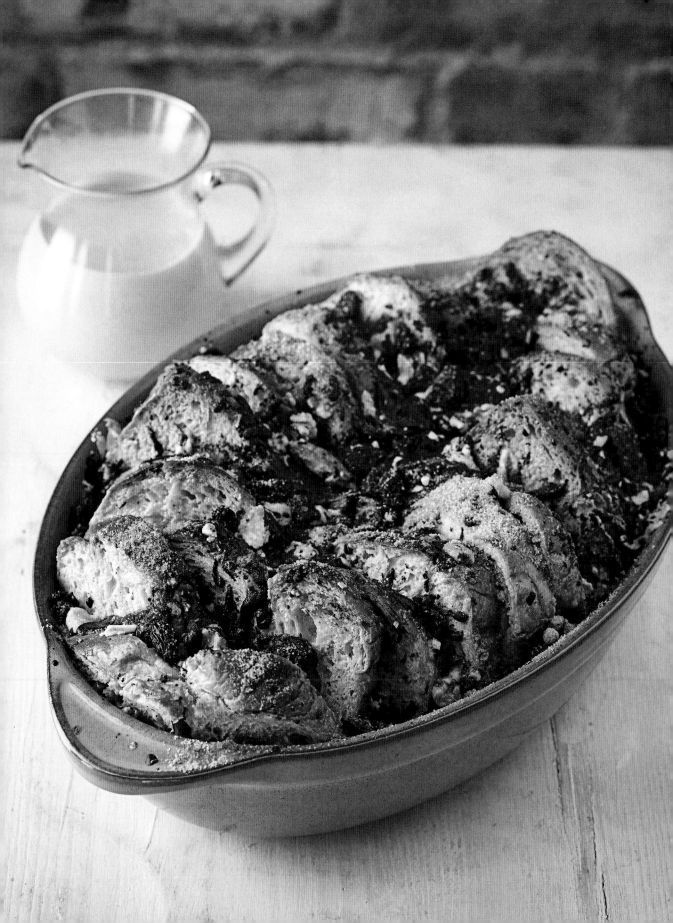

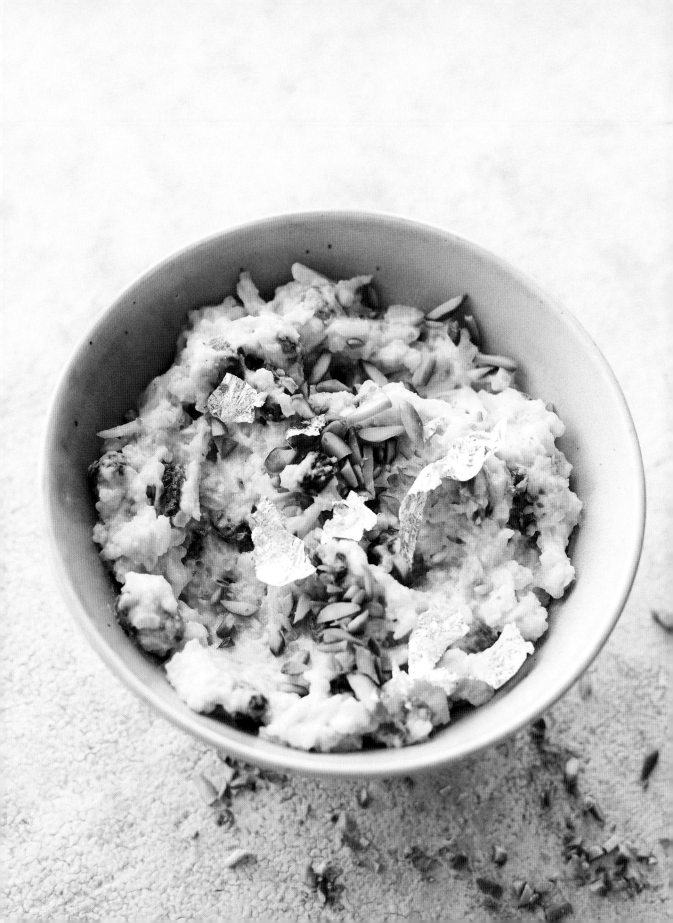

KHEER
INDIAN RICE PUDDING

70g Basmati rice
1 litre whole milk
8 cardamom pods (or 1 tsp ground cardamom)
50g slivered almonds
75g sultanas
2 tbsp caster sugar (or to taste)
a handful of pistachios, chopped, to decorate
gold or silver leaf, to decorate (optional)

1 : Wash the rice, tip into a large pan and place over a low heat for a few minutes.

2 : Pour in the milk, add the cardamom and almonds, and stir. Bring to a simmer and cook uncovered for approximately 40 minutes.

3 : Stir in the sultanas and simmer for a further 15–20 minutes, until the liquid has reduced by at least half and the mixture has thickened.

4 : Stir in the sugar, to taste, remove from the heat and allow to cool.

5 : Pour into a bowl, cover with clingfilm and chill for 1–2 hours or overnight.

6 : Garnish with crushed pistachios and gold or silver leaf, if you like, to serve.

FAMILY TIP 'This is a true family favourite that brings back many childhood memories for us.'

CHOCOLATE FONDANT

SERVES 4

For the brittle
100g flaked almonds
200g caster sugar

For the fondants
100g dark chocolate (minimum
    70 per cent cocoa solids),
    broken into pieces
100g butter
2 large eggs
100g caster sugar
100g plain flour

melted butter, for greasing
20g dark cocoa powder,
    for dusting
thick cream, to serve

1. Preheat the oven to 200°C/Fan 180°C and prepare 4 dariole moulds by brushing them with melted butter in an upwards direction. Dust each mould with the cocoa powder.

2. Make the brittle Spread the nuts out evenly on a baking sheet and toast in the oven for 5–6 minutes, checking them regularly and shaking if necessary. Once cooked, tip out evenly onto a silicon mat.

3. Tip the sugar for the brittle into a pan and gently heat, swirling until the sugar has dissolved and turned golden brown. Pour over the nuts, making sure you coat them evenly, then leave to cool.

4. Make the fondants Melt the chocolate and butter in a heatproof bowl over a pan of barely simmering water or in a microwave until just melted, taking care not to burn the chocolate. Remove the bowl from the heat and allow to cool for around 10 minutes.

5. In a separate large bowl, whisk the eggs and sugar with an electric hand whisk until pale and thickened and the whisk leaves a trail. Pour the melted chocolate mixture into the egg mixture and fold to combine. Sift in the flour and fold in.

6. Divide the mixture evenly between the moulds. Place the fondants on a baking sheet and cook for 8 minutes until the tops have formed a crust and they are just beginning to come away from the sides of their moulds. Remove from the oven and leave to sit for a couple of minutes before turning out.

7. Shatter the brittle into shards and serve with the fondants and some thick cream.

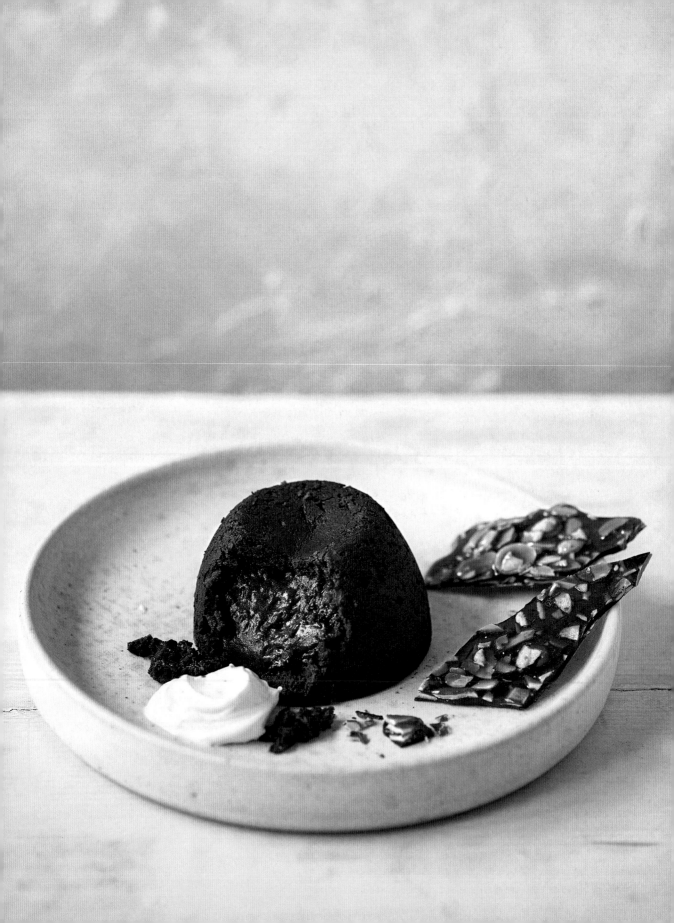

ESPRESSO MARTINI TIRAMISU

SERVES 4

4 eggs
125g caster sugar
1 tsp vanilla extract
pinch of salt
115g plain flour
3 tsp instant espresso
   coffee powder
200ml hot water
2 tbsp vodka
3 tbsp coffee liqueur
200ml double cream
125g mascarpone cheese
60g amaretti biscuits
20g dark cocoa powder, plus
   extra to decorate

1 : Preheat the oven to 190°C/Fan 170°C and line 3 x 15cm springform cake tins with greaseproof paper.

2 : Make the sponge Separate the eggs and whisk the egg yolks with half the sugar and all the vanilla. Beat until very pale; this will take about 5 minutes.

3 : In a clean bowl, beat the egg whites until they hold soft peaks. While beating, slowly add the salt and the remaining sugar until combined. Gently fold the beaten egg whites into the egg yolk mixture. Sift the flour over the egg mixture and gently fold in.

4 : Divide the sponge mixture evenly between the lined trays and bake for about 15 minutes, or until firm to the touch and golden.

5 : Place on wire racks to cool and remove the paper. (When cool, cut the cakes in half horizontally to make more layers, if desired.)

6 : Make the espresso martini Mix the coffee powder with the hot water, vodka and coffee liqueur and leave to cool. Brush the sponge discs with the coffee mixture.

7 : Make the mascarpone cream Mix a little of the double cream with the mascarpone until smooth and then add the remainder and whisk until slightly stiffened.

8 : Make the cocoa crumb Whizz the amaretti biscuits with half the cocoa powder in a food-processor.

9 : Assemble the tiramisu Place a layer of sponge in a glass trifle bowl and then spread with a layer of the mascarpone cream. Top with cocoa crumb and repeat the layers of sponge, cream and crumb until they are used up. Finish with a final layer of cream and dust with cocoa powder to serve.

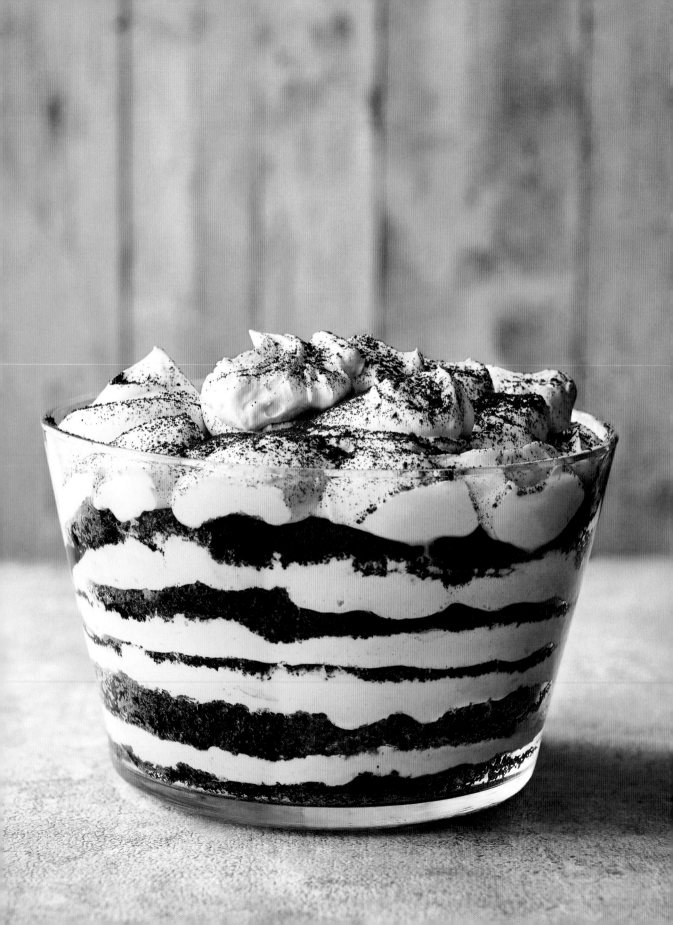

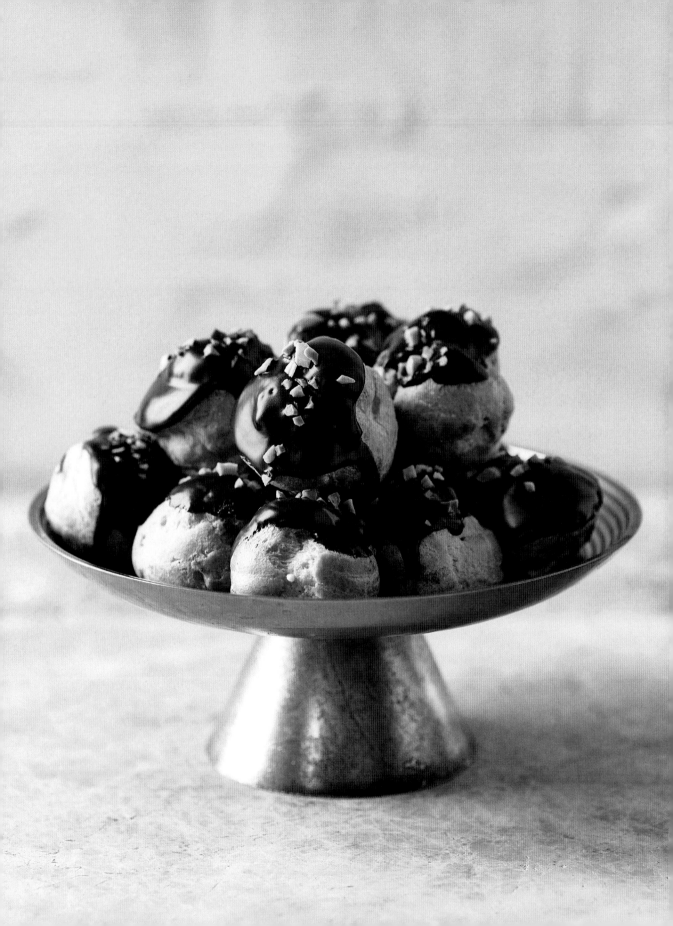

CHOCOLATE PROFITEROLES

For the choux pastry
50g butter
60g plain flour, sifted
2 large eggs, at room
    temperature
10g caster sugar

For the filling
350ml double cream
1 tbsp icing sugar
1 tsp vanilla extract

For the topping
200g dark chocolate
10g butter
100g whole almonds, toasted
    and finely chopped

1. Preheat the oven to 210°C/Fan 190°C.

2. Make the choux pastry Place 110ml water in a pan with the butter and bring up to a rolling boil. Remove from the heat and tip in all the sifted flour at once. Mix with your wooden spoon until it comes away from the sides of the pan in a cohesive ball. Return to the heat and cook out the pastry for a further 5 minutes, beating the mixture the whole time. Tip into a large bowl to cool.

3. Once the choux has cooled, beat the eggs and incorporate slowly in stages, beating until each addition is all incorporated before adding more. You may not need all the egg – you are looking for the mixture to fall from the wooden spoon in a reluctant drop (about 5–7 seconds); the mixture must not become too loose or it will just spread and not rise.

4. Place the mixture in a piping bag fitted with a plain 1cm nozzle.

5. Line a baking sheet with greaseproof paper and pipe small balls in lines across the baking sheet, making sure you give each enough room to rise. Gently rub the top of each ball with a wet finger as this will make for a crisper top.

6. Bake until a deep golden colour; they should be crisp and not soggy, about 20–30 minutes.

7. Turn the oven down to 180°C/Fan 160°C and make a small hole in the base of each choux bun with a skewer – insert it in one end and move it about in the middle – do not pierce through the other side – then place them back on the baking sheet and dry them in the oven for a further 5 minutes. Allow to cool on a wire rack.

Recipe continues

8 . **Make the filling** Lightly whisk the cream, icing sugar and vanilla until it just holds its shape and place in a piping bag with a plain straight-sided nozzle. Put the nozzle into the hole you made on one side of the choux pastry and pipe until the cavity fills with cream; the choux should feel heavy now.

9 . **Make the topping** Melt the chocolate and butter in a heatproof bowl over a pan of barely simmering water or in a microwave until just melted, taking care not to burn the chocolate. Allow to cool slightly then dip the presentation side of the choux pastry half way into the chocolate and allow the excess to drip off. It should have a lovely shine and not run down the side of the pastry.

10 . Sprinkle the chopped almonds over the chocolate before it sets.

11 . Place on a wire rack to set and then serve assembled in a stack.

APEROL BAKED RHUBARB WITH FLOATING ISLAND MERINGUES

SERVES 4

400g rhubarb, cut into
   6cm pieces
150g caster sugar
50ml Aperol liqueur
zest and juice of 1 orange
250ml whole milk
250ml double cream
1 vanilla pod, slit lengthways
   and seeds scraped out
4 egg yolks (3 whites reserved
   for the meringues)
750ml semi-skimmed milk

1 : Preheat the oven to 200°C/Fan 180°C.

2 : Prepare the rhubarb Place the rhubarb in an ovenproof dish with 30g of the sugar, the Aperol and orange zest and juice. Cover with foil and roast in the oven for 15–20 minutes, or until softened. Taste and add more sugar, if needed. Transfer to a plate and set aside. Pour the roasting juices into a pan and boil over a high heat for 1–2 minutes until it forms a thick syrup. Set aside.

3 : Make the custard Add the whole milk, cream and vanilla pod and seeds to a pan over a medium heat. Bring to the boil, stirring continuously, then remove from the heat and leave to cool slightly. Beat the egg yolks in a large bowl with 45g of the sugar until light and tripled in volume. Remove the vanilla pod from the milk and discard. Slowly whisk the warm milk mixture into the yolks. Return the custard to the pan and place over a low heat for a 2–3 minutes, stirring continuously, until it coats the back of a spoon. Strain through a sieve into a clean bowl and cover the surface with a layer of clingfilm. Set aside.

4 : Make the meringues Place the 3 reserved egg whites in a clean bowl and beat with an electric whisk until firm peaks. Continue whisking as you add the remaining caster sugar. Turn up the mixer and whisk for 7 minutes, or until glossy. Pour the semi-skimmed milk into a wide, shallow pan over a medium heat and warm through until it begins to simmer. Float heaped tablespoons of the meringue on the hot milk, making sure they are well spaced. Cook for about 30 seconds, then turn and cook for another 30 seconds, or until firm. Repeat with the remaining meringue. Use a slotted spoon to transfer the meringues to kitchen paper to absorb any milk.

5 : Spoon the custard into individual bowls and top with rhubarb, a meringue and a drizzle of the rhubarb syrup.

DESSERTS

BLACK FOREST GÂTEAU

SERVES 8

200g butter
6 medium eggs
250g caster sugar
100g plain flour
60g cocoa powder
100g Morello cherry jam
1 x tin pitted cherries, drained
500ml double cream
2 tbsp icing sugar
100g dark chocolate,
  to decorate

1 : Preheat the oven to 180°C/Fan 160°C.

2 : Melt the butter in a small pan. Weigh out 150g and put to one side to cool for the cake. Keep the remaining melted butter to grease and line the base of 3 x 20cm sandwich tins.

3 : **Make the cake** In a large bowl, whisk the eggs and caster sugar with an electric whisk until light fluffy and leaving a visible trail when you lift the whisk; this will take around 10 minutes.

4 : In a separate bowl, sift the flour and cocoa powder together before gently folding it into the egg mixture. Be careful not to overwork the mix. Once incorporated, gently pour in the cooled, melted butter and carefully fold together.

5 : Divide the mixture equally between the 3 tins and bake in the oven for 20–25 minutes.

6 : Meanwhile, heat the jam in a small pan to loosen. Reserving 8 tinned cherries for the top of the cake, add the remaining cherries to the jam, and stir to coat.

7 : **Make the filling** Whisk the cream and icing sugar together until soft peaks form and place in the fridge until you are ready to assemble.

8 : **Assemble the gâteau** When the cake is completely cooled (which should take around 30 minutes), place the cream in a piping bag fitted with a star nozzle, pipe a small amount of cream onto the first layer of sponge and spread evenly. Then pipe a ring around the edge and fill with half the cherry jam mixture. Repeat with the second layer and finish the third layer by decoratively piping on the cream and topping with the reserved cherries.

9 : Decorate the finished gâteau with grated or shaved chocolate and serve.

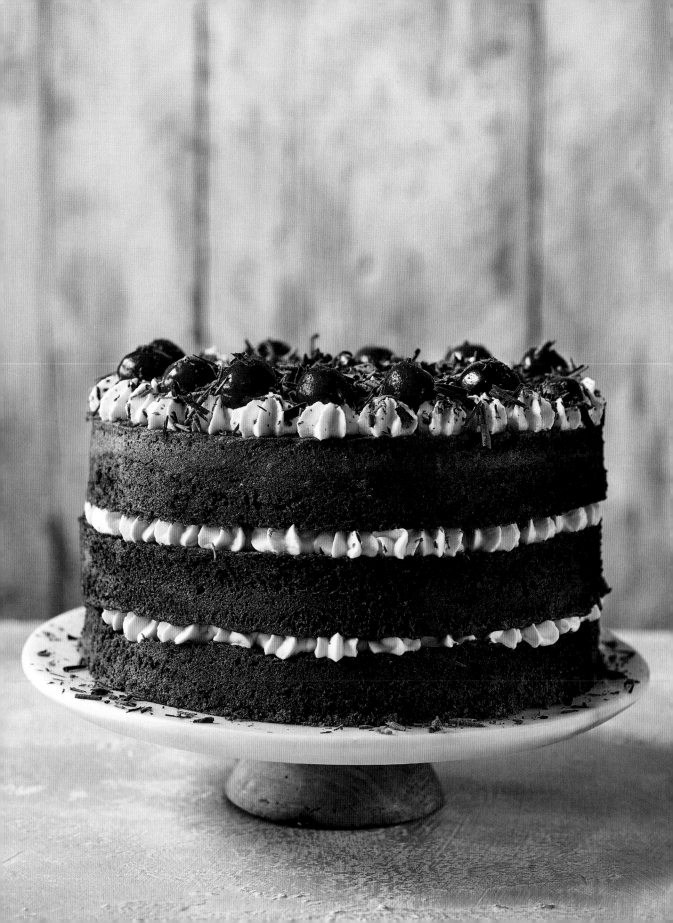

SALTED CARAMEL ICE CREAM

SERVES 6

175g caster sugar
250ml double cream
150ml whole milk
4 egg yolks
1 tsp sea salt

1. Heat 150g of the sugar in a heavy-based pan until it melts and develops a nice caramel colour. Add the cream and bring it back to the boil. Pour in the milk and then leave to cool.

2. Beat the egg yolks in a bowl with the remaining sugar. Place the bowl over a pan of boiling water and whisk continuously until the mixture is creamy and has more than quadrupled in size.

3. Take off the heat and whisk in the caramel mixture.

4. Place in the freezer to chill for at least an hour, until cold but not frozen.

5. Stir the salt into the chilled mixture and pour into an ice cream maker. Churn until frozen and then scoop into a tub and freeze completely.

6. Remove from the freezer and leave to soften slightly before serving.

BAILEYS ICE CREAM

SERVES 6

300ml whipping cream
125g sweetened condensed
    milk
2 tbsp Baileys Irish Cream
pinch of ground cinnamon

1. Whisk the cream in a large bowl until stiff.

2. Carefully fold in the condensed milk, the Baileys and cinnamon.

3. Transfer to a container and freeze for 4–6 hours, or until hard.

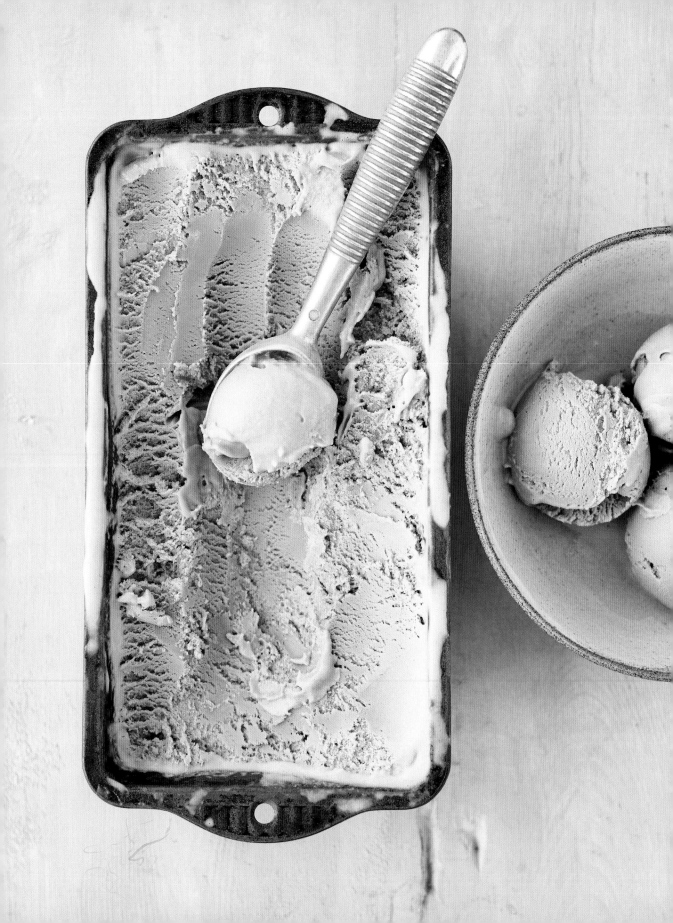

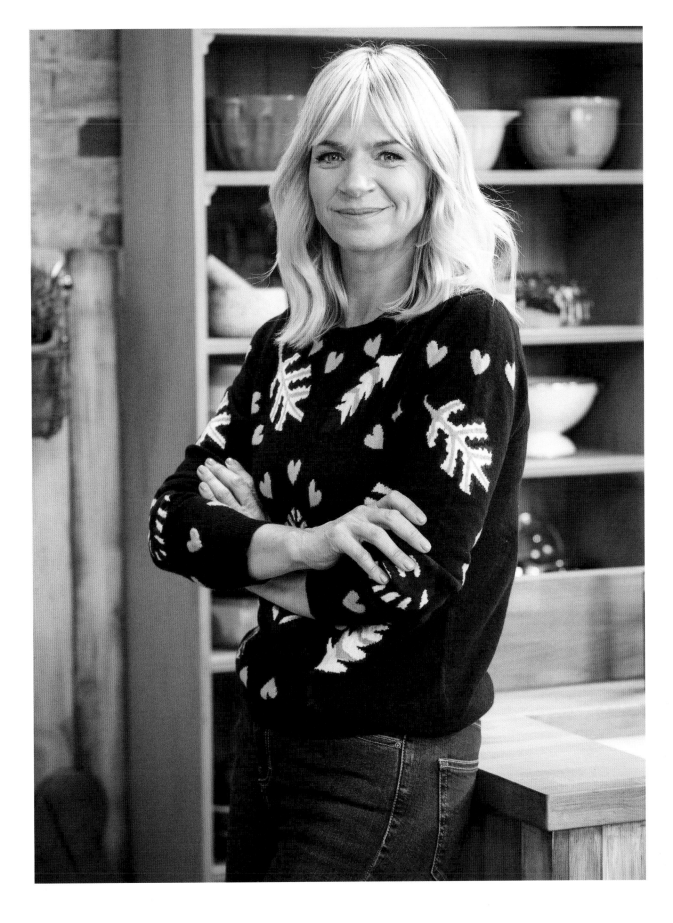

BURNT HONEY CUSTARD

100g clear honey
300ml whole milk
300ml double cream
6 large egg yolks
70g caster sugar
1 tsp cornflour
1 vanilla pod, slit lengthways
   and seeds scraped out
icing sugar (to taste)

1. Put the honey into a pan and place over a medium heat. Bring to the boil and reduce to a deep golden colour. Allow to cool slightly.

2. Pour the milk into a separate pan and add the reduced honey. Stir over a low heat until the honey has dissolved. Add the cream and bring to the boil.

3. Meanwhile, beat the egg yolks and the sugar together in a bowl with the cornflour.

4. Strain the hot milk mixture over the egg mixture and mix well.

5. Strain the custard into a clean pan and add the vanilla pod and seeds.

6. Cook over a low heat stirring continuously for 10 minutes, or until it coats the back of a spoon. Ensure the mixture doesn't boil. If needed, add icing sugar to taste.

CRÈME ANGLAISE

150ml double cream
150ml milk
3 large egg yolks
50g sugar
2 tsp vanilla extract

1. Place the double cream and milk in a pan and bring to the boil.

2. Whisk the egg yolks, sugar and vanilla extract in a bowl with an electric hand whisk until pale and fluffy.

3. Pour the hot cream mixture over the egg mixture and mix well.

4. Pour into a clean pan and cook, stirring over a low heat, until the mixture is thick and coats the back of a wooden spoon.

DESSERTS

BUÑUELOS MEXICAN FRITTERS
WITH APPLE & RASPBERRY COMPOTE

SERVES 4

140g plain flour, plus extra
    for dusting
2 tsp caster sugar
¼ tsp baking powder
pinch of salt
65ml whole milk
1 egg
pinch of anise seeds
sunflower oil, for deep-frying

**For the apple and raspberry
    compote**
500g raspberries
1 eating apple, peeled,
    cored and diced
75g icing sugar, plus
    extra for sprinkling
squeeze of lemon juice

1. **Make the dough** Sift the flour twice into a bowl and add the sugar, baking powder and salt.

2. In a second bowl, whisk the milk, egg and anise seeds together until frothy.

3. Make a well in the flour mixture and slowly add the liquid while whisking. Use your hands to bring it together into a dough. Knead on a lightly floured surface until smooth. Shape into 16 small balls and leave to rest for 20 minutes.

4. **Make the apple and raspberry compote** Put all the ingredients into a pan over a low heat and cook for 5 minutes, until soft. Blend and then pass through a sieve.

5. Roll the dough balls on a lightly floured surface into very thin rounds and leave to rest for a further 5 minutes.

6. Heat a good amount of oil in a deep pan to about 170°C, or until a crumb of bread browns in 30 seconds.

7. **Fry the buñuelos** Carefully fry 2–3 at a time in the hot oil, turning once, until puffed and golden. Drain well.

8. Sprinkle the buñuelos with icing sugar and serve with the apple and raspberry compote.

> **TIP** Serve with Baileys Ice Cream
> (see page 242).

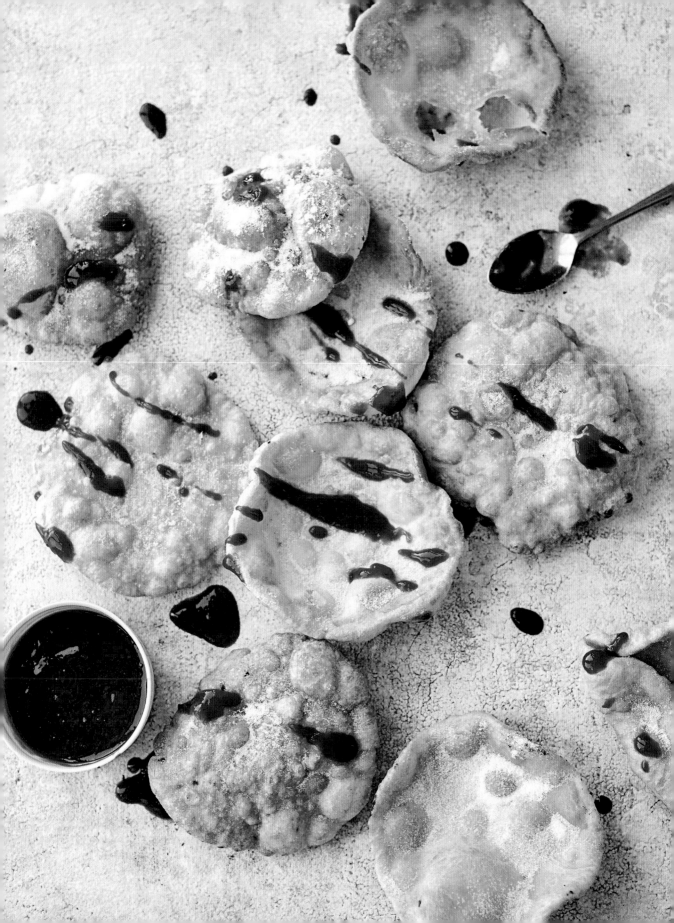

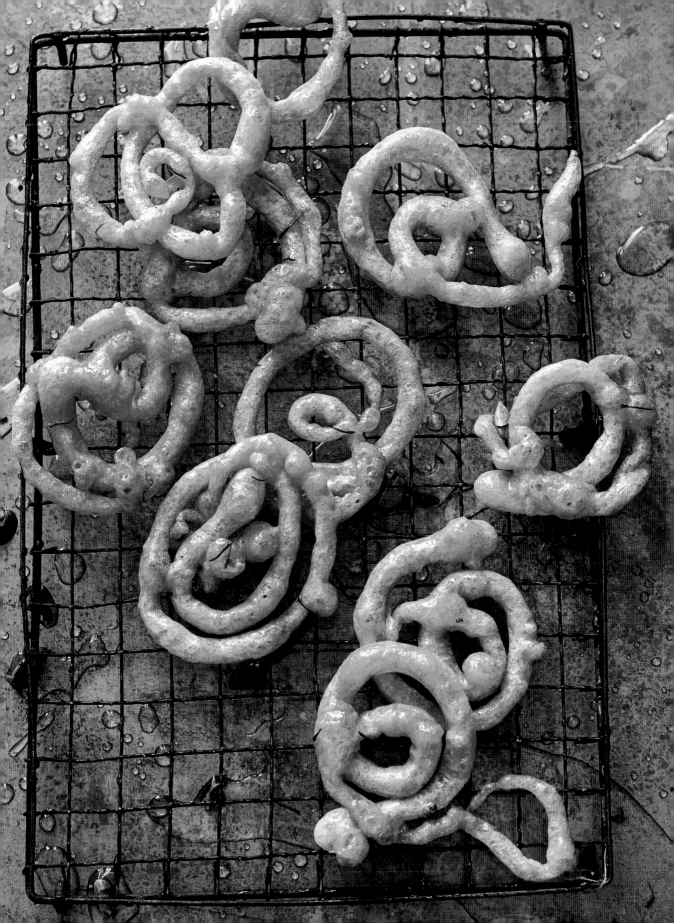

JALEBI
INDIAN SPIRAL SWEETS

SERVES 4

100g plain flour
1 tbsp gram/chickpea flour
1 tbsp cornflour
1 tsp fast action yeast
1 tsp caster sugar
about 120ml warm water
vegetable oil, for deep-frying

For the syrup
200g caster sugar
3 cloves
8 cardamon pods, cracked
pinch of saffron

1. **Make the batter** Place all the flours in a bowl and whisk together.

2. Place the yeast and sugar in a small bowl, add half the water and leave to stand for 5 minutes.

3. Add the yeast mixture to the flour mixture and mix together well. Add enough of the remaining water to get a dropping consistency.

4. Cover and leave aside in a warm place to prove for approximately 2 hours.

5. **Make the syrup** Place all the syrup ingredients in a pan with 200ml water and bring to the boil for 7 minutes, or until it coats the back of a spoon.

6. Place a good amount of vegetable oil in a deep pan and heat up to 170°C, or until a cube of bread browns in 30 seconds.

7. **Fry the jalebi** Pour the batter into a squeezy bottle and place a cooling rack over a tray lined with kitchen paper. Make spirals/jalebi shapes with the batter in the hot oil and cook for 1–2 minutes on each side.

8. Once cooked, transfer straight into the sugar syrup and leave to soak for 20–30 seconds. Remove to the wire rack to drain before serving.

> **FAMILY TIP** 'These are hot, sweet and sticky swirls of batter dipped in a cardamom, clove and saffron syrup.'

DESSERTS

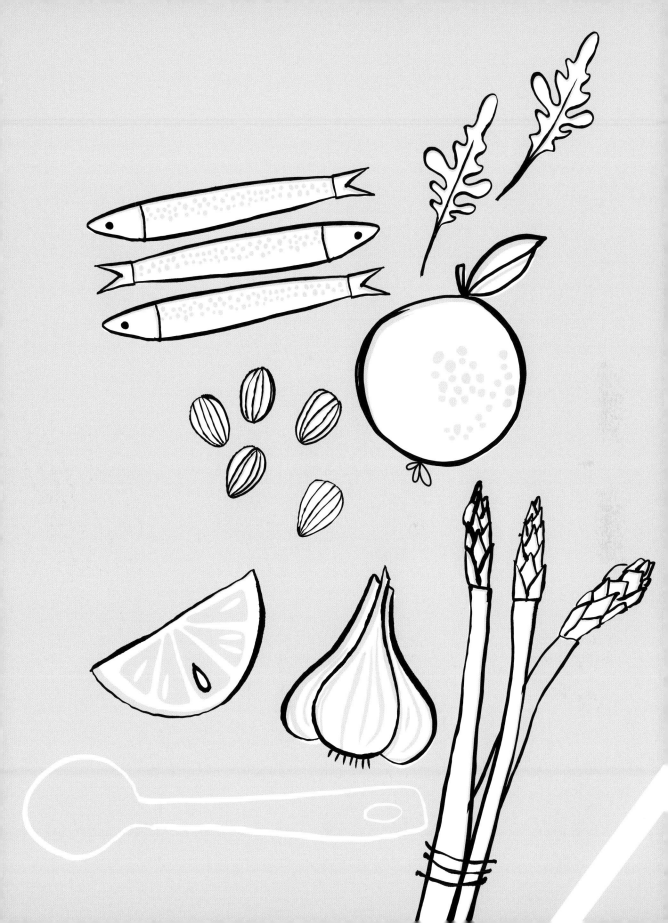

SALADS
SIDES
AND
SAUCES

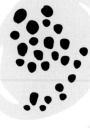

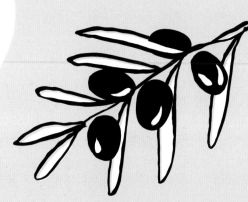

FATTOUSH SALAD

vegetable oil, for deep-frying
2 pitta breads, cut into
    8 squares
juice of 1 lemon
2–3 tbsp extra-virgin olive oil
2 tbsp pomegranate molasses
1 tsp sumac, plus extra
    to garnish
2 large vine tomatoes, chopped
    into large chunks
½ cucumber, chopped into
    large chunks
1 Little Gem lettuce, leaves
    separated and torn
2 fresh mint sprigs, leaves
    picked and chopped
a large handful of
    flat-leaf parsley
10–12 black olives, stoned
seeds of ½ pomegranate
salt and pepper

1. **Fry the pitta** Heat a good amount of oil in a high-sided pan or wok until it reaches about 170°C, or a cube of bread browns in 30 seconds.

2. Deep-fry the pitta squares for 2–3 minutes, or until golden, then drain on kitchen paper and sprinkle with sea salt.

3. **Make the dressing** Combine the lemon juice with the extra-virgin olive oil and pomegranate molasses in a small jug. Season and whisk in the sumac.

4. **Assemble the salad** Place the tomatoes and cucumber in a large bowl and toss in the dressing.

5. Add the lettuce, herbs and olives and mix well.

6. Scatter with the fried pitta and pomegranate seeds and an extra sprinkle of sumac before serving.

> **TIP** For a Syrian mezze, serve with Baba Ganoush & Mouhammara (see page 16).

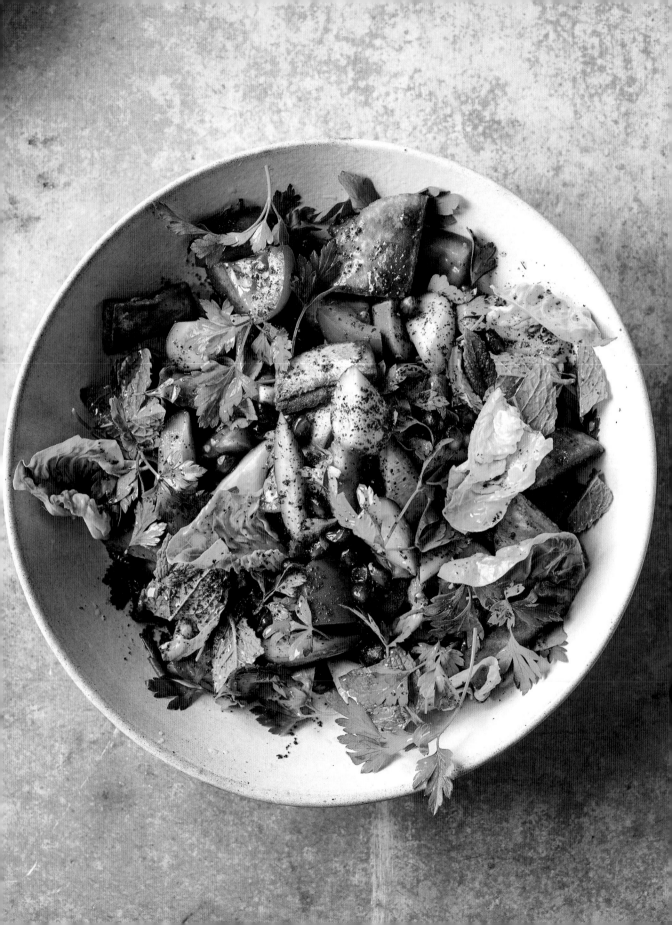

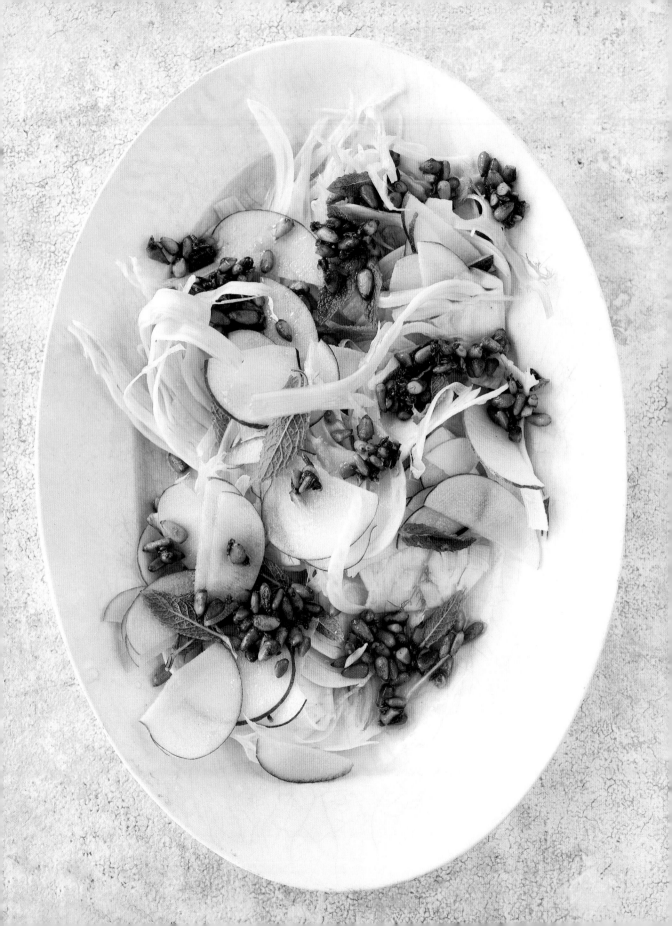

APPLE & FENNEL SALAD

1 tsp fennel seeds
3 tbsp rapeseed oil
100g pine nuts
pinch of ground ginger
1 tbsp honey
1 lemon, sliced, plus
    a squeeze of juice
2 medium fennel bulbs
2 Braeburn apples, cored
a handful of mint leaves
salt

1. Bash the fennel seeds with a pestle and mortar.

2. Heat 1 tablespoon of the oil in a pan over a medium heat and fry the pine nuts until golden. Add the fennel seeds, ginger, honey and a pinch of salt and continue to cook for 1 minute. Transfer to a plate to cool.

3. **Prepare the fennel and apples** Fill a big bowl with the lemon slices and water.

4. Slice the fennel and apples with a mandolin and put in the lemon water to stop them colouring.

5. **Assemble the salad** When you are ready to serve, drain the apple and fennel and arrange on a serving plate. Sprinkle the pine nuts over the top with the mint leaves.

6. **Make the dressing** Combine the remaining oil, lemon juice and some salt. Drizzle over the salad, toss and serve.

SALADS, SIDES AND SAUCES

GREEN BEANS & ALMONDS

SERVES 2–4

300g green beans
small handful of flaked
  almonds
knob of butter
fresh lemon juice (to taste)
salt and pepper

1 : Bring a large pan of salted water to the boil and put the green beans in to cook for about 2 minutes. Test and, when they are perfectly al dente, plunge into iced water.

2 : Dry fry the almonds until golden.

3 : Warm up the green beans in a pan with a little butter. Season and then finish by sprinkling the toasted almonds on top and a squeeze of lemon juice. Stir them in.

BRAISED LEEKS

SERVES 4–6

8 leeks (only the tender
  white part)
150ml white wine
150ml vegetable stock
30g butter
a handful of freshly chopped
  parsley, to garnish
salt and pepper

1 : Preheat the oven to 160°C/Fan 140°C.

2 : Cut the leeks into 5cm pieces and place in a medium-sized roasting dish. Pour over the wine and stock, and dot with the butter. Season with salt and pepper and cover with in foil.

3 : Cook slowly in the oven for about 30 minutes, until soft and tender but still holding their shape.

4 : Remove from the oven and sprinkle with parsley before serving.

CURRIED MUSHY PEAS

SERVES 4

3 tbsp vegetable oil
2 tbsp crushed fresh
    root ginger
3 garlic cloves, peeled and
    crushed
1 large onion, peeled and diced
3 whole green bird's-eye
    chillies, pierced with
    a small sharp knife
1 tsp garam masala
pinch of salt
200g green split peas,
    soaked overnight
3 plum tomatoes, chopped
juice of ½ lemon
a large handful of coriander
    leaves, chopped

1 : Heat the oil in a pan with the ginger, garlic, onion and whole chillies over a medium heat and fry for 5–6 minutes. Add the garam masala and salt.

2 : Drain the peas from their soaking water and add to the pan with 500ml of water. Simmer for 20 minutes, adding more water if they start to look a bit dry, until the peas are very tender.

3 : Add the tomatoes and another splash of water and cook through for a further 5 minutes.

4 : Stir in the lemon juice and fresh coriander and serve.

CHARRED CHICORY

SERVES 4

sunflower oil, for greasing
2 red chicory bulbs,
    cut in half lengthways
2 white chicory bulbs,
    cut in half lengthways
a few fresh thyme sprigs
2 tbsp olive oil
juice of 1 lemon
1 tbsp balsamic vinegar
Parmesan shavings
salt and pepper

1 : Brush a griddle pan with a bit of sunflower oil and place over a medium heat.

2 : When the pan is hot, lay the chicory cut side down and add the thyme. Cook for about 5 minutes, or until it softens and you get the charred lines. Turn over and cook for another 3 minutes.

3 : Place the chicory on a plate and drizzle with olive oil, lemon juice and balsamic vinegar. Season with salt and pepper and top with some Parmesan shavings.

SALADS, SIDES AND SAUCES

ROSEMARY'S SAUTÉ ASPARAGUS

1 tbsp olive oil
1 banana shallot, peeled
   and finely chopped
1 garlic clove, peeled
   and crushed
16 asparagus spears, trimmed
60g panko breadcrumbs,
   toasted in a pan till golden
35g Parmesan, grated
finely grated zest of 2 lemons

1. Preheat the oven to 180°C/Fan 160°C.

2. Heat the oil in a frying pan over a medium heat. Add the shallot and garlic and cook to soften for 1–2 minutes.

3. Add the asparagus and sauté for a further 2 minutes, depending on size, until just tender to the tip of a sharp knife. Place the asparagus on a baking sheet.

4. Mix together the breadcrumbs, Parmesan and lemon zest and sprinkle over the asparagus.

5. Place in the oven and cook for 2–3 minutes, or until the Parmesan has melted.

FAMILY TIP 'Cook with your instinct – we find the best dishes come from this. And stay calm – disasters will always happen at some point, but they are something you can learn from.'

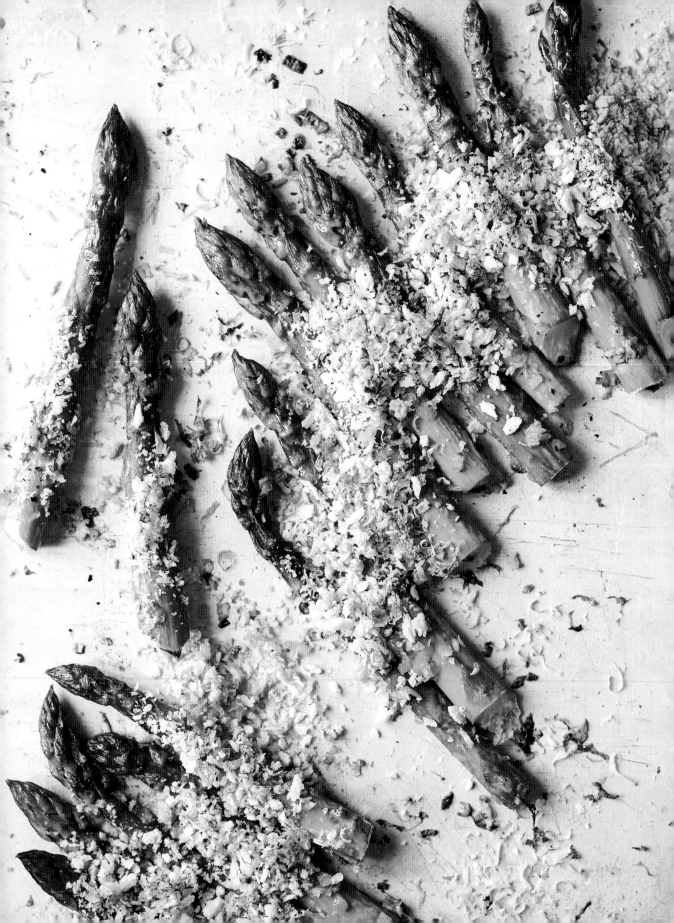

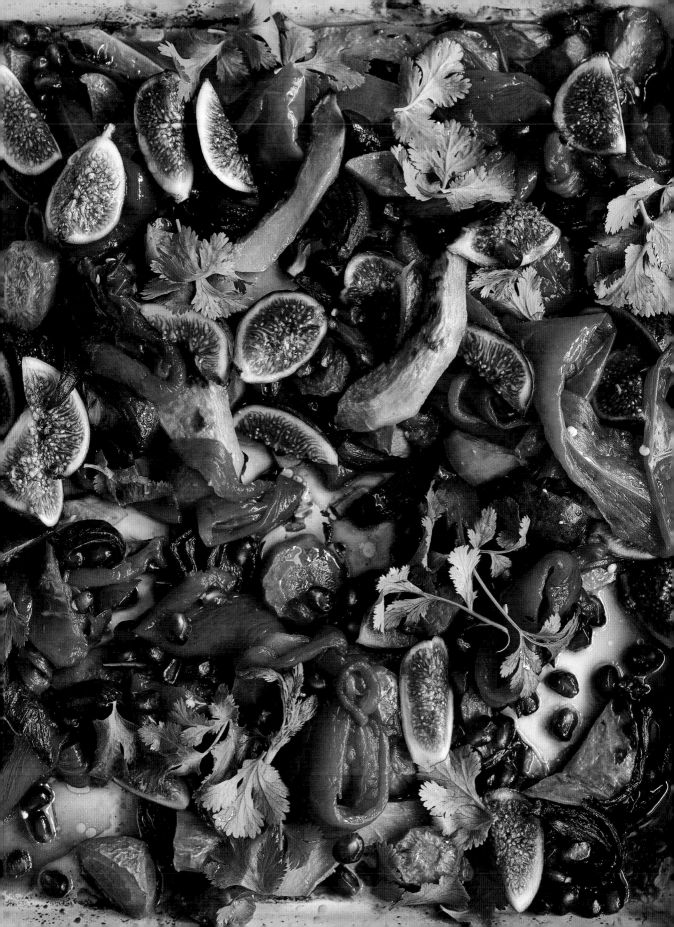

ROASTED VEGETABLES

3 long red Mediterranean
  peppers
500g long carrots, peeled
  and cut into wedges
3 red onions, peeled and
  cut into thick rounds
500g butternut squash, peeled,
  seeded and cut into wedges
3–4 tbsp olive oil
3 garlic cloves, peeled and
  very finely chopped
2 tsp cumin seeds
5 figs, cut into wedges
seeds of 1 pomegranate
juice of 1 lemon
1 bunch coriander,
  leaves picked
extra-virgin olive oil, to drizzle
salt and pepper

1. Preheat the oven to 220°C/Fan 200°C.

2. Place the peppers in the oven and let them cook
for 20 minutes.

3. Remove from the oven and place in a plastic bag
for 5 minutes. Peel the skin from the peppers and then
cut them into long pieces.

4. Reduce the oven temperature to 200°C/Fan 180°C.

5. Put the carrots, onions and squash in an oven
tray and drizzle with oil. Season and add the garlic and
cumin seeds. Roast in the oven for 40 minutes, turning
occasionally, until tender. Remove from the oven
and tip into a serving dish.

6. Mix gently with the figs, pomegranate seeds and
roasted peppers. Add the lemon juice and coriander leaves
and drizzle with extra-virgin olive oil to serve.

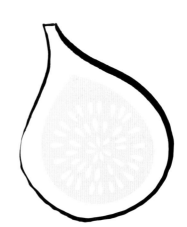

ROSEMARY'S BRAISED RED CABBAGE IN CIDER

SERVES 4

60g butter
1 medium onion, peeled
    and finely chopped
2 rashers streaky bacon,
    finely chopped (optional)
50g sultanas, chopped
good pinch of ground cloves
good grating of nutmeg
1 tsp ground cinnamon
4 garlic cloves, peeled and
    finely chopped
1 small red cabbage (or ½
    large cabbage), finely sliced
3 tbsp cider vinegar
250ml cider
50g soft light brown sugar
salt and pepper

1. Melt the butter in a large pan over a medium heat, add the onion and bacon and cook for 5–10 minutes, to soften.

2. Stir the sultanas into the onion mix, add the spices and garlic and stir well.

3. Tip in the cabbage, mix well, pour in the cider vinegar and leave to bubble for 1 minute.

4. Pour in the cider and stir in the brown sugar. Bring to the boil, then turn the heat down to very low, cover and cook, just simmering, for about 2 hours. Keep stirring every 20 minutes.

5. When ready to serve, season with salt and a lot of pepper.

> **TIP** This freezes very well – try making too much in order to have leftovers for another time. This is better cooked the day before.

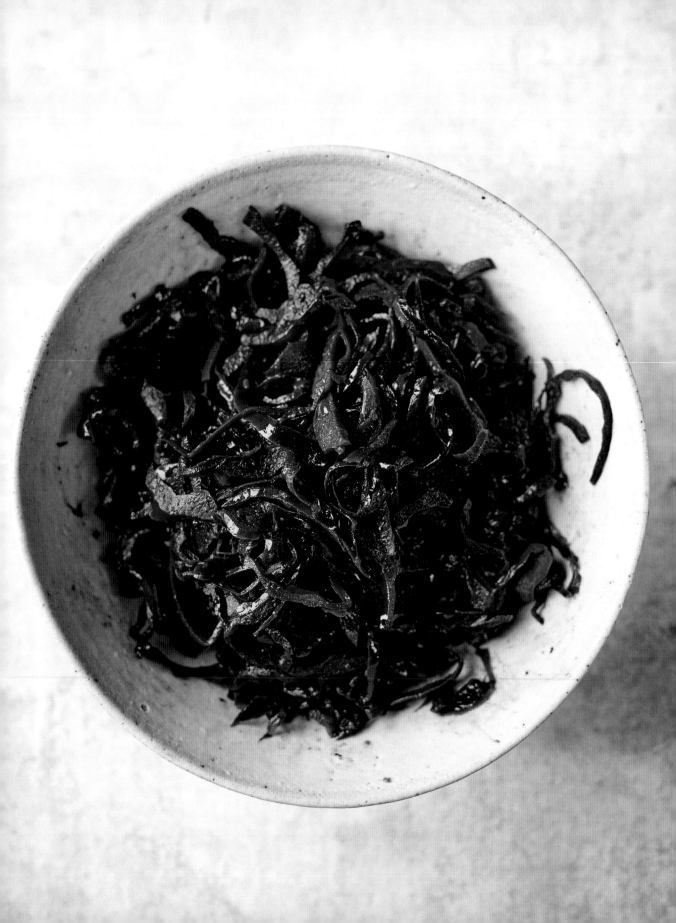

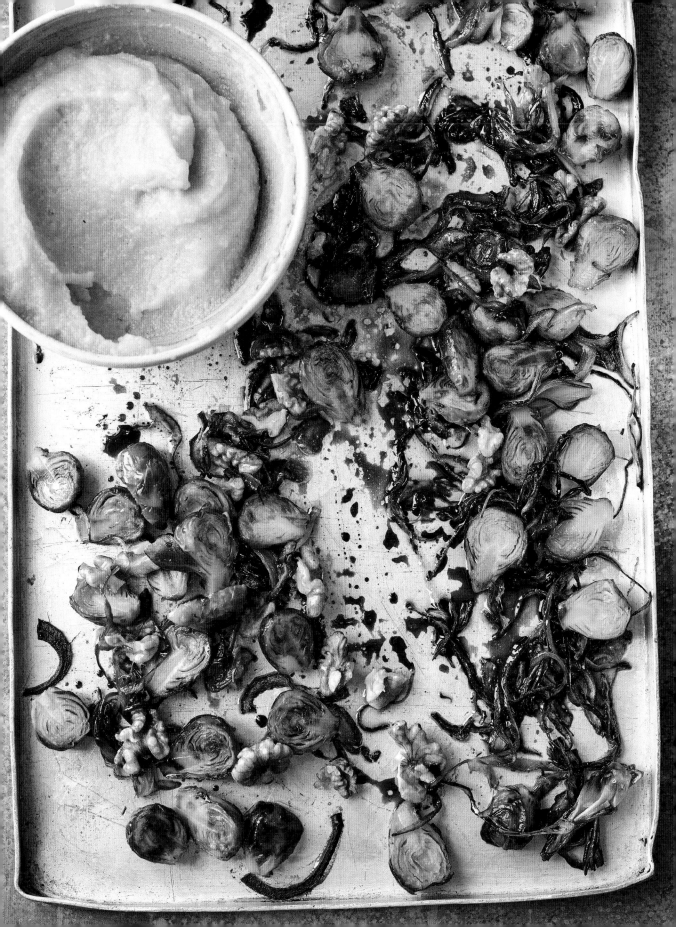

POLENTA & BALSAMIC-GLAZED BRUSSELS SPROUTS & WALNUTS

SERVES 4

250g Brussels sprouts, trimmed and cut in half
1 red onion, peeled and finely sliced
2 tbsp olive oil
100ml balsamic vinegar
1 tbsp caster sugar
750g walnut pieces
300ml vegetable stock
300g fine polenta (cornmeal, not quick cook)
50g unsalted butter
salt and pepper

1. Preheat the oven to 200°C/Fan 180°C.

2. Toss the Brussels sprouts and onion together in a bowl with the olive oil. Season with salt and pepper and then transfer to a baking sheet.

3. Cook in the oven for 15–20 minutes.

4. Meanwhile, stir the balsamic and sugar in a small pan over a medium heat and reduce down by half.

5. Toast the walnuts in a separate pan over a low heat.

6. Bring the vegetable stock and 600ml water to a boil in a medium pan. Add the polenta, whisking quite a bit, until the mixture begins to thicken. Reduce the heat to a simmer, cover, and leave to cook very gently for 20–25 minutes, stirring often, until tender.

7. Stir in the butter and season to taste.

8. Drizzle the roasted sprouts with the balsamic and the toasted walnuts and serve with the polenta.

FAMILY TIP 'It's always good to have a partner, parent, child or friend to clean up after you. If you are cooking, they should be cleaning!'

AUBERGINE SALSA

SERVES 4-6

2 aubergines
2 tbsp olive oil
6 large vine tomatoes, peeled
4 garlic cloves, peeled and
　grated
100g passata
1 rounded tbsp tomato purée
1½ tsp paprika
1½ tsp ground cumin
1 small bunch fresh coriander,
　chopped
salt and pepper

1. Preheat the oven to 200°C/Fan 180°C.

2. Pierce the aubergines a few times with a sharp knife then rub in half the oil, place in a roasting tin and roast for 40 minutes.

3. Once cooked, peel off the skin and dice the flesh.

4. Meanwhile, blend the tomatoes into a liquid. Heat the remaining olive oil in a pan, add the garlic and fry for 30 seconds. Stir in the blended tomatoes, passata and tomato purée. Finally, add the dry spices and season well. Cook over a low heat for 30 minutes until thickened.

5. Stir in the diced aubergine and fresh coriander to serve.

FAMILY TIP 'Our motto throughout the show has been – easy, simple and affordable. People with their busy lifestyles don't have the time or the energy to stand in the kitchen and cook for hours on end.'

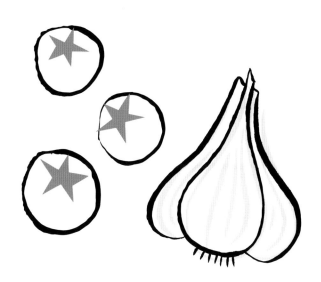

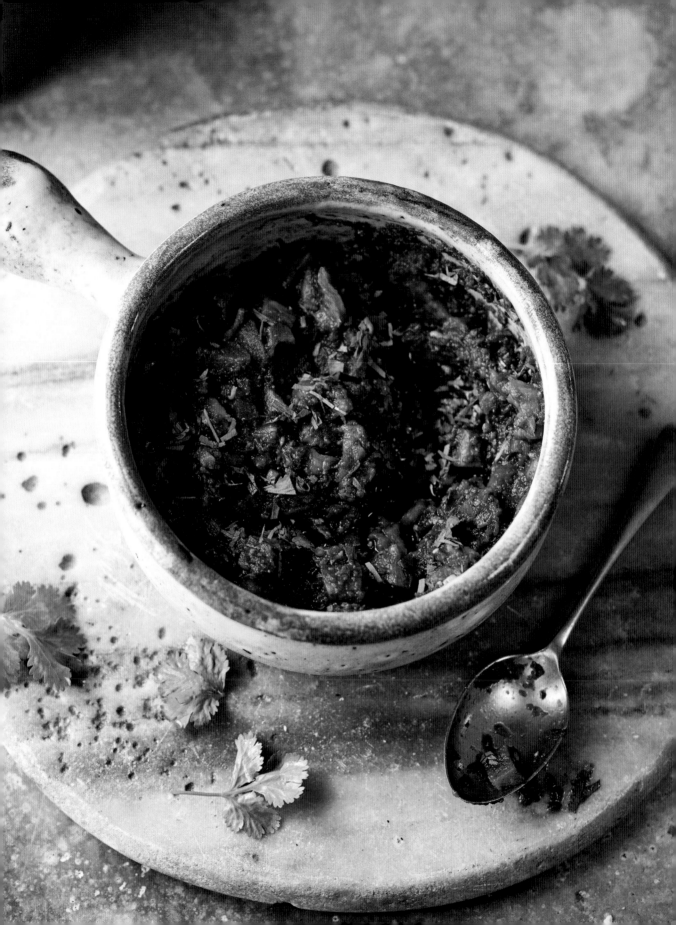

SPICY CHICKPEAS

1 tbsp unsalted butter
1 red onion, peeled and
    finely diced
1 carrot, peeled and
    finely diced
1 celery stick, finely diced
1 fresh bay leaf
1 cinnamon stick
3 dried ancho chillies,
    soaked and finely sliced
1 large red chilli, finely diced
200g fresh tomatoes, chopped
2 tbsp light brown sugar
2 garlic cloves, crushed
125g sobrassada sausage,
    sliced
100ml red wine
3 tbsp finely chopped
    fresh oregano
a large handful of freshly
    chopped basil
a handful of freshly
    chopped parsley
250ml passata
150ml fresh chicken stock
100g piquillo peppers,
    finely diced
2 x 400g tins chickpeas,
    drained and rinsed
zest and juice of 1–2 lemons
salt and pepper

1 : Melt the butter in a large pan over a low heat and fry the onion, carrot and celery for 10 minutes with the bay and cinnamon stick.

2 : Add the ancho chillies to the pan with the red chilli, tomatoes, sugar and garlic and cook for 5 minutes.

3 : Add the sobrassada and cook for 1–2 minutes then pour in the red wine and reduce by half.

4 : Add the fresh herbs, passata and stock and cook until it has reduced by about half again.

5 : Finally, stir in the piquillo peppers and chickpeas, add the lemon zest and juice and season to taste.

GAME CHIPS

100g Maris Piper potatoes,
   peeled
100g purple potatoes,
   peeled
1 parsnip, peeled
1.5 litres vegetable oil
sea salt

1. Using a mandolin with a crinkle cut, slice the potatoes and parsnips as finely as possible, turning them 90 degrees after each cut. Put into a large bowl of water to help remove the starch then drain and pat dry with kitchen paper.

2. Heat the oil in a deep pan (so it comes just under half way up) until it is 180°C, or a cube of bread browns in 20 seconds.

3. Deep-fry the chips in batches for 1–2 minutes, turning them in the hot oil with a slotted spoon, and then remove and drain on kitchen paper. Season with sea salt.

HASSELBACK POTATOES

500g new potatoes
40g butter
2 tbsp olive oil
a handful of fresh oregano,
   chopped
salt and pepper

1. Preheat the oven to 200°C/Fan 180°C.

2. Make small vertical cuts along the length of each potato, cutting only about three quarters of the way down so the potato doesn't fall apart.

3. Put the butter and oil in a roasting tin over a medium heat to melt the butter.

4. Tip in the potatoes, season, and scatter over the oregano. Give the potatoes a gentle toss so they're thoroughly coated, then roast cut-side-up on the bottom shelf of the oven for 45–60 minutes, or until golden and tender.

BOMBAY BOULANGÈRE

SERVES 4

100g butter, plus extra for
    greasing and dotting
4 small onions, peeled
    and finely sliced
1 tsp cumin seeds, plus
    extra for sprinkling
1 tsp turmeric
2 tsp ground ginger
2 tsp mustard seeds
4 tsp garam masala
4 tbsp freshly chopped
    coriander
800g potatoes, peeled
    and finely sliced
200ml fresh chicken stock
sunflower oil, for shallow
    frying
1 white onion, peeled,
    finely sliced and tossed
    in cornflour
salt and pepper

1 : Heat the oven to 180°C/Fan 160°C and butter a small metal roasting tin (20cm square).

2 : **Cook the onion** Fry the onions and spices in the butter in a pan over a medium heat for 15 minutes, or until softened. Remove from the heat and stir through the coriander.

3 : **Assemble the dish** Layer the potatoes and onion mix in the tin, pressing down after each layer.

4 : Pour the stock over the top, using enough to almost but not quite cover the potatoes.

5 : Sprinkle with a few cumin seeds and grind over black pepper.

6 : Dot with butter and bake in the oven for about 50–60 minutes, or until the potatoes are cooked through and the top is golden brown.

7 : Meanwhile, heat a good layer of oil in a pan over a medium heat and gently fry the sliced onion until deep golden brown. Drain on kitchen paper and season with sea salt.

8 : Serve the potatoes with the crispy onions.

ROSEMARY'S BOULANGÈRE POTATOES

2 tbsp rapeseed oil
1 large onion, peeled and
    finely sliced
1 tsp freshly chopped thyme
1 tsp freshly chopped rosemary
2 garlic cloves, peeled
    and chopped
60g butter
400ml chicken or
    vegetable stock
1kg Maris Piper or Desiree
    potatoes, peeled and
    finely sliced
30g freshly grated Parmesan
30g fresh white breadcrumbs
salt and pepper

1   Preheat the oven to 180°C/Fan 160°C.

2   **Cook the onion** Place the oil in a pan over a medium heat and fry the onion for 10 minutes, or until soft. When softened, leave to caramelise to a light golden colour, about another 10 minutes, then stir through the herbs and garlic. Season well with salt and pepper.

3   **Assemble the dish** Generously butter a deep round 2 litre ovenproof dish then add a tablespoon of chicken or vegetable stock to the base.

4   Start layering the potato and the onion mixture into the dish, pouring over the stock as you go.

5   Press the potatoes down so the liquid overflows, dot with the remaining butter then cook in the oven for 45–60 minutes, or until almost all the stock is absorbed.

6   Remove the potatoes from the oven and sprinkle with the Parmesan and breadcrumbs. Return to the oven and cook for a further 20–30 minutes, until golden and your knife slides through the potatoes.

ROSEMARY'S
ONE LARGE RÖSTI

500g large waxy potatoes
5 tbsp clarified butter
½ medium onion, peeled
    and finely chopped
salt and pepper

1. Cook the potatoes Ensure the potatoes have been well washed. Bring a large pan of water to the boil and put the potatoes in to cook for about 8–10 minutes, or until not quite cooked. Drain well and allow to cool.

2. Cook the onion Add 2 tablespoons of the butter to a large non-stick frying pan over a medium heat and soften the onion; this will take at least 5 minutes. Remove and allow to cool.

3. Peel the potatoes with a knife by scraping down the skins and then coarsely grate them into a large bowl. Season with salt and pepper, add the cooled onion and mix well.

4. Fry the rösti Wipe the pan clean and then add 2 tablespoons of the butter. Tip in the potato mixture and press down. Gently cook over a low heat for about 10–12 minutes.

5. Place a large plate over the pan and invert the rösti onto it. Add the last of the butter to the pan, then slide the rösti back into it, uncooked side down, and cook for a further 5 minutes or until golden brown. Cut into wedges to serve.

> **TIP** Lovely as a light lunch or dinner topped with a fried egg.

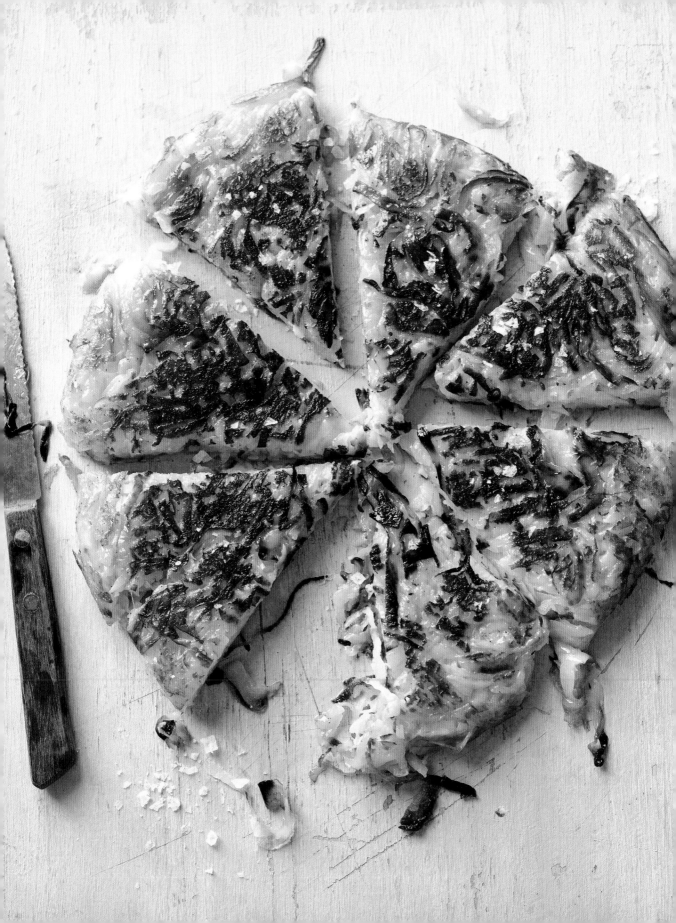

MISSI ROTI FLATBREADS

120g chapatti flour
2 tbsp vegetable oil
60g gram/chickpea flour
1 banana shallot, very
　finely chopped
2 tsp ground ginger
1 tsp ground cumin
1 green chilli, seeded and
　finely chopped
a handful of fresh fenugreek
　(methi) leaves, finely
　chopped
a handful of fresh coriander,
　including stalks,
　finely chopped
1 generous tsp salt
oil, for brushing
50g unsalted butter, melted,
　for basting

1 : Make the dough Mix all the ingredients together, except the oil for brushing and the melted butter, and add enough water to make a soft but not sticky dough. Rest for at least 10 minutes and then divide into 12 and roll out each one to a 15cm round.

2 : Cook the flatbreads Heat a heavy-based large frying pan over a medium heat. Lightly oil the base of the pan and fry the rotis one at a time for 2–3 minutes, turning, until golden brown.

3 : Brush with melted butter as they cook and serve them hot.

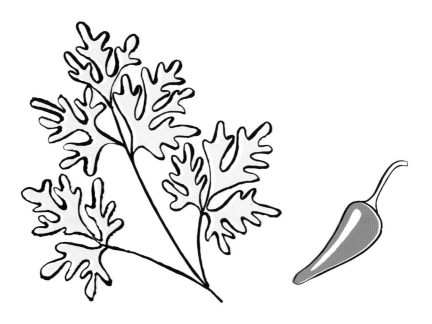

YORKSHIRE PUDDINGS

MAKES 12

180g plain flour
¼ tsp salt
3 medium eggs
140ml whole milk
120ml sparkling water
4–6 tsp goose fat or
   beef dripping

1 : Preheat the oven to 220°C/Fan 200°C.

2 : Make the batter Sift the flour and salt into a bowl and make a hollow in the centre. Add the eggs and gradually begin stirring and drawing the flour into the middle. As it starts to thicken, gradually add the milk, and slowly stir in the flour until you have a smooth, thick batter. Leave to stand until you are ready to make the puddings.

3 : Cook the puddings Place ½ teaspoon of fat in each hole of a 12-hole Yorkshire pudding tin and place in the oven for 5 minutes, or until piping hot.

4 : Gradually beat the sparkling water into the batter then carefully divide the batter between each hole. Cook in the oven for 20–25 minutes, or until well risen and golden.

5 : Remove from the oven and serve immediately.

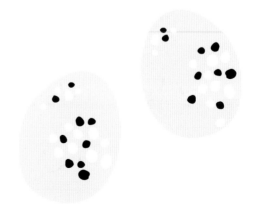

ROSEMARY'S COCONUT & ALMOND PILAF RICE

60g butter
1 small onion, peeled and
    finely chopped
150g Basmati rice, rinsed
    under cold running water
1 tsp cumin seeds
300ml chicken stock, hot
2 tbsp freshly chopped parsley
25g shredded coconut, toasted
25g flaked almonds, toasted
salt

1. Preheat the oven to 180°C/Fan 160°C.

2. Melt the butter in a small flameproof roasting tin over a low heat and add the onion, warming it through. Add the rice and cumin seeds and continue turning together over the heat for 2 minutes.

3. Pour in the hot stock, stir well, and cover with greaseproof paper, letting it rest lightly on the surface of the rice. Bake for 20–25 minutes, without stirring, until the rice is tender but still slightly nutty, topping up with stock or water as it cooks if it is drying too quickly.

4. When the pilaf is ready, remove from the oven, sprinkle with the coconut and flaked almonds, season with salt and serve.

FAMILY TIP 'Family cooking time has proved to be a real bonding session for us. We all enjoy working together.'

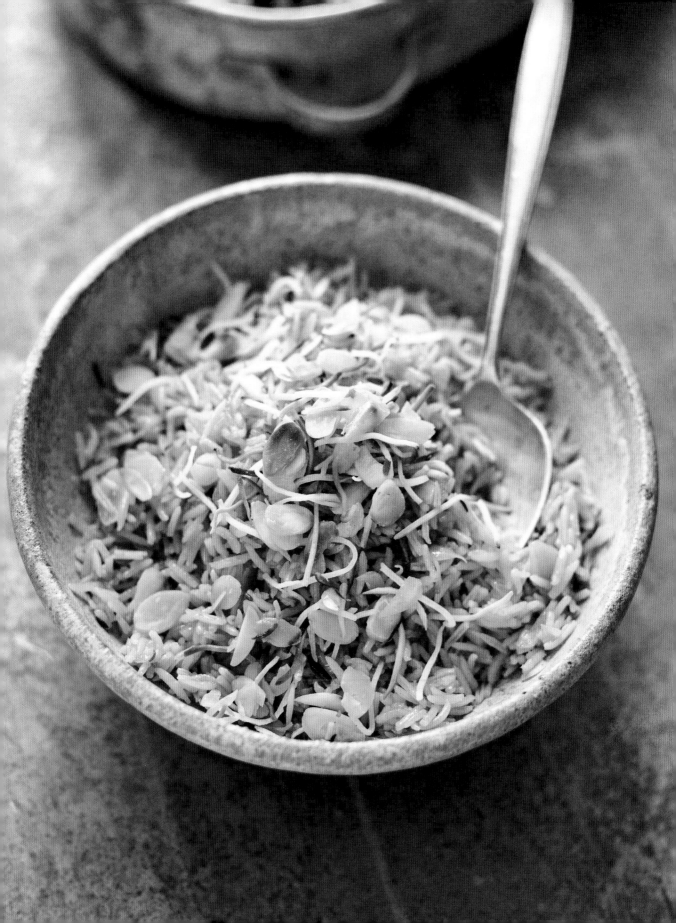

HOME-MADE KETCHUP

MAKES 400ML

2 large red peppers, seeded and cut into even-sized chunks
1 large onion, peeled and roughly chopped
500g small vine tomatoes, halved
2 tbsp rapeseed oil
2 tsp red wine vinegar
salt and pepper

1 : Preheat the oven to 200°C/Fan 180°C.

2 : Toss the peppers, onion and tomatoes in the rapeseed oil and place in a roasting tin. Season with salt and pepper and roast in the oven for 30 minutes, or until tender and the tomatoes are slightly golden.

3 : Place all the vegetables in a pan, add the vinegar and whizz with a hand blender to a thick ketchup.

4 : Check the seasoning and cool then serve with sausages or a fried breakfast. Store any unused ketchup in a sterilised jar.

RED CURRY PASTE

MAKES 150ML

5 dried red chillies, chopped
1 tsp coriander seeds
½ tsp cumin seeds
2.5cm cinnamon stick
3 coriander roots, chopped
4 garlic cloves, peeled
2–3 sticks of lemon grass, core chopped
3cm piece fresh root ginger, peeled and chopped
2.5cm piece galangal, peeled and chopped
1 tbsp chopped kaffir lime leaves
1 tsp shrimp paste
2 tbsp tomato purée
½ tsp black peppercorns
½ tsp turmeric
2–3 tbsp vegetable oil

1 : In a small pan, dry-fry the chillies for 1–2 minutes and then remove to a plate.

2 : Using the same pan, dry-fry the coriander seeds, cumin seeds and cinnamon over a low heat until fragrant. Tip into a pestle and mortar and grind to a fine powder.

3 : Combine the chillies, ground spices and the remaining ingredients and whizz to a paste, using a hand blender, with a splash of water.

SALADS, SIDES AND SAUCES

CHIPOTLE PASTE

MAKES 400ML

50g dried chipotle chillies,
   soaked until soft
1 large onion, peeled
   and quartered
4 garlic cloves, peeled
2 tbsp fresh oregano leaves
2 tbsp fresh thyme leaves
½ tsp cumin seeds
dash of Tabasco sauce
2 green chillies
200ml boiling water
2 tbsp olive oil
25ml white wine vinegar
25ml balsamic vinegar
2 tbsp tomato purée
6 tbsp demerara sugar
juice of ½ lime
salt and pepper

1 : Drain the chipotle chillies and add to a food-processor with the onion, garlic, oregano, thyme, cumin seeds, Tabasco, green chillies, boiling water, 1 tablespoon of the olive oil and a pinch of salt and freshly ground pepper. Whizz to a paste – it will take approximately 5 minutes.

2 : Spoon the chilli paste into a pan with the remaining oil. Cook for a couple of minutes over a medium heat. Stir in the vinegars, tomato purée, sugar and lime juice. Bring up to the boil, reduce the heat and simmer for about 15 minutes, or until a paste-like consistency is reached. Taste to see if more salt or sugar is needed then remove from the heat.

MUSHROOM KETCHUP

MAKES 600ML

4 banana shallots, peeled
   and finely chopped
70g unsalted butter
5 garlic cloves, peeled and
   finely sliced
400g mixed mushrooms, finely
   chopped
2 tbsp each caster sugar and
   soft light brown sugar
30ml white wine vinegar
30ml cider vinegar
500ml double cream
3 anchovy fillets in oil
1 tbsp Dijon mustard
salt and pepper

1 : Fry the shallots in the butter until soft and then add the garlic.

2 : Add the mushrooms to the pan and fry over a high heat for 10 minutes.

3 : Add the sugars and vinegars and bubble for 2–3 minutes before adding the cream.

4 : Season well, add the anchovy fillets and mustard and whizz with a hand blender.

5 : Check the seasoning then serve with sausages or a fried breakfast. Store any unused ketchup in a sterilised jar.

HOLLANDAISE SAUCE

SERVES 2-4

1 tbsp white wine vinegar
a few parsley stalks
1 shallot, peeled and sliced
2 egg yolks
250g butter, melted
tiny pinch of cayenne pepper
small squeeze of lemon juice
   (to taste)
salt and freshly ground
   white pepper

1 : Bring the vinegar to the boil in a small pan with the parsley stalks and sliced shallot. Remove from the heat and pour about 1 tablespoon through a sieve into a heatproof bowl (to remove the parsley and shallots).

2 : Place the bowl over a pan of simmering water, add the egg yolks and whisk until the yellow starts to pale and you can write an 'M' in the mixture.

3 : Remove from the heat and set the bowl on a kitchen towel. Very slowly pour the hot melted butter into the bowl with the egg yolk mixture, whisking all the time (an electric whisk is best for this). Stop pouring once the sauce reaches the correct consistency or when you reach the white solids at the bottom of the melted butter (do not add these to the sauce). If the mixture splits it can be brought together again with a drop of warm water.

4 : Taste and add the cayenne, lemon juice and seasoning, if required. Push clingfilm or greaseproof paper onto the mixture to stop a skin forming and place in a warm (not hot) place until ready to serve.

OXTAIL & BONE MARROW GRAVY

SERVES 6

1 x 200g piece marrow bone, split in half and soaked in iced water overnight
2 tbsp rapeseed oil
3 large pieces oxtail (about 600g)
2 onions, peeled and finely sliced
2 garlic cloves, peeled and finely sliced
2 bay leaves
4 fresh thyme sprigs
300ml red wine
700ml fresh beef stock
a handful of dried porcini mushroom, soaked in boiling water
2 tomatoes, chopped
1 tbsp red wine vinegar
1 tbsp Worcestershire sauce
1 tbsp soft light brown sugar

1 : Scoop the marrow from the bone with a teaspoon and dice. Keep chilled in the fridge and discard the bones.

2 : Heat the oil in a flameproof casserole dish. Season the oxtail and brown all over then set aside. Using the same pan, add the onions and fry for 10 minutes, or until softened and golden. Add the garlic and herbs and fry for a further 1–2 minutes.

3 : Return the oxtail to the pan, add the red wine and bubble until it has reduced by half.

4 : Add the beef stock, mushrooms and their strained soaking liquid, tomatoes, vinegar, Worcestershire sauce and sugar.

5 : Bring to the boil then reduce the heat. Cover with a lid and leave to simmer gently for 1½–2 hours, or until the oxtail is tender.

6 : Strain – you can keep the meat from the oxtail for another day. Strain any fat from the liquid and then return the liquid to a clean pan and bubble away until it has reduced to a light coating consistency.

7 : Whisk in the chilled bone marrow until melted, then serve.

INDEX

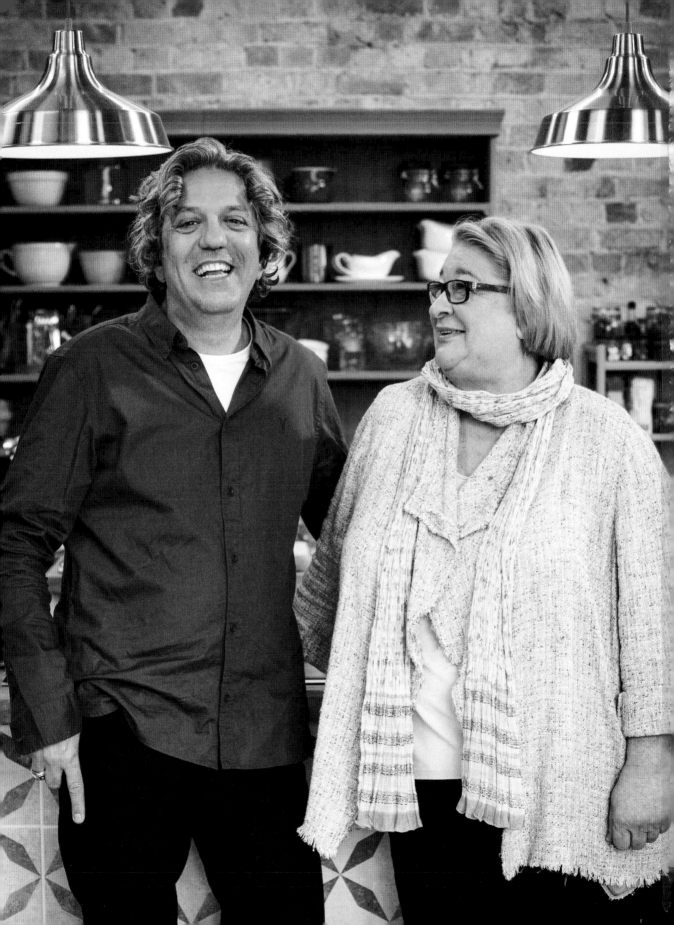